# SASQUATCH
# AND
# WHITE SPIRIT

# SASQUATCH AND WHITE SPIRIT

Fletcher McGhee

Pentland Press, Inc.
www.pentlandpressusa.com

PUBLISHED BY PENTLAND PRESS, INC.
5122 Bur Oak Circle, Raleigh, North Carolina 27612
United States of America
919-782-0281

ISBN 1-57197-247-1
Library of Congress Control Number: 00-134885



Printed in the United States of America

On August 14, 2000, the author,
Fletcher McGhee
passed from our midst to his eternal home
in heaven above. He was a beloved
husband, father, grandfather, and friend.
He will be dearly missed by all.
It is hoped this, the last of his books,
will be both a tribute to his love of writing
and a testimony to his own faith
in his Lord Jesus.


Russell Shewmaker, Pastor
Pilgrim Lutheran Church
Jonesboro, Arkansas

# Cast of Characters

| | |
|---|---|
| Joshua Langford | Teamster and wilderness pioneer |
| Angela Langford | Beautiful, devoted wife of Joshua |
| Jeremiah Langford | Son of Joshua and Angela |
| Running Brook Langford | Infant daughter of Joshua and Angela |
| Noah Langford | Father of Joshua |
| Ramona Langford | Mother of Joshua |
| Daniel Peterson | Father of Angela |
| Rising Moon Peterson | Mother of Angela |
| Pierre Benoit | Grandfather of Angela |
| Sasquatch | Sometimes known as Bigfoot |
| White Spirit | Snow-white female wolf |
| Big Thunder | Old Indian friend of Jeremiah |
| Little Flower Hatling | Daughter of Big Thunder |
| Silver Bear | Shaman grandfather of Big Thunder |
| Benjamin Ferguson | New and used boat salesman |
| Roger Nielson | Joshua's nearest neighbor |
| Kate Nielson | Roger's six-year-old daughter |

# CHAPTER

## 1

"Jer-r-r-e-e-e, Jer-r-e-e-m-m-i-i-a-a-h-h-h-h La-a-n-n-g-g-g-f-o-o-r-r-d-d. You come on home now-w-w-w. This min-n-n-u-t-te. Do you hear-r-r-r me-e-e-e-e-e?"

Angela had been desperately but unsuccessfully attempting to call her seven-year-old son home from the vast expanse of forested woodlands where he had been happily roaming and playing all afternoon. She was calling to him from the back porch of the log cabin she and Joshua had built with their own two hands, a few tools, lots of perspiration, and an enormous amount of affectionate but strenuously demanding labor. Near sundown her calls to Jeremiah had sounded a bit angry and demanding, but as the darkness of the chilly night approached, her acrimonious voice had taken on a gentler, more appealing and mournful note as she pleaded desperately for her son to come home.

Angela couldn't sit still in the kitchen. She would get up and walk to the back porch every fifteen or twenty minutes to voice her pleas to the deathly silence of the dark, thickly patterned undergrowth of trees, vines, and ferns densely obscuring the taller trees of the forest. Each time she called toward the forested hills beyond their cabin, she felt that the underbrush was simply too thick for her voice to successfully penetrate.

The sun had already gone down behind the hills toward the southwest. At some point, she would abandon her post on the back porch to approach the living room in a vain attempt to get Joshua to journey into the dark woods in hopes of locating their child.

She was beginning to get desperate to find Jeremiah, and she would have accepted help from almost any quarter. At times she would kneel by the firewood that was stacked on the back porch and earnestly pray for his return from the forlorn forest. She had come to the conclusion many times previously, that if all else failed, prayer was the most reliable solution to be used in solving any distressing problem. Prayer had always proven to be the mainstay and chief support in the Langford family's religious beliefs and moral reinforcement.

She and Joshua had chosen to locate their log cabin in a heavily forested section of an almost inaccessible spot that paralleled the secondary Grays River. This was a very sparsely populated, mountainous section of southwestern Washington. The Grays River was a small tributary of the vastly enormous and often dangerous Columbia River, which formed the boundary between the states of Oregon and Washington.

To any ordinary person it would have been just a log cabin, but to them it was truly a palace. It was in the most desirable location they could ever have dreamed of—the primeval forest wilderness, far apart from civilization. Their ultimate lifetime dream had been achieved at an early age, mainly from their skimping and saving money and then laboring incessantly while building their home. Joshua and Angela had purchased the sixty-four-acre tract of uninhabited virgin forest land in 1919, sight unseen, while they were living in Oregon.

Washington had gained statehood thirty years before, and the white population had begun to overtake the population of Native American Indians. Families were constantly settling in, and the available land was fast disappearing. Joshua figured that another thirty years would see neighbors crowding in too close for comfort. He had felt fortunate to be able to discover that precious parcel of land, which would allow them the privacy they had longed for in deciding to locate a proper place to proudly call home.

The first task that Joshua would be required to perform as they arrived on the site would be to sink a well-point into the ground that would furnish them a sufficient supply of pure water to satisfy their needs for years to come. Joshua had carefully observed his grandfather successfully dowse for water as a young man in Oregon, and he was fully confident that he could duplicate the entire process. Dowsing for water had been fast becoming an extinct occupation in that part of the country. Josh was unable to locate the slippery elm trees that he needed to make the forked dowsing rod. He was forced to substitute a green forked branch of creek willow instead.

Being in close proximity to the Grays and Columbia Rivers would ensure that the water table would be well within the limits of his ability to drive the well-point into the life-giving underground stream of clear fresh water. He would use a block-and-tackle tied with a large rope to a high tree limb to make the pile driver, which would force the sections of pump pipe into the ground. Attached to the rope would be a heavy block of western hemlock, which would strike the pipe and force it deeper into the ground with each stroke. Joshua would use the pile driver to sink the premeasured, prethreaded, ten-foot sections of pump pipe until they were driven low enough to thread on another section of pipe with a pipe coupling, then repeat the process again. He would drive the well-point down to the start of the water table and then twelve feet or more beyond that point. He would know when the pipe had reached the beginning of the water table as it would sink very quickly into the ground without being struck with the block. After fitting the pitcher pump to the last section of pipe, he would then pump some forty or fifty gallons of water until it ran clear and clean, settling in a ten-quart bucket for at least fifteen minutes.

They would then begin with the construction of the log cabin, the barn, necessary outbuildings, a root cellar under the house, and a smokehouse to cure the meat and game that Joshua would hunt and fish. During this construction they would be forced to live in a lean-to and the wagon that would be used to travel from Oregon to Washington. When they completed their new home, they fully intended to reside there until their deaths.

After the cabin was built, Joshua would attempt to sell the pair of mules, as they would only be a liability by then. He didn't intend to do any farming, and he could use the extra cash to purchase the finishing touches to the cabin. As much as he disliked selling the animals, he had already come to the conclusion that it would be impossible for him to raise enough corn and hay to feed them, and as there were no roads in that area, he couldn't really depend on them for transportation. In fact, there were no towns that were reachable by road or trail within any area that could be traversed in less than a day by wagon, even if there had been some roads.

Josh knew that it would be necessary for him to either build or buy a boat of some sort so he could travel the only byways of that region—the Grays River and the Columbia River. These would be the only roads available to him for transportation to the towns to obtain supplies and other necessities. Of course, their very remoteness is what had originally made this property so appealing to them in the first place.

He had been warned by experienced boaters from the region before buying the land that boating on the huge Columbia could be considered dangerous at best and totally disastrous at worst. A trip on this river was worthy of considerable planning and study before attempting to make a lengthy journey on or across it. One minor mistake could spell complete disaster for all those who happened to be on board. Joshua had taken that sage advice seriously and would remember it well when he eventually chose to take a trip on that monstrous river.

He was somewhat experienced in handling small boats and canoes on many of the smaller lakes and rivers, but never had he attempted a journey such as the one that would be required on a dangerous waterway like the Columbia, which violently coursed its way toward the Pacific Ocean from that area. Native Americans, who had lived and prospered here for many centuries, were well acquainted with the peculiarities of that mighty river, which they both revered and respected.

Joshua had planned well in advance of the move to include the special items of significance that would be absolutely essential for their family in a very remote section of the wilderness on the land they would eventually call home. He had plenty of time available for him to study and plan the many important details included in the construction of the log cabin. He was driving a six-mule team and wagon, hauling huge timbers from the logging camps to the river, where they would be unloaded and floated downstream to the sawmill to convert them to lumber products to be used in the construction boom then in progress in Oregon. He had ample time, as he delivered the logs, to conceive and envision the processes required for the task ahead of them, storing many blueprints of the envisioned procedures in his mind.

The additional amount of time that he had available may have contributed to his final decision ultimately to make the move to secure the only parcel of land that was available to him in the uninhabited forest. Those dreams had been embedded in his mind since he was a young boy playing in the woods near Marshfield, the town later to become named Coos Bay, Oregon. He also had the full backing from his wife and son when discussing the probability of moving to that wild area. Angela and Jeremiah were equally as excited about the venture as he was.

Josh had many pleasant memories of delightful times when he was a youth growing up along the edge of the mountains where his mother and father resided. They had reared four boys to appreciate the elements of nature. It was fairly certain that his early lifestyle around the woodlands had greatly influenced his decision to spend the remainder of his days living the style of life that he loved.

He recalled one day as a youngster of ten or eleven years old, the excited feeling he felt when his father finally allowed him the privilege of taking the muzzle-loader rifle into the woods all alone. His father had previously told him that he was too young to be handling firearms, and besides, he would only be able to fire one shot since he was not able to reload the gun. His father told him he would be required to walk home with an empty gun, humiliated by the fact that his young friends and his brothers would find out about it and tease him.

He then thought about missing his intended target with his only shot. He didn't really care about reloading. He only wanted to get one shot at some wild animal. He wanted to be able to tell his friends that he had gone hunting with a real rifle, not a toy gun like they had been used to playing with.

He remembered that it had been winter and the weather was extremely cold. He bundled up with a heavy coat and warm clothes, set off for the outdoors and headed for a place where he figured there might be some big game. He wanted to find a big bear, an elk, or a deer. Maybe a wild boar. He slipped along very quietly, as he had seen his dad doing many times. He didn't want the animal to know that he was coming toward them with a real rifle. He wanted to sneak up on it and surprise it, whatever it was, and then shoot it.

He arrived at a huge, dead tree that had been blown to the ground by the wind two or three years earlier. As he slipped along quietly, the hair on the back of his neck stood up. The moisture from his heavy breathing blew white smoke out of his lungs and condensed in the cold air.

He was shaking in his boots now, and the below-zero temperature didn't even faze him. His hot face seemed to be on fire as his footsteps froze in place, unable to move. What he had seen halted him dead in his track, momentarily. He didn't want to make any sounds, yet he wondered how he would get himself into position at the tree to be able to fire the rifle. The animal that he had frighteningly observed in front of him appeared to be asleep, and he didn't want to make any unusual sounds that could possibly wake it up and allow it to perceive how frightened he was.

Lying against a log directly in front of him was the largest wolf he had ever had the pleasure of seeing. Well, the truth of the matter was that he had never even seen a wolf, but he knew that this one was big. It seemed to be motionless, but his knees and hands wouldn't stop shaking long enough for him to cock the hammer on the muzzle-loader rifle and get it ready to aim at his prey.

This bit of luck was precisely what he had been hoping for, yet he was wondering now how he might back away without waking it up. He then wondered if anyone might eventually find out about the cowardly act that he had actually been contemplating in his frightened, insensible mind.

He finally decided against that notion, since the wolf might see him retreating and might want to catch up to him. The more he studied the situation, the more nervous he became. He finally decided to try to shoot the wolf without waking him up.

He slowly and quietly knelt down behind the tree trunk and rested the barrel of the rifle on top of it. His hands were shaking so violently that he wasn't certain if he could take good aim at the wolf. He cocked the hammer, took aim, and slowly squeezed the trigger. The black smoke billowed so thick in front of his sight that he was unable to immediately ascertain if the lead ball had struck the wolf or not.

When the smoke cleared enough for him to see clearly, he felt sure that the bullet had found it's mark because the wolf had not budged an inch as far as he could tell. He was now certain that his dad would be extremely proud of him, but his knees were shaking worse than they had been before. He didn't really want to go over and punch the animal with his rifle barrel to see if it was dead. He suspected that the wolf might jump on him if it was not completely dead. He knew that it could still be quite dangerous if it was just wounded.

He eventually summoned enough nerve to walk confidently over near the log to punch the wolf in the side with the barrel of his muzzle loader. Nothing moved. He did it again, and still the wolf did not move. He then gave a huge push with the rifle against the body of the wolf and found that it was frozen stiff and as hard as a rock. Most likely it had been dead for several days.

He was so chagrined that he actually looked behind him to see if someone had been watching him. It was several years before he summoned up enough nerve to tell anyone about his first hunting experience.

Josh first heard about the plot of land in the forest being for sale from a teamster and fellow worker whose father owned over a thousand acres of timber land in Washington near the Columbia River. Josh's eyes got as big as half-dollars when he first heard about this distant retreat far back in the wooded hills on a dead-end trail that terminated at the water's edge of the Grays River.

He told Josh that the old trail had undoubtedly grown over and might not even be recognizable at that time since it had been many years ago that his father had acquired it from an older brother. Josh's heart started thumping wildly as he first heard the son describing the parcel of land that was commonly referred to as land's end.

That was the one thing in life that he had been earnestly praying for since his early youth, and he could scarcely wait to tell

Angela of the paradise on the river that he had learned about. He knew they were going to investigate the possibilities for acquiring this exciting-sounding parcel although he didn't allow the fellow to suspect how thrilled and excited he was to find out more about it. He was fully aware, though, that many things in life did not actually turn out as they first appeared. He anxiously hoped this would not be one of those times.

When Josh finally broke the news to Angela about the land, she was even more thrilled about the potential for that golden opportunity than Josh was. Angela's long bloodline of American Indian ancestry mixed with French Canadian forebears had most likely played a very important role in her being able to accept living the lifestyle such as the one they would be embarking upon. If only they could save the amount of money needed to strike a deal that would be acceptable to the land owner!

They both agreed that it was going to put a strain on their budget if they were to save the required payment for that parcel. They had also considered having enough money to make a trip there to inspect the property, since they felt highly uncertain about purchasing sixty-four acres sight unseen.

The next day Josh's colleague informed him that his father would be willing to sacrifice heavily on the distant plot of land to be rid of it. His father was getting old, and he would never have any occasion to use it. The son informed his dad that he, too, would never be interested in settling on it. So the old man decided that if a family would be willing to settle and live on it, he would be happy to make them a very good deal for the land. Josh had wanted to rush home to tell Angela about the good news, but he knew if he left before completing his workday hauling logs to the river he would be fired.

Josh and Angela had started saving their money seriously and skimping to get by on the barest of essentials, yet desiring to be somewhat comfortable. Skimping to get by was really nothing new to either of them, as they had accepted that as their normal lifestyle while children. They were both adept at squeezing a buffalo nickel until the animal bellowed. It wasn't much fun being poor children, but they were both thankful for having learned that very important lesson of stretching their dollars early in life. It didn't really seem to be a hassle to them because they were convinced in their own minds that the results would be well worth the inconvenience and discomfort of waiting for the eventual outcome. Being extremely frugal seemed to make both of them pleased with each other. Their happy and proud faces proved that fact.

Each Saturday night after supper they would get the heavy cookie jar down from the top of the pantry to count the money that had been saved. Angela was appointed treasurer and bookkeeper. She took her job seriously. It was a ritual of extreme importance to them. They enjoyed the observance of that celebrated occasion each week. It was a means of securing their hopes for the future. The role of performing that act of saving their money would be the manifestation of their magnificent dream. The heavy clay cookie jar containing gold coins, silver coins, and paper bills was getting much too heavy to be placed on top of the pantry. Angela would try to locate a safer hiding place for it. Josh told her he would see about getting some of the silver coins exchanged for paper money or even for lighter twenty-dollar gold coins. That would make it much easier for them to transport on the trip north.

It finally became necessary for them to make up their minds to proceed to acquire the parcel of land unseen because they were unable to make the trip to inspect the property and the owner had verbally promised them that he would refund their money if they decided they didn't like it or felt that he had misrepresented it. Angela told Joshua that she was absolutely certain that they would want to keep the land, and she felt that it would be satisfactory to buy without seeing it. She was afraid someone else might snatch it away from them before they had saved enough money to purchase it. Josh agreed with her that he already knew enough about the parcel to want to buy it, and he couldn't think of a thing that could make him change his mind.

Angela said, "Well, it's settled, then. We will tell the gentleman that we want the property and that we expect him to hold it for us until we can come up with the entire sum of money he is asking for it."

Their skimping and saving had finally paid off. They had not only saved enough money to buy the sixty-four acres but would have sufficient funds left over to purchase many of the needed materials for the construction of the cabin and other structures that they would require, as well as the fencing around their vegetable garden plot.

Josh knew that the hard work of hauling and lifting the logs during the construction of the log cabin would have to be accomplished with only the help of his trusted mules, plus Angela and Jeremiah. There were no neighbors living close enough to call on for help. Angela was so intent on getting her own cabin that she would work her fingers to the bone if necessary. She kept insisting to Josh that she would be able to do it. She was as excited as a schoolgirl who had just fallen for her first crush.

Jeremiah was then four years old and would be five when they finally started with the actual construction of their mansion in the woods. He was a brilliant kid and learned quickly. He would be much help to his father and mother. It would be necessary for him to be a fast learner because it would be up to his mother and father (mostly his mother) to do the school teaching, since there were no schools around that area for miles. Angela would bring many textbooks along with them when they moved. She would give him the best education that she knew how to teach. She would have made a wonderful schoolteacher in the public school system. She was level-headed but imposed the necessary discipline to maintain a wholesome classroom atmosphere that would require her only pupil to have an intense desire to want to learn. She was always patient, yet persevering. She had the ability as well as the knack for teaching.

Angela's father, Daniel Peterson, had met her mother, Rising Moon Benoit, a half-French and half–Yakima Indian girl at the trading post and general store near The Dalles. Rising Moon was a beautiful and well-proportioned girl who was used to doing heavy manual work almost as well as a man. She had helped her husband build a log cabin, as well as the trading post building, there on the Columbia River in Oregon.

Angela was the spitting image of her mother and just as beautiful. She had made up her mind and decided that if her own mother had been able to help build a log cabin, so could she.

Rising Moon had been born somewhere in the foothills of the Rocky Mountains in the southeastern corner of Washington, but her family had crossed the Columbia to settle in Oregon when they had become pressured to leave their homeland territory. Although they were forced to leave, that move across the Columbia to Oregon had served them well. Pierre Benoit had prospered significantly, building up the trading post clientele from the white men as well as the Indian traders. Pierre would have been considered to be an extremely shrewd businessman when it came to trading with the white men. His French ancestry had been passed down to him from a line of French-Canadian fur trappers, traders and suppliers of the wagon trains that were headed west for the gold fields of California, Alaska, and Canada. The majority of his customers were headed for some of the wild river tributaries of the Yukon River in Canada. He felt that it was highly unlikely that he would ever see any of them again. Most would end up broke. Many of them would die trying to reach their bonanza. A very few might strike it rich as they searched with great effort for the gold that was always somewhere just beyond the next bend in the river.

Angela had continued to call from the back porch for her son, but her voice was not as strong as it was before it started getting dark. She would rest for a short time and then resume calling out his name again to the dark forest. The gloomy forest had not yet responded to her pleas.

There were times when she would call with anger in her voice and at other times she would beckon him with an appealing, forgiving voice. She only wished for him to return safe to home. She would welcome him with open arms and a huge embrace. She now felt that she was no longer angry at him. Lord, if only he would just come on home to me, she thought, as she looked up toward the heavens and held her damp face in her hands.

# CHAPTER

## 2

The day had finally come when they would be moving to their new home. The wagon had been packed to the point where it would not hold another item. However, Angela's highly prized Red Mountain wood cookstove had not yet been loaded. She gave strict orders that the load would just have to be rearranged because she did not intend to leave her precious cookstove behind, even if it meant something else would be left instead.

Joshua and Angela's father had been attempting to explain to her that it would be impossible to make room for it on the wagon. It appeared certain that she was going to lose her greatly cherished, irreplaceable cookstove, but not without a fight. Her begging and pleading was in vain. She would be forced to resort to introducing some serious consequences that could occur should her precious cookstove be prevented from being loaded as cargo on the wagon.

She saw her father speaking with Joshua's father and mother, Noah and Ramona Langford, in the back yard near the barn. She approached them with tears in her eyes and, her teeth clenched, imploring them to do something that would prevent the loss of her stove. She fully convinced them that she would be unable to leave Oregon without it. She would sit on the porch until her stove was loaded.

They attempted to calm her and told her they would try to think of some way for it to be loaded on the wagon even if they had to leave something else behind. She wasn't in favor of that idea, either. She insisted that they tell her what it might be that they were contemplating on leaving behind.

They had packed bags, boxes, and trunks all afternoon. They had intended to be ready to leave early the next morning by sunrise. Brothers, sisters, cousins, aunts, uncles, and neighbors had come to wish them well and help them pack their belongings before their departure the next morning. Josh had wanted to leave by daybreak so as to have a lot of distance covered after traveling a full day, but Angela was adamant about not leaving at all until she could bring her stove along with her.

Noah and Ramona Langford came around the corner of the house, where Angela had Joshua's undivided attention with both hands wrapped tightly around his right arm. They informed Angela that Noah had finally figured out a way for them to carry her stove with them. The blank look on her face showed that she wondered what might have to be sacrificed. Noah then told Josh and Angela that they could have the two-wheeled cart that had been stored in the barn. He said it could be pulled behind the wagon, and he advised them that in all probability he would never need the use of it again.

He warned them that it would be necessary to grease the axle hubs before dark and to soak the wooden wheels with water. That would swell them sufficiently so that the iron tires wouldn't roll off the wooden rims. He said the mules should have no problem with the slight extra weight since the cart wheels would roll very easily.

Angela threw her arms around old Noah's neck and thanked him for figuring out a way to save her valuable stove. She was laughing now that her one monumental problem had been solved. She assured Josh that she would now be able to cook some fine meals when they got their cabin built. She was bursting with tears and laughter. She took Josh by the arm and gaily danced around the wagon with him.

All the ladies had repaired to the kitchen to commence preparing the supper meal while the men set to work restoring the ancient cart that had been donated to the cause. They would restore that piece of equipment almost to its original traveling condition for its final journey to the distant hills far away.

Angela couldn't thank Noah enough for contributing the cart to save her magnificent stove, He told her that it would have just lain there in the barn taking up space until it eventually dry-rotted to the point where it would be destroyed. He was actually thankful that some benefit could be derived from it. He had once thought about dumping it, as he considered that it would be useless to him.

Supper was ready. Friends and neighbors had furnished the chicken casserole, the ham, country fried potatoes, baked sweet potatoes, potato salad, relish, pickles, onions, cakes, pies, and many other items so the Langfords would have a banquet supper for a joyous remembrance prior to their exodus to the north woods. It was an elaborate feast to commemorate their departure.

They celebrated and reminisced until half-past ten, when it was decided that it was going to be a short night if the Langfords didn't get to bed soon. All of the guests finally trickled out and allowed them the luxury of some much-needed sleep in preparation for the lengthy, tiresome, and possibly troublesome trip ahead of them.

The previous few days had been hectic with all the paperwork that was required to close the sale. Much of the paperwork needed to be mailed to the Wahkiakurn County courthouse in Washington. It was necessary for the tax stamps to be mailed back to Scottsburt to be placed on the deed prior to filing it at the courthouse there. Angela didn't realize how much paperwork was involved in buying or selling a parcel of land. She was glad to see that portion of it over with.

They awoke the following morning to the arousing aroma of freshly ground coffee perking on the wood stove. Both sets of parents had already arrived in the kitchen when they entered. The ladies were preparing a delicious breakfast of smoked ham, fried eggs, biscuits, hand-churned butter, crabapple jelly, and coffee.

After a very satisfying breakfast and all of the melancholy good-byes were said and the hugging, hand shaking, back slapping, and praises were shared by all the family members and friends, Angela said, "Folks, we really need to be on our way. We love all of you and would love to visit longer with you but it's time for us to leave. You have all been so kind to us, and we do hate to leave, but we must go. Thank you for everything. If you ever happen to be near the Grays River, stop by and see us."

She hugged her mother one last time and stepped up on the wagon wheel to reach for Josh's hand to assist her in getting into the spring seat. The tears were welling up in her eyes as she smiled and said, "Good-bye, wonderful friends. Thank you for being so nice to us. We will never forget you."

Joshua flipped the reins on the backs of the mules and clicked his tongue. They were beginning a long journey toward a new horizon. The tears were flowing freely as she looked back to wave at her family and friends one last time before the wagon rolled out of sight. One final glance at the old home where she had been born and recalling the wonderful memories of her childhood had caused the tears to flow down her cheeks in rivulets, yet she was smiling and waving still as they moved out of sight of the wonderful old homeplace.

Jeremiah acted as though he was quite happy that all of the fuss had finally ended and that the hugging and kissing by his grandparents, aunts, uncles, and cousins had ended. Now he could have some peace and quiet again.

Angela asked him to lie down on some quilts to rest since he was up late the night before. He was sound asleep before they had traveled a mile. That was to be his only bed until they reached their final destination and built a cabin.

They were now beginning to observe some of the most beautiful country that Angela had ever witnessed as they traveled toward the north. They only stopped long enough to water the mules and allow themselves a few minutes to eat and drink from the huge quantity of foodstuff that had been left over from the feast from the night before. They each picked out a tree to hide behind to relieve themselves, and then Josh told them it was time to hit the trail again.

Things were going well so far, although this was only the first leg of their trip to paradise. Things could change, however, and often did. Josh was well aware of this eventuality, although he did not mention it to his family since he felt it might jinx them.

The sun was already beginning to hide behind the mountain peaks on the south side of the valley. Angela felt that it was impossible to be that late already. She guessed that it might possibly be mid-afternoon, so she asked Josh what time it was.

He took out his pocket watch, opened the dial cover, and told her, "It's a quarter to three, Angela."

He closed the cover, placed the watch in his overall bib, and continued on silently as though his mind was in deep concentration about something much more important.

Angela took note of the fact that he acted as though he was unconcerned about the time of day and may have had more important considerations on his mind at that time. She was aware of the fact that he didn't intentionally intend to be rude toward her, so she decided not to disturb him until he resumed a conversation with her.

She found it hard to believe that it was only mid-afternoon, yet the sun had disappeared behind the mountain toward the southwest. She could feel the chill in the air once her body had been deprived of the sunlight. Josh drove on another three or four miles, when all of a sudden the sun was shining brilliantly again. It felt good to sense the warmth of the sun's rays against their faces to dispel the chill in the air.

Angela hadn't really meant to initiate a conversation with Josh, but she forgot and remarked, "This country is certainly peculiar. A few moments ago it was beginning to get dark and now the sun is shining brightly. How odd."

Joshua answered, "Yes, it may be peculiar, but it certainly is beautiful country. I'd love to have a huge picture of this painted to hang on the wall of the living room when we get our cabin built."

Angela said, "It truly would make a beautiful picture if we could get an artist to paint it for us, but I'm sure we will be able to look out the living room window and see the most beautiful picture for real that we could ever imagine. Just think, we will have our own palace to survey the remainder of the world."

"I know we'll be happy there, Angela," Josh said. "I couldn't tell if you said place or palace. I thought you said palace," he told her.

"I did say palace, dear, and that's what I meant to say," she answered. "It truly is going to be our own palace, fit for a king, when we finally get it built."

Josh said, "Angela, this is going to be one trip that we can tell our grandchildren about. I can hardly wait to behold the majestic Columbia River. You won't believe your eyes when we start across it on the ferry. I just hope the mules don't get frightened when we load them aboard," he expressed a slight concern.

"They've been on a ferry boat before," he said to Angela as he was attempting to convince himself that this might credit them as having had experience.

He was actually speaking to himself, but loud enough for the others to hear when he said, "I'll just have to stand in front of them and hold their bridles as we start across at Westport. I think if I talk to them the whole time we're on the river it will soothe their nerves so they will barely notice we're on the ferry. I don't really have any doubts about their dependability," he stated in a low voice. "I trust them completely," he said.

He stated to his wife and son in a louder voice, "I am convinced that they will make the river crossing just fine."

Josh spotted a perfect spot to pull into up ahead. He decided they would prepare to spend the night there. Someone had obviously camped there before, as he witnessed the remains of a campfire and some flattened grass. Josh fed and watered the mules while Angela prepared their supper. They hardly knew which party-leftover goodies to sample first.

Josh rustled up some branches and small logs to build a fire. He found one large log that he painstakingly heaved on the pile of wood. It would probably burn most of the night, removing the chill of damp night air that would inevitably come after midnight. Josh told them that he couldn't swallow another bite of food and suggested they should get to bed early for a good night's rest, since the following day could possibly be harder than the one they had just finished. He assumed they were probably as tired as he was from traveling all day in a bouncing, steel-tired wagon.

Josh was the first to arise the next morning.

"It's five o'clock," he yelled. "Time to get up and hit the trail, again. Looks like a premium day for traveling," he told them as he started a small fire to make coffee. That was one necessity that Josh couldn't do without.

Josh wanted to check out the two-wheeled cart first. He needed to know if it was going to make that long haul successfully. It hadn't been used for years, and he had ample cause to wonder about it since this trip wasn't to be confused with a short pleasure trip to the trading post.

After careful examination he concluded that it was probably in just as good condition as the wagon; maybe even better. It was not necessary to pour any more water on the wooden wheels since they had run the wagon and cart through several small puddles of water the previous day.

After a breakfast of cold cakes and hot coffee, Josh completed getting the rest of the equipment prepared for travel, and he concluded that they were ready once more to set out on the epic journey.

Each succeeding day had gone as well or better than they had expected. Angela and Jeremiah were making it just fine and beginning to enjoy the trip. Jeremiah was taking to the wild outdoors like a duck takes to water. He seemed to have some of the qualities of a real mountain man. Much of his liking for the wilderness was probably inherited from his mother's side of the family. After all, he was partly an Indian, too.

The mules had performed magnificently thus far. They seemed to be enjoying the duties that they were volunteered to do. Joshua had nothing but praise for them as they dutifully pulled the wagon and cart without any problems.

During the early afternoon of the fourth day the ferry landing was in sight ahead of them near Westport. Josh told Angela and Jere to be alert because they were closing in on the Columbia River. After they had approached close enough for them to see it, Josh yelled, "What a spectacular sight! Angela, I never would have dreamed that the Columbia would be this huge and breathtaking. It's like seeing something unreal. I don't seem to be able to find the proper words to fully describe it."

After seeing the terribly awesome size of the river, he was beginning to wonder anew if his team of mules would make the trip across without raising a ruckus.

"Oh well," he said. "I suppose we'll just have to wait and see. I'll spend my time talking to them as we cross the river," he muttered to himself.

When the skipper of the ferry boat helped Josh load the mules and wagon aboard he instructed Josh to lead them to the bow against the chain and to stand there in front of them for the whole trip across the river. He also told Josh that he wanted him to talk to them constantly in a pleasant tone of voice to keep them calm the whole trip as they ferried the dangerous currents in the river. The skipper said he had witnessed many animals discard all signs of their distress when they had someone talking to them in a pleasing, confident voice. He predicted a safe crossing.

Josh was surprised to learn that there could be more than one destination that could be chosen when a person boarded on of their ferries. Some of them traversed the entire stretch of river, whereas others went to an island where it was possible to transfer to another boat and travel to another point on the opposite shore. Josh had previously told the captain their destination, so he loaded them aboard the ferry that would take them across the river in one sweep. Josh was relieved that he would not be required to reboard another ferry and transfer in the middle of the river. He didn't think the mules would like that. When they reached mid-river, they might think they were done for the day and would not have to board another ferry.

The entire ferry crossing was made without incident. Josh and Angela were happy to be on the trail again, although they still had a long trip ahead of them with only an obscure trail to follow. He was trusting that the directions he was given from the owner were reliable enough for him to follow without getting lost. He didn't tell his wife or son, but he reckoned that if they accidentally took the wrong trail, it might take two or three days for them to finally figure out where they were and then get back on the proper logging trail leading to their land.

Joshua's map showed that when he came to a fork in the logging road it would be necessary for him to take the right leg. He would proceed on that trail for three more miles until they saw a yellow piece of cloth tied high to a tree limb. That would indicate that he should continue straight and not take the left nor the right trails. That would then be the one that would lead them to the Grays River.

Another yellow flag tied high on a tree limb would indicate the starting boundary of their parcel, and it reached from there to the Grays River. The other boundaries had been marked with steel pipe stakes and piles of boulders denoting property lines and corners where it had been surveyed.

Angela spotted the first yellow flag, although it had been bleached out by sun and rain until it was almost white. She called out to Jeremiah that they had come home. Josh hoped that she would not be disappointed with what they were going to see for the very first time. She felt a certainty in her heart that their hopes would not be thwarted. She had faith in the old man who had sold them the property, and she trusted his word. Of course, they would not be able to do much of anything about it if it didn't meet their expectations. After all, they had bought the place sight unseen, but she figured that a man's word should be his bond. That's what her mother had always told her.

They would soon realize if they had been duped or if they had made an important purchase of sufficient worthiness. Their hearts were pumping harder as they closed the distance to their promised land. Jeremiah had made the trip in excellent shape and his eyelids were peeled while watching and waiting for the second yellow flag.

"There's the second flag," Angela yelled so loudly that it not only startled Joshua and Jeremiah but the mules as well. It was quite obvious that she was thoroughly elated at the sight of her new homestead there in the hilly wilderness. Joshua found it necessary to cut some tree saplings in the middle of the trail before they could proceed further. It was quite obvious that the logging trail had not been used for many years owing to the almost impassable condition it had been allowed to deteriorate to. He found it necessary to detour around some areas that had trees growing in the wagon route.

"We're coming home darling," she said as she kissed and hugged her husband. "I am so happy I could cry," she said as she smiled the most beautiful smile that Josh had noticed in several months.

"Well, it appears that it is exactly as the man told us it would be," Joshua said. He felt all along that it would be precisely so. He had no doubt that it would be anything except as the way it was described to him and Angela. His word of assurance had convinced both of them that this is what they had dreamed of, and they had felt no need to make an earlier trip to examine it.

Joshua guided the team of mules up to a clearing in the woods that appeared as if it had been purposely cleared and designated for the building of some structure, possibly a family dwelling. He stood up in the wagon and said, "This is it, Angela. We couldn't have picked a better place to build our log cabin. It is perfectly situated on a south slope, where it will take advantage of the full sun in the winter while warding off the cold north wind which will blow from the other side of the ridge."

Angela replied, "Dear, we couldn't have picked a better spot if we had ordered it out of a catalog, I am completely satisfied with it," she said to him, seeming to be more than satisfied with their new homeplace, if her smile was any indication.

"So am I," he replied to his beautiful, raven-haired wife.

Angela was smiling from ear to ear with happiness and pleasurable satisfaction as she surveyed the beautiful hillside before her eyes. Josh knew that she was as happy as a clam at high tide.

Joshua dismounted from the wagon and helped Angela to the ground. "I think it's the most desirable homesite that we could have ever hoped for, Josh," she beamed as she hopped down out of the wagon to inspect it better. After making a short tour of the site she informed him, "I don't think we could have found anything better if we had looked for years. It looks absolutely perfect to me. The general area around here makes me wonder if someone had planned to build a cabin in this exact location," she expressed an observation to her husband.

Jeremiah had already jumped out and headed straight for the river bank. Josh placed his hands on his hips, looked down toward the water in the Grays River and said, "Angela, this is the place we have been waiting all our lives for. I can truthfully say that I am completely happy with the deal that we made with the owner."

"It couldn't have been any more perfect," she agreed.

It was an easy decision to make about the location of their cabin, but the more serious and extremely tedious work would soon be beginning. They had known and accepted that it would not be easy, but it would be fun planning the dream home that would last them the remainder of their lives. They finally realized the tremendous magnitude of the situation—they had finally discovered the perfect place to fulfill the dreams they had both envisioned since that lucky day when Josh took Angela for his lifetime wedded partner.

Angela walked up to where he was standing, wrapped her thin arms around his neck, kissed him, and said, "Dear, I want to thank you so much for presenting me with this wonderful present. You've made me extremely happy, ," she told him.

# CHAPTER
## 3

They had begun construction on the cabin. Day after day, they continued to cut, haul, trim, fit, trim again, adjust a bit here and a bit there, and then start all over again with another log. It seemed to be advancing at a snail's pace, yet when they stood back and observed the results of only two weeks' work, they were amazed to recognize the definite appearance of a log cabin taking shape. They were pleased that it had progressed that well, although they knew it was still a long way from being completed.

The blisters on their hands, sore muscles, and tired backs were beginning to be a bit bothersome, but their ambitions to witness the fulfillment of their achievements and their eager desire to own their personal mansion kept them in an optimistic mood that would not pass. They ran cold water over their blisters; rubbed and massaged their sore backs, necks, and arms; and gave each other words of encouragement as they ended each day by telling one another how much they loved each other and their son. Each morning as they awoke, they vowed their love and gave thanks to the Lord for another beautiful day to build their log cabin.

Josh told Angela that he was also thankful that he had a fine set of mules to haul the logs from the place where he had cut them down to the cabin site where they would be assembled into the cabin structure. He told her he could never have completed the cabin or barn without them. The mules actually seemed to enjoy the job of pulling the logs.

After six weeks their log cabin was mostly complete. They all breathed a sigh of relief and ran some more cold water over their blisters. Angela was continually thanking Josh for building her such a beautiful log cabin out there in the woods.

Josh answered, "You're welcome, dear. I'm just as happy as you are about our land. Three years ago I would never have believed that we would one day be moving into our own log cabin far off here in the wilderness," he told her.

He gave her a big hug and kiss. Jeremiah always turned his head away from them and told them that he couldn't understand why grown-ups acted like that.

They had finally succeeded in building a functional, four-room cabin, complete with fieldstone fireplace and a small barn to store things in and dry the garden produce, such as peanuts, beans, and the like. He had also dug a root cellar under the cabin and added a smokehouse for curing the meat and fish they would catch.

He left the two upstairs rooms unfinished until he would have enough money to be able to complete them. He felt that he would be able to finish them to a livable state within a year or two, when and if the family increased in size to the point where they would need the additional space.

Angela was extremely proud of her fieldstone fireplace. She had once thought that only rich people would be able to afford a genuine fieldstone fireplace, but she was proven to be wrong. And then, maybe it could be said that she was rich.

He had built a bear-proof log smokehouse that was strong and sturdy. He would use it to smoke deer, elk, salmon, beaver, and any other types of game that he killed while hunting and fishing. He might kill a bear in the winter, but all of that meat would be cooked up as fresh or frozen meat before the weather got warm. The bear meat would be good frozen during the midwinter months, hung on the barn rafters with wire. That be their only means of refrigerating meats. Bear meat just did not accept curing and smoking very well. It was much better when eaten fresh or after it had been frozen. Many of the other meats and fish would stay good for several months without refrigeration after it had been smoked and fully salt cured.

Angela had not been overly fond of smoked salmon when she had first tried it, but had since developed a liking for it. She had then gotten to the point where she actually anticipated the flavor of the gourmet type of smoked and dried salmon. She had even gotten to the point where she enjoyed another delicacy that she had once totally ignored—salmon roe, the American Indian substitute for sturgeon caviar.

She had also mastered the technique of substituting and adjusting the many Indian recipes, she had acquired from her mother, for preparing much of the wild game that had been harvested out of the wilderness by her dad in Oregon. Many of her dishes had turned out to be delicious culinary treats for Josh and Jere as she adjusted the game recipes to her and their liking, making them even better than when her mother had prepared them years ago for her family.

Josh told her that if he had to eat the same fare all the time, it would get boring. That was precisely what made it necessary for Angela to start making variations and to commence to be more innovative in her ability to correct and adjust recipes that had been possibly handed down to her from her grandmother. In planning the variety of meals that were available to them, Angela not only pleased the men, but herself as well. She actually enjoyed cooking for them when it became quite evident that her time spent in the kitchen was favorably appreciated by her husband and son as they continued to devour her magnificent meals. This ensured that the effort of her labor was made worthwhile, giving her ample incentive to continue serving gourmet meals that would test her ability as a master chef.

An occasional visitor might turn up at the cabin to require food, as they so often did when Josh was a lad living in Oregon. His mother had never turned away anyone who was hungry, and they always had room for one more person to sleep in the barn out of the cold, damp weather. He would make certain that he and Angela would continue this tradition for unfortunates who might get lost or possibly just be down on their luck.

The log cabin had been completed, the outside structures that were mandatory for a home in the backwoods were now in place. It was early November 1921. Just in time for the Thanksgiving feast in their new home. They did celebrate and gave thanks for all of the bountiful blessings that the Lord had bestowed on their family during the past months in that mountain wilderness land of their dreams.

A man who lived five or six miles to the west of them had heard a hammering noise one day when the wind was blowing from the southeast and decided to trek over the hills to inquire as to who it was that was making all of the unusual noises.

After admiring the handiwork that Josh, Angela, and Jere had accomplished on the construction of the log cabin, he noticed the pair of mules in the barnlot. He inquired if Josh might be interested in selling them since he could use one more pair of mules in his operation if he were able to find a team for the right price.

Josh didn't have to think about that proposition very long as he had wondered how he was going to feed them through the winter. It was already beginning to get cold, and the available grazing pasture was just about gone. He didn't have any hay or corn, so he decided to make the man an offer he wouldn't be able to refuse.

Josh put a price of twenty dollars a head on the pair, and before he could clear his throat the man had placed a pair of twenty-dollar gold coins in his hand and said, "Sir, you have yourself a deal. That's a mighty fine-lookin' team o' mules you have there, and I'll just be willin' to take 'em off your hands for that price. Oh, I forgot to ask you, mister. Are their harnesses included in that price?" he asked.

"Absolutely," Josh told him. "The bridles, the sets of harness including the reins, trace chains, and collars. If you can't take the harnesses with you now, you can come back any time and pick them up."

"My name is Roger Nielson, and I live just west of here about five or six miles," he told Josh. "Me and my wife and our six-year-old daughter, Kate, have lived there for nigh on four years. I occasionally do some log hauling for a timber company located about ten miles further north of my spread."

Josh said, "My name is Joshua Langford, and I live here with my wife, Angela, and my son, Jeremiah. You folks come to visit us sometime. I'm certainly glad to know that I have a neighbor in fairly close proximity here," he said. "If you ever should need us for anything, please let us know."

"Thanks, I will," he told Josh. "Likewise, if you should ever have need of me or my missus to help you with something, please let us know."

He told Josh he would come back in a week or ten days to pick up the rest of the equipment. He was so happy to get the team that he had them bridled and was on his way by the time Josh realized that he had just taken care of his winter feeding problem. Josh could hear the man whistling a tune over the next two ridges as he rode one mule and led the other.

Like Angela, Josh was trying to think about other things in order to keep his mind from the fact that their young son was somewhere out there in the dark woods alone—maybe lost or possibly even injured.

Jere had been going into the woods by himself for many months, and though it was against his mother's wishes for him to traipse through the wilderness alone, Joshua felt that Jere actually had enough prudent forethought for him to play sensibly in the forest. He really did enjoy going on the journeys and outings so much that Joshua didn't wish to prevent him from exploring the woods. He felt that it was probably good for him.

He had become acclimated to the woodland and forests. He felt as though it was his second home. He had some unusual stories to tell to his mother sometimes, and she didn't quite know whether to believe them. She felt that his stories must be true because she had never caught him in a lie. He promised her that he would always tell the truth.

"Josh, it's getting dark and our son is not home yet," she told him in a sad voice that fully expressed her grief.

"Let's give him a little more time, dear. Let's try not worry about him for the time being," Josh tried to set her mind more at ease. "I'm sure he'll be coming home almost any minute now."

Angela was having some serious doubts and misgivings about her son being all alone out there in the forest at night. She felt that he may have had the misfortune to unexpectedly encounter something sinister during his expedition. She was getting to be more genuinely concerned now because of some of the wild stories that Jeremiah had been telling her lately about several strange creatures that he had encountered and some he had actually made friends with.

At one time she had seriously questioned the authenticity of one of the stories he had related to her, but he had assured her that it was an honest-to-goodness truthful story and he would swear by it on a stack of Bibles. Angela allowed their conversation to stop there, and told him she believed him, although she was not sure that some portion of it could not have come from a very powerful imagination.

"Joshua, I'm beginning to get terribly worried about Jere," she said again. "He has never stayed out this late before. Suppose you go out and try to find him; he might need some help," she begged.

Josh didn't answer right away. He was stalling for time because he felt the boy was just running late and would be home shortly.

"Lord only knows what kind of trouble he may have come up against out there in the dark. Please go and try to find him, Josh. Please," Angela pleaded with him. She was attempting to fight back the tears that were now welling up in her eyes, but it was no use. She was straining to be very brave and reasonable.

"I realize the boy is only seven years old, Angela, but he has been traveling all over those woods out there for nearly two years," Josh answered, trying to appease and comfort her. That only caused her to cry harder.

"To tell you the truth, hon, I'm not really worried about Jeremiah," he said to her rather calmly and convincingly. "I don't know why but this is one of the few times that he has taken Old Blue with him, and I'm sure thankful that he did," Josh told her in a calm and steady voice.

That bit was actually meant to relieve some of the anxiety from Angela's mind, because Josh knew full well that if a bear was bent on harming Jeremiah, then his dog would just fight to his death to try to protect the boy, but it would be in vain. An angry bear would then just turn on the boy after he had finished with the dog. He felt that it might possibly give Jeremiah time to get away, but he also knew that Jere would never abandon his dog. Anyway, his purpose for telling Angela about Old Blue had succeeded and that had caused her to brighten up some after Josh told her about the dog.

Angela was still dissatisfied with the obvious answer that Josh had given her about going out to find their son. Her son. She was reluctantly agreeable about going into the woods to look for Jere and she was somewhat willing to relent to his sage advice for the time being.

Josh was again attempting to console his distressed wife. He told her, "Angela, if he's not home by nine o'clock, I'll go out behind the house and start firing my shotgun every twenty minutes in order to give him a direction of sound to home in on and follow it to safety. I wouldn't have any idea where to start looking for him, anyway. He could already be home by the time I made it back two miles into the woods and I would never know it. It's just not a good idea," he stated rather firmly to his now distraught wife, who was wringing her hands.

"Oh, all right, Josh, I suppose you know best," she finally conceded to him and consented to the proposal that he had just put to her.

She knew, of course, that her husband was equally as concerned about the safety of their son as she was, but it was also her contention that he probably didn't intend to reveal his anxieties in her presence. Likewise, when his son returned home, he would probably decline to reveal his concerns in his presence. She was of the opinion that Josh would act as though he were convinced all along that Jere would be home as soon as he had completed doing whatever it was that was so important. But then, it could be that he did actually feel that way since Jere had been tutored and schooled in much the same manner that Josh's own father had schooled him and his brothers in the ways of life in the woods and mountain wilderness.

Jeremiah was a fast learner. He had studied hard and learned well the lessons that he had been taught because he was intensely interested in receiving a valuable education. He wanted to learn about the earth and its secrets, and no institution of higher learning could ever hope to match what his parents knew. Feelings of intuition, correct evaluation of indistinct signs, and a sharp eye for the smallest indication are things that the schools would never be able to teach a student. This is what Jeremiah was learning in the outdoor classroom of nature's wild grapevine league university.

If any one of them would have been considered to have already received the total value of the purchase price that was paid for the parcel of land, it would certainly have to be Jeremiah. He had already received more joy and satisfaction from the numerous jaunts through the back door to the woods for many countless surprises, delightful memories of unusual contacts, and communications with his secret pals and creatures than he had ever expected. He had already considered this section of the forest a paradise for him. He had already partially admitted to his mother that his ultimate desire in life was to be a real mountain man.

The Native Americans had lived off that land and those rivers for countless centuries and had enjoyed many privileges of fishing, hunting, farming, and trapping in order to sustain their way of life and clothe and feed themselves. This was their utopia, and they thought it would last as long as the sun would rise in the east. It might have, too, if the white men had not migrated there to spoil it for them.

Josh had an intense desire to duplicate the living standards and conditions of the Native Americans, who had enjoyed the privileges of sustaining themselves by living off the very plot of ground that he had recently bargained for. He had a warranty deed stating that he owned the land now, as well as a bill of sale duly signed and notarized. Yet in his own mind, he knew that his property, its game, and wildlife actually belonged to the Indians in spite of the documents that he held in his possession. He wanted to fish the rivers and hunt the woods for enough food to feed his family and to trap enough fur-bearing animals for their pelts to enable him to purchase other necessities for them to sustain a normal livelihood there in the wilderness. He had wanted to live that type of life since he was a young lad growing up in the woodlands of the Oregon countryside, and now it was finally his to enjoy. It had finally become a reality as he had dreamed and prayed for.

Joshua had no doubts whatsoever that his family would survive and prosper in that environment. He recalled the story in the Bible about God telling Moses to take his people from Israel and to depart and go into the wilderness. God told him that He would furnish them whatever was necessary for them to survive in order to sustain Moses and the Israelites. They had nothing when they went into the wilderness except their faith, yet they survived for forty years in the desert because God gave them their water and the manna from heaven.

Josh's mother took the responsibility for the moral and religious teachings that he and his brothers had been blessed with. Josh had been taught that if he had a strong enough faith in something he desired that he would be able to succeed in whatever virtuous endeavor he might choose to select, and he believed it. As Joshua's mother had taught them about moral objectives and religious beliefs, she also nurtured them in a profound interest in the arts, literature, mathematics, music, and history. His father had taught them the essential and fundamental skills of discipline, hard work, and achievement of success in life as well as detailing for them also the pleasures and joys of life and setting attainable goals for achieving them.

He and his brothers were grateful that their bodies and minds had been properly tuned to the condition where they could successfully achieve the energetic goals they had set. They actually felt that there was no feasible task too great for them to accomplish should they put their minds together and cooperate with one another on the task at hand.

Some of their neighbors had felt that their father may have been too harsh on the boys as they were growing up, but they had always loved him for offering them challenges that they could be proud of. They did their utmost to meet Old Noah's standards. If he had set goals for them that were easily attainable, it might have destroyed their desire to attempt to succeed beyond their expectations. An important step in the ladder of life is to reach high enough so that you will not be considered an underachiever by your peers.

# CHAPTER
## 4

It was getting dark enough in the kitchen for Joshua to decide to light the kerosene lamp as he and Angela sat on the wooden bench of a picnic-style homemade dining table that had a bench attached to either side. He had just tossed a small lighted splinter of wood into the stove after he used it to light the kerosene lamp when they both heard the sounds of someone stepping onto the back porch. Josh remained sitting, but Angela couldn't keep from running to the back door hoping to see that it was her precious son who had finally come home after scaring his mother out of her wits.

"Well, it's about time you finally decided to come home, young man; we were beginning to get worried about you," Angela spoke reproachfully after she had determined that nothing appeared to be wrong with him. She had been both angry and genuinely thankful when she heard his footsteps on the back porch. She didn't know whether to spank him or to put her arms around his neck and lovingly hug him.

"Hi Mom, hi Dad. Got anything to eat?" Jere asked more or less nonchalantly with an air of pomposity in his voice that defied censure from his mother. "I sure am hungry," he stated flatly. "I'll bet Old Blue is beginning to get mighty hungry, too," he hinted. "We sure have traveled a long way in the woods this afternoon," he said matter-of-factly as he flashed a winning smile to his parents that immediately melted his mother's heart to the point where she had already decided to forgo any censure she had pondered.

Josh still hadn't moved from his seat on the picnic bench and hadn't uttered a word.

Angela thought silently to herself, "Now, how could anyone be angry at a darling little boy like my sweet son? His smile would melt anyone's heart." The uptight feeling of rigidity and nervous tension had already left her. She was now relaxed and amiable. She was her old self again, and she felt appreciably better.

"Well, yes son," his mother replied to his question. "I have a pot of venison stew that has been warming on the stove for over an hour," she told him. "We haven't eaten our supper yet, so if you will go wash your hands and face I will set the table for us," she said to him. "I baked some homemade bread this afternoon. It should go very well with the stew and hoop cheese," she told them in a pleasant manner. She had brought up the hoop cheese from the root cellar where it was stored to keep it cool. She sliced off a hefty slab from the hoop and cut it into quarters with her butcher knife.

"I saved some scraps from the dinner table at noon for you to feed Old Blue," she said to Jere. "I'm sure he will enjoy his meal."

"Thanks, Mom," he replied. "I know he'll enjoy them."

Joshua finally spoke. "Did you have a good time this afternoon, son?" he wanted to know, but really he had spoken just to engage in a conversation with his son. He was really interested in finding out what the boy had been doing out in the wilderness all afternoon and why he had been so late coming home. Josh felt that his smug and complacent demeanor held some secret that he seemed reluctant to share with his family. He appeared normal, as if everything was all right with him. He seemed to be unshaken and to not be disturbed about anything, and he also seemed to be in fine spirits, as far as Josh could tell.

"Yes sir, I had a great time this afternoon," he replied to his dad. "I went back farther into the woods today than I ever had before, and I saw a lot of new wild country back there," he stated simply but enthusiastically. "I even found a cave back there, and I went part of the way in but got kinda scared and came on out," he admitted to his dad.

"I never did get to see White Spirit though," he told his dad. "I suppose she must have been in another section of the woods today," he said as though his mom and dad knew exactly what he was talking about. "It's just as well, though, because she probably would have been afraid of Old Blue. Well, really, Old Blue might have been afraid of her, also," he added.

Angela was showing an interest in the direction their conversation had taken.

"Do you get to see White Spirit very often?" she wanted to know.

"Oh yes," he said. "I've actually seen her quite a bit lately. She's much friendlier toward me than she used to be," he explained. "I think she's gettin' used to me. She stands with her tail up in the air instead of letting it hang down like she used to do when I first got to know her. She lets me get pretty close now. Of course, that's when I don't have Old Blue with me," he clarified.

"Of course," his mother replied. "Well, how did you come to get to know her and how did you come to name her White Spirit?" Angela asked.

"Well—I didn't really name her," he answered. "I had always called her a 'him' until Big Thunder told me that she was a female. I had always called her the Ghost when I would see her running around in the woods. I tried to be friendly, but she wouldn't let me come close to her. I kept calling out, 'Ghost come here,' but she wouldn't come close to me. After several encounters with her she finally allowed me to get within a few feet of her but still wouldn't let me touch her," he told them.

Angela and Josh were all ears listening to the unbelievable tale that their son was telling them. They hadn't yet figured out if he was telling the truth or not.

"Big Thunder told me that she was just like a vapor and could disappear in a matter of seconds if she wanted to," he told them. "He said that she just appeared to be real," Jeremiah explained to his mother and father.

They had all become so engrossed with Jeremiah's story that they had forgotten about being hungry. This story of encounters with White Spirit had their undivided attention and completely occupied their minds for the time being. Angela felt that those stories were too intriguing to be completely true and attributed part of it to the boy's vivid imagination. She wanted to believe in him completely, yet she felt it highly unlikely that he could actually become friends with a wild wolf.

"Let's eat our stew, son," Angela said. "You can finish telling us about your friends of the forest after supper. I'll cut some bread.

I'm kinda hungry myself," she admitted. "Are you still hungry?" she asked.

"I'm starved, Mama," he answered. "I can't wait to dig into that venison stew and homemade bread."

The look of anticipation on his face indicated that he really was a hungry lad. He hadn't eaten for about seven hours. The gusto with which he approached his bowl of stew was ample proof of his mother's ability to serve up a wholesome as well as delicious meal to a family worthy of grateful appreciation.

"Mama, those are true stories that I have been telling you and Dad," he stated very seriously after he had partially satisfied some of his hunger pangs. "I would not tell you a lie, Mama," he vouched. "Honest, I wouldn't," he sincerely said.

"Big Thunder told me that the white wolf was only an apparition," he continued. "I asked him what he meant and he said she was not real; that what we were seeing was only a phantom. He explained that she was a spirit from one of his ancestors who had come back to check on him to see if he was all right," Jere told them.

"Finish your stew, son," she said softly. "You can finish telling about your friends as I'm washing the dishes. I'm sure your father will want to hear all about your experiences in the woodland, won't you, Dad?" she asked Josh. "Have a slice of cheese to go with your bread," she said as she served each of them a slice.

"Son, I will always be interested in hearing you tell about your friends," Joshua confirmed what Angela had just said. "From what you have told us, it sounds as though you had an wonderful time in the woods this afternoon. Several afternoons, in fact," he added.

Jere was still so excited about the happenings that afternoon that he was gulping down the last of his stew and had to be reminded to eat slowly. He apologized and said he would try to remember. He was sitting on the edge of his chair and was wound up tight. He had told them many times before of his enjoyment from roaming the woods behind the cabin, but he had never been so emotionally intoxicated as he was that night. His euphoric exhilaration was beyond anything his mother had ever observed from him before, but she still had a question in the back of her mind about the absolute authenticity of the tales that he had told them. She realized that some boys were prone to making up weird stories in their own minds. They were not really worried about the condition of his mind, as they knew that he was a very brilliant young student and an excellent learner in all subjects. He had never shown any tendencies before of wanting to exaggerate.

When Jere had first stepped in the kitchen door that night he appeared to act as if it was just like any other afternoon, similar to many that he had spent in the woods, with nothing much happening that would stir his emotions, but as he started eating he began to exhibit an intense excitement that he had not shown prior and that he was unable to restrain. In fact, he was unable to contain the desire to share with his mom or dad the exciting and unexpected occurrences and fortunate encounters that had evidently taken place that very afternoon. He wanted so much to share that compelling information that he had stored in the recesses of his brain. He wanted to be able to distribute that information to some interested listeners who would not make a joke of his conversations about his outings in the woods. He wanted to be sure of being taken seriously. Otherwise he might not tell everything that they wanted him to tell or that he actually knew.

Josh recognized that and attempted to demonstrate an intense interest in the things that Jere wanted to tell him and his mother. He certainly did not want the boy to clam up and keep this highly significant information bottled up inside. Josh could sense that Jeremiah could scarcely contain his distress until the time when he could relate that sensational information about his experiences of the day.

Jere had no male friends of his age in that area that he could share stories with and confide in. They had no close neighbors, so it would be up to Josh to be not only a father to Jere but also his best friend, if he were to mature properly. He felt that it was most important to keep the meaningful lines of communication open between father and son.

After supper Josh and Jere moved into the living room to sit on the sofa. Angela brought Josh a cup of coffee, dumped the remainder out of the pot, and began to wash the supper dishes.

Josh hadn't said much to his son except maybe to talk about the weather. He was giving him ample time to think about where he wanted to start with the events of the afternoon, and Jere seemed not to know exactly where to begin. He had so many important things to relay to his father. He wished he could tell all of them at one time. He had a hard time trying to figure out what was most important.

"Dad, have you ever been close friends with any Indians?" he asked his father, finally starting the conversation.

"Well, yes son," he answered. "I have known several Indians in my lifetime. In fact, I suppose the one I have come to know best is your mother. She has one-quarter Indian blood flowing in her veins. I think I know her pretty well," his father answered. "Her mother, Rising Moon, is half-French and half-Indian," Josh said.

"Aw, dad," he said. "I mean real Indians, like—well, you know. I don't mean the ones like my mom. I mean a real Indian that lives in the forest, hunts wild game, fishes for salmon, and lives completely off the land," Jere explained more fully to his father. "Do you know what I'm talking about?" he asked.

"Okay, I understand what you mean, Jere," he answered. "Yes, when I was a lad in Oregon there was an old Indian who lived far back in the woods. We didn't know exactly how far. We would see him occasionally," Josh continued with his story.

"He was always very friendly and liked to say hello to us. If we had the time to talk he would tell us stories of the mountains and about his life as a small boy when there were no roads, no logging trails or other man-made pathways through the wilderness and backwoods," he told his son.

"He told us that the only trails through the woods that one might follow would be the ones made by wild animals on their way to feeding grounds or places to water or else the ones made by Indians that were traveled as they rode their horses through the woods," he related to Jere.

"We really enjoyed talking to him, but we seldom had time to engage in a long conversation," Josh continued. "Some of the wild stories he told us about many of the Indians were pretty far fetched," he said. "That's not meant to infer that your mother is not a real Indian," he explained, "She certainly has Indian ancestors that can be traced back for many generations, maybe even centuries. She is a real Indian, that's for certain. Why are you asking me, son? Is there some compelling reason why you are asking me this?" he wanted to know.

"Well, Dad," Jere slowly picked up the conversation. "You see, I have this old Indian friend who is a very old man with a reddish-brown, wrinkled face. I sometimes see him when I go out there in the woods. We have a great time talking to one another, and we really enjoy one another's company. Dad, I really do like him very much. He's a friend of mine even though his face looks like leather and he's a lot older than I am," he reluctantly told his father. "He likes me just as much as I like him, too," Jere told his dad.

"I see," Josh said, and it was obvious that he was in deep thought. "So you two really hit it off, in other words?" he asked. "And you two really have a swell time together when you are out in the woods and you enjoy having a conversation with one another, and you like having him for a good friend? Right?" Josh asked his son.

"Dad, we are not only just friends, we are great friends, and we trust each other like I've never trusted anyone in my life," he confided to his father. "It's like we understand one another completely. We just—we just—well, it seems like he is the best friend I would ever want to have in the whole world," Jere confessed. "It just seems like we have known each other for hundreds of years," he explained.

Jeremiah didn't want his dad to think that he had allowed someone else to take his place as the greatest friend that ever was, but he wanted his dad to understand that Big Thunder was really someone special to him and he felt at ease talking with him about the secrets of the forests and rivers. He intended to convey information to his dad that Big Thunder was a fascinating man who evidently loved to share his stories and tales of the Northwestern territory before statehood with his newfound friend and that the feeling was definitely mutual.

Angela was deliberately washing the dishes very slowly and quietly in order to grasp every word as they were engaged in a serious though quiet conversation in the living room just a few feet away from her in the kitchen.

She wasn't about to interfere in their private conversation. They talked as though they felt they were alone, although they knew that she was washing dishes just a few feet away. They must have thought that she would be fully occupied and wouldn't pay them any attention, but she had latched onto every word that had been said between them.

Josh said, "I can understand your feelings for this old man, and I don't fault you one bit for liking him and having him for a trusted friend. Your mother and I would like very much to have him for our friend, also. We would love to have you bring him home with you sometime to have supper with us and allow us get fully acquainted with him," Josh told him. "I'm certain we would like him, also.

"Suppose you invite him home with you some afternoon when you run across him again. Ask him to come and have supper with us," Josh suggested. "I feel sure that he would enjoy having a home-cooked meal occasionally. It's almost a certainty that anyone would soon grow tired of eating roots and wild vegetables all the time. Anyway, I'm sure that he would be pleased to meet me and your mother since he likes you so well," Joshua surmised, as he pleaded with his son to allow them to meet his friend.

"I'll try, Dad," he promised. "But I don't think he will want to come here. I invited him to come home with me once and he said he'd rather not become close to someone again. He left his family to go to the woods to live out his final days so as not to be a burden on his daughter. He just roams the woods, living off the land. Since he doesn't have a home he just stops wherever he happens to be when it gets dark," Jere explained.

Jere was in a talking mood. The longer he talked, the more interested he became in telling his dad the information that he had so desperately desired to share with him.

"Big Thunder told me that he would continue to live there in the woods until it was time to leave this earth and go to his home up yonder. He has a daughter and son-in-law living some miles back across a lake somewhere. He admitted that his daughter would probably like to see him, but it seems that he is too proud to place a burden on her in his final days, as he would become unable to care for himself," he told his dad.

Josh kept nodding his head as he listened intently to his son's narration about his old Indian friend in the forest.

"Jere, it's going to be too cold in a couple of months for a man to survive out there in the damp woods," he said. "It would be no bother at all to allow him to come here and sleep in the barn at night," Josh said as he tried to convince his son to make a forceful appeal to the old Indian to come and stay with them at least temporarily.

"Tell you what," Josh said. "Why don't you ask him to come and see me so we can talk it over? Maybe I can convince him to come and sleep in the barn. After he meets us he may like us well enough to want to stay. Tell him that I look forward to talking to him about my younger days in the wilderness of Oregon. That might get him interested enough to want to come and talk to me and your mother," he said to Jere.

"All right, Dad. I'll try," Jere promised. "I'll see if I can talk him into it, but I can almost guarantee you that he won't accept any charity from you or from anyone," he stated emphatically to his dad.

"Son, try to convince him that there is no earthly need for him to have to suffer out there in the cold, damp woods this winter when he could stay comfortable in a dry barn here with us," Josh said.

"Try to convince him also that having someone to talk to would be far better than the loneliness of that solitary isolation in the woods," he added further. "Tell him that we have extra blankets that he can use to cover up with on snowy and icy nights and the barn will certainly be good and dry," Josh implored him.

"I will, Dad," he answered.

Jere didn't think he was quite ready just yet to tell his mother and father about performing the ritual that made him a blood brother with Big Thunder. He wasn't certain they would understand. He knew it was wrong to keep it from them, but he was just doubtful that it would be in anyone's best interests to divulge that information. The old Indian man was his closest friend in the whole world, and he didn't want to say or do anything that could increase their chances of being separated.

When his mother had asked him how he had cut his hand, he admitted to her that he had cut it with his knife. That was the truth, although it was not the whole truth. He didn't relate the rest of the story, and he wasn't sure if that would be considered a lie or not. He wasn't going to try to figure out the finer points of that issue. It would have to suffice for now that his secret should remain between him and his blood brother.

Angela enjoyed listening to the men having such serious talk, just as two grownups would do. She sometimes felt that her son was already grown, the way he acted. She knew that he felt he was almost on the same level as the grown people, also.

Angela had plucked each word of the conversation out of the air as it was being spoken in the adjacent room. She caught herself leaning her ear toward the living room when their voices were lowered. She couldn't keep from smiling at some points; at other times a small frown would form on her face. She did thoroughly enjoy listening to her special men carry on with an enlightening and interesting dialogue as she stealthily eavesdropped on them from the protective security of her kitchen.

Their conversation had just about come to a standstill, so Angela entered the living room and announced, "All right fellows, it's time to go to bed. It's been a long day for all of us. When you two get up in the morning I want you to pump enough water to fill the cast-iron wash kettle in the back yard and then build a hot fire under it," she commanded. "I will also need two number-three wash tubs filled with water," she continued with her orders. "I'm going to wash clothes tomorrow, so throw all of your dirty clothes and underwear on the kitchen floor near the back door and get you some clean duds to wear in the morning. Get a good night's sleep 'cause we're going to be busy tomorrow," she directed.

After they had gone to bed and were certain Jere was asleep, Angela asked Josh why he had not questioned the truth of some of the stories the boy had told. Josh told her he had no right to insinuate to Jere that his stories were anything other than true. He assured her that they would be much better off to listen with great interest to what he wished to tell them and take a positive attitude about his outings in the forest. To do otherwise would jeopardize forcing him to remain completely silent. Josh explained to his wife that it was absolutely imperative that they keep strong lines of communication open between them and Jeremiah, if at all possible.

Josh said, "Angela, I believe the story of the old Indian man. There is no way possible that Jere would have known enough about something like that to make up a false story nearly as convincing. He was too excited about the whole thing to have made it up. I believe every word that he has told me," he said to his wife.

"Now that you put it that way, I'm certain you must be right," she told him. "I really should have known that he would not willingly tell a lie," she corroborated what Josh had concluded about his story being the absolute truth.

Josh said, "That boy was so excited and emotionally kindled that he would have stayed up all night telling us about his journeys through the forest. I hoped you would let us to stay up a little later. He may have had something that was very important to tell me and was just taking a breather when you told us to go to bed. He knew he wouldn't have time to tell all of it, so he thought he hadn't better start telling it," Josh said to her. "I think it is important that we find enough time to allow Jere to tell us in detail these events. He did seem to actually want to tell more of his secrets of the wilderness tonight, but we chose not to allow him enough time to get it completed."

"I'm sorry, dear," Angela told him. She agreed with her husband that it would be best for them to encourage him to elucidate more thoroughly about his unusual new friends that he had been fortunate enough to encounter on his various expeditions.

"We won't be able to do it for the next two days because I had already planned to dig the peanuts," he told her. "But we will make some time soon to have that important conversation with our son," he promised her.

"After I get the peanuts dug with a grubbing fork, I will need your and Jere's help to put them in the barn to dry," he told her. "If we don't put them in the barn after they're dug, the crows and jaybirds will carry them off to the woods. After they have dried enough, we will pull the peanuts off the vines, place them in tow sacks, and hang them from the rafters with a strand of baling wire so the mice won't be able to get near them," he explained.

She figured Josh was getting sleepy because the words of his conversation seemed to be getting slower.

They loved to sit around the fireplace in the cold winter months and eat parched peanuts while they told stories. They would throw the peanut hulls into the fireplace and watch them disintegrate into a flaming ball of fire for just an instant. Sometimes they would also pop a screen popper full of popcorn over the flames in the fireplace. If they had popcorn and peanuts left over, it would be made into popcorn and peanut molasses balls, covered with butter from Angela's buttered hands and placed on wax paper bread wrappers to cool. Jere called them cracker-jacks.

Angela had said something else to Josh while waiting to fall asleep, but when she heard him snoring she knew she would be wasting her breath to attempt to have a sensible conversation with him.

She said, "Goodnight, Josh, I love you." She fluffed her goosedown pillow and laid her head on it. She didn't recall saying anything after that.

# CHAPTER 5

The sun was barely showing some red in the east when Angela told Jere to get up and have some breakfast so he could help his dad with the wood and water for her wash. Jere was anxious to get started because he thought he might be able to go off into the woods that afternoon when she finished washing and drying the clothes.

Before he could tell his mother of his intentions, she told him that Josh also wanted them to help pick up the peanut vines when he finished grubbing them. She then told him that it was going to be necessary to do some schooling after that. That didn't go over too well with Jeremiah, since he had really wanted to return to the woods to be with his friends.

Angela attempted to convince him that it would be very beneficial for him to cram some more mathematics into his cranium. She wanted for him to excel, particularly in math.

She said to him, "Math is one subject that will take you wherever you want to be if you are much better than an average student. You can get a job almost anywhere in the country when you master the subject. The opportunities are almost limitless for a person who is schooled and talented in that one subject, especially," she expounded forcefully to him.

"Mama, do you mean to tell me I'm going to have to read some more books?" he queried. He was hoping to receive a reply to his question that would be to his liking.

"Of course you will need to read more books, son," she tried to remind him gently so as to not upset him. She figured that he was just trying to test her by trying to bargain with her so he could slide by with fewer books to read and study. His mother wasn't about to buy any of his malarkey that day. Or next week, either.

"Jeremiah, you will need to study history, geography, mathematics, the sciences, music, art, and literature as you get older," Angela told him. "The only way you can accomplish that is to study constantly and enjoy it. If you are unable to enjoy broadening your mind you will never grow up to appreciate life to the fullest," she told him, and she meant every word of it.

"I don't mean that you have to learn all of Shakespeare's plays to be a bright, talented, and contented scholar, but you do need to study art and literature to some extent," she told him. "Just to be able to recite 'To A Waterfowl' by Edgar Allan Poe gives me a great deal of self-satisfaction, and I'm certain that when you get to the point where you can recite a poem or other such works that you will be proud of your accomplishment, also."

She continued, "Jere, you might even want to attend the university later in order for you to further enhance and polish your education skills. There is much more enjoyment in living than just being able to read and write sufficiently to be able to post a letter to your mother," she advised him.

"I want to be a mountain man, Mama," he told her. "I just want to be able to read and write so I can get along in the world. I want to be able to read and study the Holy Bible and be able to understand it," he said.

Angela knew what it was to have childhood dreams, and she knew that being a mountain man was what he had his sights set on right now. But that would change, and she knew it. She would not push him very hard right now.

"Son, when you become older and smarter you will realize that your success could only have come about as a result of your parents loving you enough to want you to have a well-rounded education, and you will be very thankful for the many hours that we have spent studying and testing in scholastic subjects that really do matter," she assured him.

"Jere, I do realize that you would love to take a hike in the woods today," she said. "But it will be too late when we finish with our studies for you to do so, and I also feel that we should study again in the morning to bring you up past the level where you should be at your age," she said. "Well, really you are already past that level now, but I don't intend for you to fall behind in the progress you have been making," Angela smiled and placed her arm around his shoulder, giving him a caring type of motherly hug.

"If your father doesn't have anything planned for you after lunch the day after tomorrow, you might be able to take a stroll in the woods then," she told him. "But I won't promise that he doesn't have something lined up for you," she cautioned.

"Aw shucks, I don't see why I have to always be helping out here instead of being able to go into the woods where I can have more fun," he muttered softly in discontent.

"Jeremiah Langford, you should be thankful that your father and mother allow you to go traipsing off into those dangerous woods at all!" she reminded him. "Just remember, son," she said a bit harshly. "You are only seven years old, and most boys are not allowed to go into the woods by themselves until they are eleven or twelve. You should be thankful that we allow you to go there at all, Jere," she stated sternly.

"You should be extremely grateful to your father that he doesn't have you working steadily with him when you are not busy with your lessons," she continued with her mild attack on his apparent opposition to her anticipated plans for him. "Many boys your age are required to work with their parents to help them make a living," she chided him slightly for seeming to be ungrateful.

She reminded him that they did allow him some time to do as he wished out there among his friends, which was more than some boys were allowed.

"I'm sorry, Mom," he sheepishly told her. "I'm really sorry, and I do appreciate the time that you and Dad allow me to go see my friends," he apologized.

"I wouldn't mind working harder around here if it meant that I could spend a little more time with them," he said.

"I haven't seen Harry for several weeks, now, and I'm not certain if she's even still around here," he told her.

"Excuse me, son," she said, with one eyebrow raised. "I must have misunderstood you. I thought you said Harry was a she," Angela said quizzically.

"Well, several times when I would just be sitting on a log, watching the chipmunks and squirrels playing," he started explaining to his mother, "I noticed a big hairy animal off in the distance but I could never get close to him," Jere told her. "I kept calling it 'hairy' because it had lots of dark brown hair all over its body," he said, as Angela edged closer to hear all of the story that Jere was beginning to tell.

"But when Big Thunder was with me one day, we saw it together and he said it was a female and her name was Sasquatch," he continued with the story. "Back then it was hard for me to say 'Sasquatch' so I just kept calling her 'hairy.' Big Thunder and I went to the place where she crossed the creek, and you never saw such huge footprints in all your life," he told his mother who was then getting to be wide-eyed and excited herself. Jere indicated to her the size of the footprints in the mud with his outstretched hands, which she thought were being stretched for her amazement. She felt that his young mind believed that they were much larger than they actually were.

"Big Thunder told me if I couldn't say 'Sasquatch' to call her 'Bigfoot' instead," he continued. "I've been calling her Bigfoot ever since until I finally learned to say 'Sasquatch'. I just forgot and said 'hairy' a few moments ago," he explained.

Jeremiah's eyes were as big as half-dollars as he continued to tell about the encounters he had made with Bigfoot, White Spirit, and all of the other friends that he had encountered in the forest.

Angela was completely surprised by some of the stories he told about Sasquatch, although she had thoroughly enjoyed listening to her son very confidently and excitedly relating all of those exhilarating and rousing incidents to her.

"Son, I have heard about Sasquatch and Bigfoot animals all of my life. Even when we lived in prime Bigfoot country in Oregon, I never did get to see even a tiny glimpse of one of those creatures that whole time," she told him. "And you mean to tell me that you have already had the occasion to see one at your young age?" she asked, amazed at hearing about his encounters. She could barely contain her curiosity about this unusual story of her son encountering a living Sasquatch there in the woods so near to their cabin.

"Yes, Mom," he answered nonchalantly. "Several times, in fact."

"Jeremiah," his mother said nervously, "I don't really think that you should go out into those woods alone any more if there is a Sasquatch roaming those hills. There is no telling what that wild animal might do to you when you're alone. It's just not safe for you to be in the forest gadding about aimlessly with no protection whatever against a sudden attack from a Bigfoot, or any other type of wild animal, for that matter," Angela said to him rather heatedly, intending to be very firm with him this time.

"Mama, she will not harm me," Jere insisted. "I have seen her several times. She just looks at me and then goes on her merry way as quick as she can. I know that she does not mean any harm to me whatsoever," he stressed to her with much emphasis.

He meant to stop her from worrying about the friendly animals that he had encountered in the woods adjacent to their cabin home. Evidently he had not yet succeeded in calming her down to the point where she would grant him free access to the woods at any time he wanted.

He clarified his mother's statement, "You said that it was near here, Mama. It's not really that near. I would guess that it's at least three or four miles to the closest place where I have seen her," he explained to his mother. "I don't really think that the Bigfoot animals intend to get very close to civilization or any place where people live and work."

Angela was still indicating her displeasure at having her only son, her very young son, assuming that cohabitation and making friends with a wild animal such as Bigfoot would be acceptable to her. She was obviously concerned for his safety, as any loving mother would and should be.

"Mama, all she wants is to be left alone out there with her baby, just like any other loving mom would want for her family," he was earnestly seeking her understanding of the matter. "I saw her one day with a little one cradled in her arms. That's when I found out it was a she. She doesn't want anyone getting close to her or her baby.

"I haven't seen her husband yet; if she has one," Jere confided to his mother. "Big Thunder told me that it would be an absolute certainty that it would be necessary for her to have a mate running around out there somewhere, but he explained to me that male Sasquatch animals will not allow themselves to be easily observed by a human being," Jere told her, but evidently he had still not convinced her that a close relationship with one would be healthy or even desirable for any human being, including him.

"Jeremiah Langford, I can scarcely believe this," she reiterated. "Are telling me the honest-to-goodness truth, young man?" she asked in a demanding manner.

"Yes ma'am. I told you before that I will swear on a stack of Bibles that all of the stories that I have told you and Dad are absolutely true, Mama," he firmly stated. "You know that I would not lie to you. You know that," he acted as though he was hurt when she questioned the sincerity and truthfulness of his stories.

His mother finally decided that since he was so adamantly unyielding to alter the accounts of those unusual encounters with strange animals of the forest, then she would be forced to believe his explanations of those encounters, which she had heretofore considered highly unlikely.

"Mama, if I can get Big Thunder to come here and talk to you and Dad, he will verify everything that I have told you. He will say that I've been telling you the truth about everything," he assured her. "He is a virtuous man living a decent, moral, and honorable life," Jere added to the Indian's credentials.

"All right son, I believe you," his mother finally told him. "I've never caught you telling me a lie, and so—I believe you," she said. "It is rather hard for me to accept that you have now observed a Sasquatch more than once, while I have never seen one in my entire life," she acknowledged to him.

"They were supposed to have been rather plentiful there in the backwoods where we lived in Oregon, but I am not acquainted with any individual who had ever seen one in his or her entire life,—except you, of course," she added. "It is certainly uncanny to say the least," she told him. "I can't wait to tell your dad about this. It will just about blow his mind, young man," his mother suspected.

"By the way, son," she said to him. "How did you come to learn such exemplary words as moral, honorable, and sincere in your vocabulary?" she inquired.

Jere chuckled when his mother asked that question. He replied, "Well, Mama, I picked up many of them from Big Thunder, and a lot of them from you and Dad when you were talking about things and carrying on a conversation.

"Mom, I'd rather you didn't tell Dad about Sasquatch just yet," he pleaded with his mother. "I'm not quite sure that I'm ready to tell him yet. I'm afraid he might not believe me and would go out there to make certain she was there. I'm almost sure if he went out there that she would not show herself. Big Thunder said there was no telling how many times she had observed me and him without allowing us to see her. She refused to allow herself to be seen by us until she was sure that we would not harm her," he carefully explained.

"Big Thunder told me that the Sasquatch animals have a very keen sixth sense for ascertaining when someone may have intentions of harming them," he told Angela. "If they suspect that someone is intent on doing them harm, they just don't allow themselves to be seen by those people. Mama, I know you don't like to keep secrets from Dad, but could we keep this between just the two of us for a while, please?" he begged.

Angela thought for a moment before giving a reply to his pleading request. She said, "Son, I have never kept anything from your father, and I certainly don't like keeping a secret from him at this time, but in the interest of safety for you and for your friends, I'm going to agree to your unusual request," she promised.

Jeremiah questioned, "Does that mean 'yes,' Mama?"

"Yes, son," she answered. "I will agree to hold off telling your dad, temporarily." Angela stressed the word *temporarily* to him.

"Gee thanks, Mom," he said. "I sure wouldn't want any harm to come to Sasquatch, even though she won't let me come within close range of her. I still feel that she likes me and trusts me, now. There was a time when she didn't. The old Indian said that evidently she trusts me more than him because he never got a glimpse of her before he met me. Since I have known Big Thunder we have already seen her four times, but only one time that was very close," Jere excitedly said to his mother.

"Jere, I will try to live up to my promise that I gave you," she told him. "But if you should accidentally spill the beans about it to someone and your father finds out that I knew about it and didn't tell him, he is going to be furious," Angela warned him. "You do understand that he is going to be angry with both of us, don't you?"

"Yes," he said. "I do understand. And I'm sorry to have to put you through this, but I'm thinking about the harm that could possibly be done to Bigfoot.

"Let me tell you about one of the times that I went out looking for Bigfoot," Jere continued. I still called her 'hairy' then, not knowing that it was a she and that her name was Sasquatch. One afternoon after we had finished with our schooling I noticed a shotgun shell on the apple crate you and dad use for a nightstand. I picked it up and put it in my overalls pocket and went to the place where I had seen Bigfoot before. I waited a long time for her to show up, but she never came. Big Thunder finally came by and sat down on the log beside me. I told him I had been looking for Bigfoot, but she hadn't shown yet. He asked me if I might have anything on my person that would make her wary of me and not want to reveal herself to me. I happened to think about the shell in my pocket and showed it to him. Big Thunder told me that was the very reason that she was not going to let me see her that afternoon," Jere was excitedly telling his mom.

"It took her several days before she could begin to trust me again, and I swore never to carry anything like that in my pocket. Please don't tell Dad about this either, okay?" he asked her once again to promise to keep his secret.

"I put the shotgun shell back where I found it. I promise you faithfully, Mom, I will never take another shell or bullet with me again unless I ask you or Dad for it," he solemnly vowed to her.

"All right, Jere," she answered. "I won't say anything to your dad about this until you decide that it's time to tell him or if he finds out from some other source. I'm glad you told me about the shotgun shell," she said. "Because I need to warn you about how dangerous that could have been to you. You could have been maimed for life or killed if it had somehow accidentally detonated," she cautioned. "You also said that Bigfoot would not appear and show herself if she sensed that there was some dangerous object nearby?" Angela asked.

"That's right," he verified. "Big Thunder said that he used to carry a knife in his pocket as he journeyed through the woods and he never once saw a Sasquatch until one time after he had lost his knife and then twice after he met me. That's the only reason that we see her occasionally, now," he told his mom.

"Big Thunder didn't realize that his knife was keeping him from observing the Sasquatch that his ancestors had observed and talked about for many generations past," he further explained to his mother, whose ears were eagerly receptive to every tidbit of the information.

"His grandfather, the old shaman, had told him stories about the Sasquatch people when he was a little boy," Jere said to her. "He said that they had lived in the far distant mountains where humans had feared to go.

"Big Thunder said he had been told that the male was more cautionary than the female and would observe humans without being seen themselves," he explained. "Males have an intuitive fear that humans will want to inflict harm on them," Jere explained assiduously to his mother as she listened attentively.

"Jere, I fully understand how well you like being with your special friend, Big Thunder. I know that you really care about him and enjoy talking to him," she said. "I also know that you trust him completely," she approached the subject of her conversation with him very carefully.

"But I am hoping that you don't become so emotionally involved and attached to him that you will be terribly hurt and mentally affected by it when his life finally comes to an end," his mother lovingly related to him in terms that she felt that he would be able to understand.

Angela was attempting to prepare him for that assured certainty of Big Thunder's death when it would eventually come to pass. She felt that it might be in the not-too-distant future since he was a very old man. She also knew that her son was becoming emotionally attached to the kind and gentle old man, and she wanted to attempt to avoid the shock that would undoubtedly come on his passing.

"Mama, I am old enough to understand that everything in the world must die at some time or another," he assured her. "I also know that Big Thunder must die some day and he knows it, too. That is precisely why he spends so much time in the forest; so he can enjoy his final days on earth doing what he likes before going to that heavenly home in the sky, which he knows will be someday soon," Jere made clear that he understood completely about life, living and dying.

"Big Thunder told me that he actually looks forward to the joyous time when he will be called from this earth to be with God in heaven and to be with all of his ancestors who have passed on before him," he continued. "That was one of his reasons for leaving his daughter's house; so he could go to the forest and die in peace."

She had now come to the conclusion that her son was much more intelligent than she had previously thought. She could only guess that being with Big Thunder had done wonders of broadening and developing his education to the point where she was amazed at the reasoning in her young son at that tender age.

She patted him on the back and said, "You have a good head on your shoulders, son. Just make certain that you use your mental and physical skills for the good of our people and for the ultimate benefit of our precious environment so that our children and grandchildren will be able to enjoy many of the same things we ourselves enjoy," she cautioned him of that necessity.

"Those are almost the exact words that Big Thunder used when he told me that, mama," he said, surprised. "I can't believe that you both said the very same thing."

Jere continued, "And I made him a solemn promise that I would not mistreat the earth or the animals or any living thing, and that I would take enough game for me and my family to live on and that I would not waste anything foolishly," he related with a significant zest.

"Son, I am beginning to love your friend, Big Thunder more and more, as I find out about his likes, his dislikes, his habits, and his moral beliefs from some of the things you have been telling me," she confided to him.

"I'm beginning to think that he is not only an outstanding person for you to be associated with for your moral and behavioral edification but also for the sharpening of your education as well. He seems like a person to be admired for his positive and realistic outlook on life," she admitted.

"Do you think it would be possible to for you to encourage him enough so that he would want to visit us sometime soon?" she asked. "We would definitely enjoy having his company for supper some night. Perhaps he would like to tell us more of the exciting stories that he has learned, about his ancestors and of the way he grew up in the wilderness," his mother pleaded. "Please tell him that it would be an honor for us to have him to visit with us and share a meal with his other family."

Jere's eyes quickly flashed at hearing his mother say "other family." He wondered if she might suspect that he and Big Thunder were blood brothers. She didn't pursue the family subject any further, though; "thank goodness," he thought.

"I'm not sure he will come, Mom," he told her. "I'll do my best 'cause I'd like for him to come and meet you and Dad. He seems reluctant to be with others since he had made up his mind to go the Great Beyond, as he calls it. He doesn't enjoy being close to lots of people any more. He doesn't even visit his own daughter," Jere told her.

Angela said to him, "I know that he lives off the land, son, but I can't imagine how he gets enough food to keep from starving. What does he eat to keep up his energy?"

"He told me that he eats nuts, berries, edible roots, seeds, and wild fruits and would occasionally catch a fish to supplement his food in the summer. But I suppose he hasn't yet spent a winter in the woods," Jere told her.

"He told me once that he didn't expect to live to see another spring," Jere said. "But he said he would be able to find plenty of pine nuts and roots and catch a fish now and then to wrap in clay and bake under the live coals of fire in the campfire. He said there was lots of food for those who knew where to look. He said that many people would starve in the woods because they didn't know how to look for food," Jere explained.

"He knows how to build a simple fish trap to set in the small creek to catch his supper," he told her. "If he catches more than one fish he turns the other one loose and only keeps what he intends to eat. He said he had learned to eat fish without any salt since living in the woods, and he found that it tasted better since he was used to it.

"He confessed to me that the only thing that he really missed in the white man's world was a cup of good, hot coffee early in the morning. He has been unable to get anything out in the woods that would come close to serving as a substitute for that one small weakness, if that would be considered one," he said.

"Big Thunder has already told me not to worry about him if he didn't survive the winter," Jere told his mother. "He said this is what life is all about: we are on this earth only for a very short time in our present form, and then we will go to be with our loved ones who have already crossed over to the other side," he told her.

"It made me kinda sad when he told me that, but he convinced me that it should be a happy thing instead of a sad thing. He said that he wanted me to celebrate his reaching the far beyond instead of mourning him," he revealed.

"He said we will live eternally there, where there will be no hunger, no sadness, no sorrows, no anger, and no illnesses," Jere said softly. "He also said the angels would sing beautiful songs constantly for everyone to enjoy."

Angela was amazed at the total amount of knowledge that Jere and the old Indian had shared with one another. Big Thunder had evidently acquired that knowledge and accomplished his feats of intelligence without any type of formal schooling, although she was not about to encourage her young son to do the same thing.

Big Thunder had told his little blood brother about the place where he spent a lot of time, but he had never taken him to it. He told him it was two ridges over toward the south and halfway down the far slope. He had wanted Jere to come with him some day and see the spring where he got his drinking water. He also wanted to show him the little creek where he sometimes set out his fish trap. He didn't want Jere to visit and get into trouble with his parents, though. He said if he could get them to agree to let him spend the day with him, he would show him how to wrap a fish with clay to cook it under the hot coals of fire. He convinced Jeremiah that it would be more delicious than anything he could ever imagine, except maybe ice cream. The scales and skin would come off with the clay when it was broken from around it, leaving the tender meat to be savored.

Jere told his mother that he longed to see White Spirit again and he also wanted to get a glimpse of the mother Sasquatch. He missed Big Thunder most of all. He wanted to see the squirrels and chipmunks playing around the log where he would sit. He wished to see the mother raccoon peek out from behind a tree trunk to find out if he was still there. He missed all of them a lot.

He had lots of friends in the forest. He thought about them at night while lying in bed. He wanted to tell his family lots of things, but he wasn't certain that his father would fully understand the situation. He felt his mother would probably understand his decision to become a blood brother with Big Thunder, but he wasn't sure if his dad would accept it. He certainly didn't want to be barred from going into the forest. There wouldn't be anything worthwhile for him to do if he were forced to stop meeting in the woods with his friends.

Jere had ceased talking to his mom and had sat silent for a few minutes, seeming to be engrossed in his thoughts. She had thoroughly enjoyed listening to his stories of the wilderness and the enlightening tales of his friends, and she allowed him the privilege of meditating and reminiscing about his innermost thoughts. She understood.

Josh had come into the kitchen from the garden area, where he had been mending fence that was supposed to keep out intruders. Gardening season had almost gone until the following year, except for turnips, rutabagas, parsnips, and winter onions, which were still available for harvesting and consumption until a hard freeze came. Before then, Josh would dig them and properly store them in the root cellar.

He said, "Angela, I will need you and Jere to help me pile up the turnips and parsnips tomorrow. I will cut the tops off to get them ready for storage. I have already cut the vines away from the sweet potatoes, and I will need to get them dug in the next two or three days."

"All right, Josh," she answered. "We should be able to help you for the next couple of days. We did some schooling yesterday and today. We're in pretty good shape there." Angela was hoping that Jeremiah would mention to his dad that he would be willing to volunteer but instead he remained silent.

"Is that all right with you, son?" his dad asked point blank, as though he thought Jere didn't understand what he had said.

"Oh sure, Dad," he said. "That'll be just fine with me," although the tone of his voice didn't indicate that he was absolutely thrilled about it. Josh guessed as much but didn't push it.

Jeremiah had much rather be roaming the woods than working in the garden, but he didn't dare mention it to his father. He didn't want to disappoint Big Thunder. He wanted to be in the woods at their favorite spot on the log by the little brook where rippling water seemed to sing a lullaby as they sat and talked about the Indians of long ago who lived there in those same woods. It was a gesture of friendship from God and the mother earth to allow them to live in harmony with nature and the environment, multiplying their kind in the forests and along the rivers of that area. It was a wonderful life for those Native Americans of long ago, before the white men arrived on the scene to invade and destroy their precious hunting and fishing grounds.

Jeremiah wondered if White Spirit had missed him recently. He hoped that she did not think that he had purposely stayed away because he was unhappy with her. The old Indian had told him that she was only an apparition, anyway. But he knew better. He had seen her outline against the early morning sky on top of the hill as the sun was rising and her breath was producing the smoke-like vapor as she exhaled air from her lungs. She had run to the point on the hill where she could see him in the valley below. He could tell that she was not an apparition. She was real.

She appeared to be just like any other wild wolf in the forest except that her fur was snowy white, extremely full and beautiful. She actually did look like a white ghost, but she was his good friend and he loved her.

He doubted that Bigfoot would miss him if he didn't show up. She would probably be much happier if no humans ever showed up in the vicinity of where she resided. He never did see the little one again after she was carrying it in her arms. He had by now seen her five times; three of those times were at a great distance from him. If he hadn't had very sharp eyesight, he might have missed her altogether. It was absolutely necessary to watch very closely or one would not be able to see her. She was very adept at keeping herself hidden from view. Big Thunder had probably missed seeing her because of his failing vision. He wouldn't have seen them if Jere hadn't pointed them out.

Big Thunder had told Jere that he had been beginning to doubt the truth in the old stories about the elusive Sasquatch. His family had told them about the furry and hairy mountain men for ages, but he had never seen one until Jere had shown him one. He had lived in that same area for decades and had never had a glimpse of one. He didn't doubt them any more. He was now convinced that they did exist, and now he was certain that they were multiplying. This was proven by the fact that a mother was carrying a baby cradled in her arm one day.

Big Thunder told Jere that his grandfather, Silver Bear, had been a shaman for the Suquamish tribe, which had lived in the area of Washington now known as Puget Sound. Silver Bear told him that the Sasquatch people had dropped out of the sky to come to earth to attempt to get the earth people to quit destroying their precious land and water on earth. Earth people were terribly mean to the Sasquatch and chased them to the farthest reaches back in the forests. The Sasquatch then gave up on trying to help the humans. Some of them went back up into the clouds, never to return, and the rest of them moved deep into the woods, vowing never to try to help people again. He told Jere that this story had been handed down verbally through many generations of Indians from the shamans and their ancestors who had no written history.

Jere had no idea of what a shaman might be, so he asked Big Thunder if his grandfather was a prophet. He told Jere that it was something similar to that in that he was a religious leader of the tribe and that his word was law in that tribe. He advised them of all the rituals, dances, and practices that were to be carried out to comply with the law.

Silver Bear had taught him that good and evil could be separated by how they lived, and he would then advise them how to live and what to eat so that no evil entities would come into their lives. He said that the shaman received his powers from the Great Spirit above, who had been responsible for giving us our land, our great waters, the forests, and the plants and animals that were put here for food and clothing. Big Thunder said a shaman was similar to a high priest. All the members of the tribe were completely responsible to him for everything.

He said many great shamans were given the power from the Great Spirit above to prophesy and foretell future events prior to them happening. Many of them had foretold of the hordes of white men who would come to the land of the Indians to plunder, pillage, ruin, and kill the Native Americans who owned the land and the rivers and then eventually drive them from their own lands that rightfully belonged to them since the beginning of time.

Big Thunder told him that the Indians did not have shamans any more since the white men had come into the territory and put a stop to it. They hated the shaman rulers and would often put them to death by hanging them or shooting them. They told them that if they were so powerful that they should be able to save themselves. All the leaders were frightened to study to become shamans any more, and the old faith had all but died out.

"All right, you two," Angela said, and disturbed the thoughts and daydreaming that Jeremiah had been totally engrossed in at the time. He was startled by the voice of his mother breaking the silence because he wasn't aware that anyone was in ten miles of him as she made the announcement for supper. Jere and his father went to the back porch to wash up and returned to the kitchen table. All of a sudden, Jere had the feeling that he was terribly hungry. Angela had baked biscuits, made gravy from the pan drippings where she had fried the venison sausage, baked some potatoes in the oven of her cookstove, and even made some sugar cookies. Jere could hardly wait until his father had given thanks to the Lord for the food and everything else they had. Jere thought his dad would never finish with prayers, but he eventually resounded with a loud *A-men* to which Angela and Jeremiah each responded with their own a-men at the conclusion.

After they had finished their delicious supper, Josh indicated to Jere that he would be interested in hearing more about his exciting journeys into the backwoods. Jere put him off with a flimsy excuse that he had eaten too much and was too full to talk much.

Evidently, he was not quite ready to discuss his secrets with his father just yet. He was afraid that his dad intended to lead him into the type of conversation that he didn't want to discuss. In order to safely remove himself from that situation, it became necessary for him to feign the appearance of being sleepy by starting to yawn and placing his hand over his mouth.

"Are you getting sleepy, Jeremiah?" his mother wanted to know.

"Yes ma'am, I'm kinda tired and sleepy for some reason or other," he answered. "I think I will turn in now so I can get a good night's sleep to be ready to work in the garden tomorrow," he said.

Angela felt it a bit unusual for Jere to be considering in advance the work that he would be doing the next day, but she didn't say anything to him. Josh had a pretty good idea that Jere was putting him on by pretending to be sleepy, but he didn't mention it either. He was of the opinion that Jere didn't wish to discuss the personal activities that had transpired out in the woods, but he wouldn't pursue it. He felt that if he pushed Jere for answers that it would only make him clam up even more. Josh decided he would wait until Jere was ready to discuss it with him.

Joshua said, "Well, I'm a bit tired myself. I believe Jere has a good idea. I think I will turn in and get some much needed rest, also."

"Well, if you think I'm going to stay up by myself and twiddle my thumbs, you're mistaken," Angela announced to them. "I'll just blow out the lamp and come to bed, too. I can use the rest and extra sleep just about as much as anyone else around this house," she bluntly stated. "Goodnight, all."

"G'night, Mom and Dad," Jeremiah said to them.

"'Night, son," they replied in unison. "We love you," Angela told him.

"Love you both," Jere replied, went to bed and pulled the covers up over his head.

Sleep was very slow in coming that night for Jeremiah. He had at least a thousand important things to think of and ponder and mull over carefully in his mind. He tried to quit thinking about some of the things so he could go to sleep, but it was no use. He lay awake in bed, tossing and turning. He didn't know what time it was, but it must have been well after midnight. It was very late when he finally quit thrashing around in bed and dropped off to sleep.

The next morning when Angela went to wake him, she noticed that his covers were strewn all over the bed and halfway touching the floor.

She said, "Jere, you must have had a terrible nightmare last night, considering the way your bed is totally destroyed and judging from the way your quilt is on the floor."

"Oh, no ma'am," he replied. "I slept real well, and I feel just fine. I had a real good night's sleep last night. I'm rested and rarin' to go," he said enthusiastically.

"Well, good," she said. "I have a hot bowl of oatmeal waiting for you at the table. Your father has already finished his and picked up the tools to go to the garden. You and I will go help him as soon as we finish our breakfast," she said.

When they arrived in the garden Josh already had many of the vegetables dug and lying on top of the rows. He said, "Shake the dirt off the roots of the rutabagas, turnips, carrots, and parsnips and pile them separately. I'll use the butcher knife to trim the tops off and carry them in the wheelbarrow to the root cellar," he told them.

"We still have some peanut vines in the barn that need the nuts picked off," he told them. "But we can always wait until the weather turns cold to do that."

It was important to remove the tops from the roots because the leaves would draw nutrients from the root vegetables and cause them to shrivel up and dry out. It appeared they would have sufficient vegetables to last throughout the winter and with the wild game and fish that Josh would furnish, it appeared that they should have ample food until warm weather next year.

Josh still hadn't dug the Irish potatoes yet and that would ensure an even greater amount of food that would be available for the family when stored in their root cellar during the winter.

Jere said, "Dad, why do we have to have so many potatoes? We made a big crop of them last spring and still have a bunch of them left in the cellar. Now, we will have too many when we get these dug."

"Oh no, son," his father said. "We will never have too many potatoes. You have probably not heard about it, but millions of people died of starvation in Ireland when a disease invaded their potato crops and devastated their food supply."

Angela corroborated his story and said, "Son, he's right. If we think we might have too many potatoes, we can always give some to our neighbor to the west of us. In fact we could probably sell some to the grocery store this winter."

Angela had placed an iron kettle of beans on the rod in the fireplace that morning as they were leaving to go to the garden. She added a sizable chunk of salt pork, also. She had surmised that it was about time for her to go to the cabin and check on the noon meal. Since they had all worked hard that morning, everyone would be ravenous.

"We've done a fine job this morning," Josh complimented them, "If we work hard at it this afternoon and get the things done that I want to accomplish, then Jeremiah should be allowed to go back out into the woods tomorrow to visit his friends, again," Joshua said.

Those were the precise words that Jere had been waiting to hear. He didn't mind working hard if he knew that he would be rewarded by being allowed to journey out into his favorite surroundings in the woods.

It had become quite apparent to Josh and Angela from the expressions of his moods that Jere would much rather be out there in his favorite element among his animal friends and Big Thunder than to be almost anywhere else. While it was not his mother's wishes that he be allowed to continue to meander and roam about the woods and wilderness uninhibited and at his own discretion, she did agree that his outings had seemed to offer him untold satisfaction. She might even agree that he was receiving a substantial education on his jaunts. It also seemed that Big Thunder was helping him obtaining a great amount of knowledge through his close association. From what little Angela knew about him, it seemed that he was a wise old Indian who knew the ropes about many things other than just being a wanderer in the wilderness.

Angela was hesitant to revoke his privileges of going to the woods. She was afraid that it might cause him some mental harm. But she knew that if she restricted him he would likely rebel and cause more problems. She weighed the two alternatives and concluded that all concerned would definitely be better off if Jere were allowed to continue part of his education out in the forest.

After they had finished eating, Jere willingly headed down the hill to the garden to help finish the chores. At the end of an hour he was on one end of the rows and his parents were on the other end. Jeremiah was whistling a tune, a skill that neither of them had noticed in him before. Evidently he was happy. Angela asked Josh if he had taught Jere to whistle.

Josh replied, "No, not that I'm aware of, anyway. I do, however, sometimes start whistling though when I am busy working. I hardly even notice it or realize that I'm doing it until I stop, or else look up. Then I may notice it."

Angela said, "Now that's cute. He's whistling, 'I Was Seeing Nellie Home.' Where in the world did he learn that tune?" Angela wanted to know.

Josh corrected her, "Well, the real name of that tune is 'Quilting Party' and I've been whistling it quite a bit recently. I suppose that's how he came to pick it up," he replied.

Jeremiah had been working hard all afternoon, obviously with much enthusiasm. He seemed to work harder when he was whistling. His newfound skill was as pleasing to his mother as it was to himself, evidently. When he was whistling he pretended to be in another universe where no other person was nearby. Even as a baby he had enjoyed his solitude; now he tended to be a loner, except when he was with Big Thunder.

The afternoon passed as quickly as a sunny breeze. When the sun started getting low to the horizon in the southwest, Joshua said, "Fine job; well done!"

Joshua seldom handed out praise voluntarily, so this was an occasion to be proudly remembered. Evidently he was well pleased with the way the harvest of the vegetable crops had been accomplished. He was satisfied that much of their staple diet had been provided and their tasty victuals would be plentiful during the winter.

Josh said, "Son, if your mother can let you loose after you complete your schooling tomorrow, then you may have the rest of the day off to do as you wish."

"Yippeeee," Jere yelled. "Thanks Dad, I really appreciate that. I can hardly wait to get started back out on the trail that leads to the little creek where Big Thunder meets me sometimes and we have a powwow. Boy, he really tells me about some great stuff, sometimes; like about when he was a boy growing up and living in the wild country, kind of like what we're doing now. He said he really enjoys talking to me and I am more like a grandson to him than anything else. He told me that he is really proud to have me as a good friend and he has always enjoyed the conversations we have. He sometimes uses me as an extra pair of eyes since his eyesight is failing and he can't see too well," Jeremiah confided to his parents, who were absorbing every word that their son had spoken to them.

"Jere, I think we might be able to skip our lessons for tomorrow and make them up another time," she said to her son. "This will let you get an even earlier start in the woods so that you can enjoy a full day of it," she told him.

"Aw gee, Mom," he said. "That's really swell of you. Are you sure we'll be able to do this?" he inquired. Jeremiah had not been known to be very affectionate with his mother, but he actually walked up to her, put his arms around her neck, and hugged her. This completely surprised her, but it greatly endeared him to her.

"Go ahead and have a good time," she told him. "I want you to promise me one thing, though. Promise me that you will be extremely careful so that you don't get hurt. Promise?"

"I promise that I will be extra-careful, Mom," he declared.

Jeremiah felt that he had great parents. He knew that he was a lucky boy to have parents who understood his desires as they did. He was very grateful to them for being so good to him. He had known some children who didn't really enjoy the parents they were forced to live with.

"Mom, do you think I might be able to take a small picture of you and Dad to show to Big Thunder tomorrow?" he asked politely. "He had asked me once if I carried a picture of you. I told him that I didn't. He said he would like to see what you two looked like, and he told me that he had already pictured in his mind what he thought you would look like but figured he could be wrong."

"Yes, I suppose you may," she answered. "I have one photo of your dad and me sitting on a rail fence at my father's place in Oregon that is a very good likeness of both of us. He might enjoy seeing it," she told him. "I certainly wouldn't want it to get lost, however," she warned him.

"Thanks Mom," he told her. "I'll be certain to take good care of it for you," he promised her. "I just know that Big Thunder will be real proud of you both. He told me that since I was proud of both of you that he knew that he would be, too. He said that he thought I had enough sense to be a good judge of character in people."

Jere didn't have to be reminded to go to bed that night. After he finished supper he washed his hands, face, and body extra well, dried off, and told his mother and father good night. He wanted to be well rested so he would be able to explore the woods all day long the following day.

Angela told him, "I'll fix you two peanut butter sandwiches on biscuits to carry with you. Don't forget to carry my picture in your shirt pocket under the bib of your overalls so that it doesn't fall out and get lost," she warned. "That picture has much sentimental value to me and your dad. We treasure it, son."

"Okay Mom, I'll take good care of it, don't worry," Jere promised and then hurried off to bed smiling.

"'Night, Mom and Dad," he told them. "I love you," he said.

"We love you too, son," Angela told him. "Good night."

"Sleep tight, son, see you in the morning," Josh said.

# CHAPTER
## 7

Jere didn't need to be called the next morning. He got up, rushed to the back porch, washed his hands, and sat down to breakfast in a very good frame of mind, wearing a wide smile and bidding both of his parents a good morning. He ate his oatmeal in a hurry, snatched up the two biscuit sandwiches that his mother had made, and impatiently rushed for the back door. The sandwiches were safely stowed in a paper bag, and the picture of his parents was safely in his shirt pocket. Just as he took a step off the back porch, his mother called out to him, "Aren't you going to give your mother a good-bye kiss, son?" she asked him in a hurt voice.

"Aw Mom, I'm gettin' too big for that," he answered.

"You come here, young man, and give your mother a kiss," she commanded. "You will never be too big to give your mother a good-bye kiss when you leave me to go off somewhere," she scolded. He returned to the back porch and gave her a kiss before she let him leave to begin his exploratory journey into the outback of the wilderness.

"Too old, my foot," she muttered as he scampered hastily away from the cabin. In a much louder voice she yelled, "You be extremely careful while you are out there today and don't get into any meanness. Tell your friend we said hello and to come and visit us. Tell him we want to meet him. Bye, now," she said as he was getting close to being out of earshot.

He yelled, "Bye, Mom and Dad, see you tonight."

Angela watched him progress swiftly along the small trail into the woods until he was completely out of sight.

Jere normally ambled along the small trail into the woods at a relaxed pace when he left the cabin, but that morning he was in a much greater hurry than ever before. For him, it had been much too long since he had seen his friends of the forest, and he was wondering if they could be nearly so glad to see him as he would be to see them.

He stopped to check on a couple of crows that had spotted him and started cawing loudly at him for intruding into their territory. The sun was just beginning to pop through the trees in the southeast. It was cool enough that the brisk walk had made him feel nice and warm. He checked his shirt pocket to make certain he still had the picture.

An owl suddenly and silently darted by close to his head, startling him. He didn't know that she was in the vicinity, but she was just being inquisitive, not meaning any harm. An owl can move so effortlessly, freely, and silently through the woods that one can't know they are around at all until they fly past.

A rapid movement ahead caught his attention as a raccoon darted behind a tree to hide from him. He knew she would sneak another peek at him as he approached closer. Jere laughed out loud, "Go on you mama coon, I'm not going to bother you."

He was beginning to get thirsty. He found a brook of clear water near the trail and got down on all fours to drink from the cold, clear trickle until his thirst was eased. Water from a snowmelt stream in the mountains just seemed to taste better to him than any well water.

He sat down on a fallen tree trunk and rested several minutes while taking in the grandeur of the most beautiful scenery he could imagine. He thought to himself, "How could anything be more beautiful and heavenly than this? Surely God must have put that here for all of us to enjoy, so we should be thankful to Him for giving us this place to behold."

After a moment, he continued on at a more leisurely pace, taking in all the grand works of the natural forest that had the helping hand of God. Jere fully realized the importance of the precious solitude, the awesome beauty, and the many friends that he had, probably more than any other seven-year-old boy could.

He had already approached and passed one of the places that Big Thunder had been known to frequent, but his friend was nowhere in sight. However, he didn't consider this to be unusual because Big Thunder pretty much wandered continuously over the hills and valleys of this region from dawn to dusk if he was feeling well.

Jere had no way of knowing where his friend could be. Perhaps he wasn't feeling well. After all, he was an old man, and that could mean that he would be ill more frequently. Big Thunder had once shown him a small cave that was just over the next ridge, but he hadn't said anything about spending any time in it. Anyway, it looked too small to be frequented by humans and appeared to be used by smaller animals.

Jere sat down on a log and decided to rest again, so he could straighten out his thoughts concerning the old Indian. He sat for a long time, and it crossed his mind that he had not seen Sasquatch or White Spirit, either. But, of course, he didn't expect to see all of his friends each time he came to the woods.

He slowly turned his body around on the log to take in a full sweep of the hillside above him, hoping to catch sight of some small movement in the underbrush at the top of the hill. He squinted his eyes diligently for something that would suddenly alert him to an old Indian coming his way, but no such luck. He was sorely disappointed that this day had thus far turned out to be something of a failure.

Jere finally decided that it might be better if he walked some more in order to find a clue of some kind that could lead to the whereabouts of his blood brother. He was getting tired of sitting, and the walk would do him good. But then, he thought, the old Indian had no way of knowing that he was even in the forest that day and may not have made any preparations to seek him out. He may have been looking for him the past several days and when Jere didn't show up he may have become disheartened and reconciled to the fact that Jere's mother and father might not allow him come to the woods.

He knew that there would be no way he could tell what Big Thunder might be thinking at this time. He couldn't blame Big Thunder if he had grown tired of waiting and looking for him and had probably given up on finding him again, although he hoped that this was not the case. He now wished that his friend had shown him where he spent his nights, but evidently he had desired to keep it a secret from everyone.

Jere walked for another hour and found a suitable stump to sit on while hoping to see a familiar sight. He was beginning to get hungry. He began unwrapping one of his peanut butter sandwiches. Before he got it completely unwrapped, a chipmunk appeared close by. It must have scented the peanuts in the biscuit sandwich. He began begging for a bite of it, so Jere pinched off a small bit and tossed it among the leaves. The chipmunk scampered over quickly and gobbled it up. Jere took one bite, and before he could take another, four more little rascals had shown up and were scrambling to get close enough for a handout from him.

Jere was having lots of fun watching and listening to them as they scampered to get in position for the next tidbit he would pinch off his biscuit and peanut butter sandwich. They acted as though they had never known such tasty morsels before.

"Oh well, I had two bites of it anyway," he said to them, as though he thought they might be able to understand him.

Jere almost jumped out of his skin when he was startled by a husky voice from over his shoulder behind the stump that said, "That's very kind and generous of you, my little brother, to share your dinner with the little animals of the forest."

Jere could hardly believe his eyes when he turned around and caught sight of his good friend and blood brother standing within two feet of him. He smiled and offered his hand to Big Thunder. Big Thunder shook his hand so hard that he thought it would fall off. He was so glad and proud to see him, though, that he didn't care. Evidently his friend was glad to see him, too.

"Little Brother, you will never know how glad I am to finally find you out here in the woods," he said with a visible twinkle in his eyes, a seldom seen huge smile on his face, and a cheery tone in his husky voice.

"I was beginning to wonder if I had lost my little friend forever," he said. "You cannot imagine the pleasure I felt when I saw you sitting on the stump as I came over the ridge. I almost thought you might have been an apparition, but as I got closer and saw you feeding the chipmunks, I knew you were real," he told Jere.

"I was really beginning to wonder if perhaps you might not like me any more, or maybe that your mom and dad might not let you come out here any more. I could just imagine all kinds of bad things that could have happened to you," he told his little brother.

"Oh, that reminds me," Jere told Big Thunder while reaching into his shirt pocket to pull out the picture that he had carried there that morning intending to show his friend.

He handed it to Big Thunder and said proudly, "This is my mom and dad. They said for me to tell you hello and that they would like to meet you. They want you to come home with me sometime to visit with them and have supper. Mom said she would like to know a little ahead of time so she could prepare a good meal for you," Jere said to him as they sat side by side on the edge of the stump.

"Little Brother you have some fine-looking parents," he told him. "I knew beforehand that they would be. I'd certainly like to meet them, but I would hate to bother your mother with cooking a meal for me," he said. "I can get by on the foods that I find here in the forest, and they are extra good and healthy for me," he explained.

Big Thunder said, "I know you're very proud of your mother and father. I can tell by the picture and by what you have told me that they are very fine, upstanding people. This is a good likeness of them," he said as he held the picture sideways to catch the full light from the sun on it. He was having trouble seeing it clearly in the shade.

"I feel very close to them," Big Thunder continued. "Especially now since I know they are the parents of my blood brother. I feel like I have known them for a long time from what you have told me about them."

Big Thunder held the picture close to his eyes, rotating it from side to side for quite some time, squinting his eyes and studying the likenesses of Angela and Joshua on the print. His eyesight wasn't very good, and it was necessary for him to get all of the available sunlight shining through the tree limbs to strike it directly to see it at all. He acted as though he might not want to give the picture up to Jere at all. He was totally enthralled with it, but he finally handed it over to and said, "You do have every right to be proud of your parents. I know they are fine people, Little Brother, and they have raised a fine lad. I'm as proud of you as they are," he admitted.

"Thank you, Big Thunder," he acknowledged the compliment. I will tell them what you have said," Jere promised. "But it would not be any trouble at all for my mother to fix supper for us some night. She told me to tell you that. My mom and dad would be thrilled to have you come and eat with us. They really do want to meet you, and I think you owe it to them to come and let them see who their son's best friend in the world is," he begged the old Indian man. "We haven't had any company at all since we built the cabin and moved in. My mom and dad would consider it an honor for you to come and see us. I would also consider it an honor," he pleaded.

"Well, I certainly want to thank you for inviting me, and I'd like for you to tell your mother and father thanks, also," he said to Jere. "I really do feel that I have known you and your family all of my life. That's a fact," he certified to Jeremiah. "I feel like you are as much a relative to me as any brothers or sisters I have ever had. I'll tell you what, Little Brother," he said. "The next time you make a trip into the woods I will let you know at that time when I will be able to come and visit with you," he promised.

Big Thunder said, "I almost missed seeing you this time because I was walking on the other side of the ridge and going away from you when I heard this commotion and noise, sounding like animals fighting and coming from over the ridge behind me. I couldn't imagine what had stirred them up to such a frenzy as that. I decided to meander up to the top of the ridge to see what the excitement was all about. That's when I found out that it was the little chipmunks making all that noise as you were feeding them," he told his blood brother. "I was very happy to find you feeding them and I know they were happy to get a delicious meal from you, too," he said. "They will remember you for the favor you did for them, and the next time you come by they will beg you for some more food.

"You can't possibly realize how happy it made me when I saw you sitting on that stump," he told Jere. "I will always be grateful that I did not miss you this time. I think I would have been totally devastated if you had not been here today. I was almost ready to give up on you ever coming back to see me," he sadly said to him.

"I am also glad to find out that everything is well with you and your family and I am thankful to the little animals for leading me to you today," he said. "Without them I might have missed you completely and that would have made me very, very sad," he admitted.

"I'm proud that you have proven to me that you are kind to the little animals," he told him. "We must always be kind to them as they have a way of paying us back. They are our friends, also," he reminded Jeremiah.

"Big Thunder, I have not yet told my dad about seeing Sasquatch," Jere said, "I'm not sure that he's ready to be told about my wandering in the forest. He might want me to quit coming into the woods completely if he heard about Sasquatch and that would be terrible for me," he indicated to Big Thunder.

"I have already told my mother about coming in contact with the Bigfoot three or four times, and she was greatly impressed," he said excitedly. "She said that she had not seen one in all of the years she lived in Oregon. They had told them in Oregon that the creature was half-man and half-animal," he said to the old Indian.

"Little Brother, I had gone eighty years in the wilderness without seeing even one Sasquatch that I had heard so much about from my kinsmen," Big Thunder exclaimed. "I had almost made up my mind that the shaman and others were making up and telling us tall tales about them and wanted everyone to believe there was such a creature when it didn't even exist," he said to his young friend.

"However, I will tell you that these creatures are not half-man and half-animal like your mother heard in Oregon," he assured the boy. "They are a completely different species of animal in the forest and are not related to human beings," he stressed.

"Big Thunder, I have one peanut butter sandwich left," Jere told him. "We can share it now." Jere took the sandwich out of the bag and unwrapped it. He broke it in half and handed half to Big Thunder.

"Oh no, Little Brother," he objected. "I am not hungry. You go ahead and eat all of your sandwich that your mother fixed for you.

I wouldn't care for anything to eat. I eat very little, anyway," he told Jeremiah.

Jere begged him, "Please, Big Thunder, take half of this sandwich and make me happy. I have already eaten one and I would be unable to eat all of this one, anyway," he told his friend. "So you just go ahead and take this half so you can help me eat it up," he begged again. He handed the half of a biscuit sandwich to Big Thunder.

Big Thunder finally took it and the two of them ate the sandwich.

The old Indian said, "Little Brother, I had forgotten how good a peanut butter sandwich could taste. I want to thank you for allowing me to remember the taste and to have some wonderful, pleasant memories of times past. I must say, that your mother certainly knows how to bake a tasty biscuit. This is the best biscuit that I have ever eaten in my entire life, bar none," he asserted.

"I am very grateful to you and your mother for sharing this delicious treat with me," he stated to his friend. "I will thank you to tell her for me that I sincerely appreciate her thoughtfulness," he stated firmly. "Tell her that I said thanks, and I mean it very sincerely, my friend.

"Little Brother, we should pick a spot in the woods where the two of us can meet in the future so that we will not miss one another," Big Thunder said. "We came very close to missing each other today, and each of us would have thought that the other one might not have wanted to be seen," he explained.

"I agree," Jere replied. "Yes, we really would have missed each other today if it had not been for our animal friends raising such a ruckus."

"Why don't we agree to meet each time here by the little creek from now on since this stump and the log over there will make a perfect place for us to sit and wait for each other," he suggested. "It will also make a good sitting place where we can talk when we meet again in the woods," he suggested.

Jere told him, "In case I can't come here some day, I don't want you to wait past one o'clock. That will mean that I'm not coming that day. I know you can tell time by the sun," he concluded. "I wouldn't want you to wait unnecessarily one day, thinking that I might come and then I wouldn't be able to show up that day at all" Jere said.

"That's a very good idea, Little Brother," he agreed. "You are a very smart little boy to be only seven years old. We will certainly abide by your rules on our meeting place from now on," he said.

Big Thunder said, "I'm thirsty now after eating that delicious peanut butter sandwich. I think we should get a cool drink of water from the brook."

"Me too," Jere agreed. They both got down by the edge of the brook and drank their fill. It was very satisfying and thirst quenching.

They got up and went to sit on the fallen log. They had only been sitting for a few moments when, out of the corner of his eye, Jere noticed something moving. He turned his head slowly to see it better and saw that it was White Spirit coming in a direction that would bring her very close to the log where they were sitting if she didn't change her course.

"Sssssshhhh," Jere warned Big Thunder. "Don't move and don't make a sound," he whispered to the old Indian, who had not yet seen her. Jere spotted White Spirit as soon as she topped the ridge, and she hadn't even noticed them yet.

"White Spirit is coming to pay us a visit," he told Big Thunder. "But she doesn't know that we're here. She will be surprised when she finds out that we're close by when she gets nearer," he said in a very low voice.

Big Thunder said, "If she truly is a spirit and not a real wolf, then she will know for certain that we are here, without any question."

Jere whispered, "Let's be perfectly still and not move a muscle. She won't know that we are here until she smells us, and then it will probably frighten her. Sssshhh, she's getting closer," he whispered to Big Thunder, who still couldn't see her.

White Spirit was walking along at a leisurely pace and was beginning to get closer to the old Indian's side of the log. She stopped, put her nose up in the air and sniffed. She took another step, stopped again, lifted her nose high in the air, and sniffed again, rotating her head very slowly. She knew that something was nearby that shouldn't be there. She must have noticed the old

Indian about that time, because she let out a soft whoof that could barely be heard. Evidently she was trying to get one of them to move so she could see if it was something dangerous. She thought she might frighten them with a little whoof, but it didn't work. She was still puzzled and didn't know quite what to do about the alien odor that had permeated her nostrils. She gingerly took a few more steps, being very precise and cautious about where she planted her feet. She stared at the two of them, straight on, studying them, sniffing the air and attempting to determine where that strange scent was emanating from.

She was only about ten feet from them now and breathing heavily, wondering what was causing the hair to stand up on the nape of her neck and the top of her shoulders. She was probably a young female, since an older wolf would have bolted instantly and left nothing to chance in a situation as questionable as this one. An older female would have been over the top of the next ridge five minutes earlier.

Jere decided to see how far he could go with her before frightening her enough for her to bolt. She had been slightly accustomed to their odor before, and she may have recognized it. Jere let out a low whistle but didn't move a muscle. White Spirit's ears shot straight up and her glassy looking eyes took on a glow that was weird looking. She was a true albino, and her eyes were pink. Jere was getting slightly uneasy from the stare she was piercing him with. He wondered if she was getting ready to charge toward them. He had never heard of a wolf causing harm to any human before, but White Spirit didn't appear to be any ordinary wolf, and these weren't any ordinary circumstances.

Just then, Big Thunder made a strange, guttural sound that seemed to emanate from deep within his throat. It must have astounded White Spirit as much as it did Jere. She lowered her tail and head and came over to where Big Thunder was sitting on the log and muzzled the back of his hand momentarily.

She was still rather uneasy about the friends she had found sitting on the log and began slowly walking off in the general direction from where she had originally come. She may have had a date with a male over on the next ridge or maybe she was just out for an afternoon walk. She trotted along slowly for ten or twelve steps, stopped, then looked around to see if they were still watching her, and then finally disappeared over the top of the next ridge.

"Well, that's quite an experience that we have just had, Little Brother," the old man told him. "That is something that you will be proud to tell your grandchildren someday in the future that should interest them a great deal," Big Thunder said.

"I've never had anything like that happen to me in my lifetime," the Indian attested. "But I had heard the sound of a mother wolf talking to her little ones, so I tried to imitate the sound as best as I could by making that sound in my throat. It must have sounded very familiar to White Spirit because it aroused some memories and got her full attention," Big Thunder told his friend.

"Little Brother, you have now proven to me, without a doubt, that White Spirit is a real wolf and not an apparition as I once thought," he admitted. "I want to thank you for allowing me the opportunity to witness that outstanding event. Without your eyes to locate her it would have been impossible for me to ever have seen her, and it would have been a golden opportunity missed. I am very thankful to have you as a blood brother, and I want you to know that I hold you in very high esteem," he confessed to Jeremiah.

"There have been so many things that we have witnessed together since we became blood brothers," he reminded Jere. "Just think of all the things we would have missed if we had never decided to become good friends back when we first met," he said. "Just think of all the wonderful times we have spent together in the forest since we have known one another. I am amazed when I think of all the exciting experiences. Do you think that it might have been divine providence that interceded in our behalf to show us all of the great wonders in the world?" he asked.

"I don't really know, Big Thunder," he answered. "I only know that I am certainly glad to be your friend and blood brother. I am very thankful that you came into my life when you did and caused me to have such great times and lots of wonderful trips with you. There's one thing I am still worried about though," Jere said. "I haven't yet told my parents about being initiated to be your blood brother because I'm wondering what they might think if I told them," he said.

"My mom noticed the cut on my hand that day, and I told her I had cut it with a knife," he continued. "I didn't actually lie to her, because that's what really happened, but I didn't tell her all of it. I quit carrying my knife, though. The main reason I quit carrying it was on account of Sasquatch being able to sense that it was in my pocket," he explained to Big Thunder.

"Little Brother, that secret will be known only by you and me," he promised. "I will carry that secret to my grave without ever telling a soul. It will be yours and mine alone, and the one up yonder who looks down on us constantly. I will never allow our secret to pass from my lips. You may do the same," he said to Jere.

"Thanks. I really appreciate that," Jere told him. "I'm certainly glad to be one of your friends," Jere said again.

"You are not one of my valued friends, you are my only greatly valued friend, and I cherish your friendship and that of your family very highly," he acknowledged.

"This has been a very enjoyable day for me, Big Thunder," Jere reminded him. "I am so glad that we found each other so we could talk and visit each other again. I'm going home now, and I hope to see you again soon. I'm not certain what I will have to do tomorrow, except that I know that I will have to do schooling in the morning. My mom is my teacher, you know," he explained.

"That's fine," Big Thunder told him. "I'm glad that your mother loves you enough and takes enough interest in you to give you a quality education. I'm real proud of your mom and dad for teaching you the most important things in life. I will now leave you and go back to the place where I spend my nights. May God go with you and keep you until I see you again," he said as they parted and went their separate ways.

"Bye, Big Brother," Jere said. "And may God bless you, also," Jere told him as he waved his hand in a salute and headed through the woods toward his home. Jere turned around to look and wave at Big Thunder and noticed the tears rolling down the side of Big Thunder's face. He, too, was smiling and waving his hand good-bye to his best friend and little blood brother.

✦ ✦ ✦

Angela was well pleased that her Jeremiah had come home in plenty of time to keep her from worrying about what might have happened to him. It was not necessary for her to ask him if he had enjoyed his day. It was written all over his face, and she recognized it the moment she saw him. He couldn't have been more satisfied. He was unable to contain his enthusiasm about the happenings of the day, but he feared that if he told his mother about their encounter with White Spirit that she might think that he had made up the story and decide that it wasn't true. He wasn't even sure that he would have believed another seven-year-old boy if he had been told that story.

When supper was finally ready he didn't have to be called twice. He was famished, and his mother was glad to see that he had a healthy appetite. She smiled at him and his dad constantly during the supper meal. Evidently she was happy, also.

Angela was up early the next morning making a fire in the cookstove. She was frying flapjacks when Jeremiah arrived in the kitchen. Angela said, "Good morning, son. And how are you this fine morning?" she asked.

"I'm fine, Mom," he answered simply.

Again, she smiled one of her beautiful smiles, pulled him to her, and hugged him very hard until he said, "Mom!" She smiled at him, held his face in her hands, and kissed him on the cheek. She was still smiling when she resumed frying the flapjacks in the skillet.

Jere hadn't said very much to his mom or dad about his journey into the woods the day before, except to tell them that he was really happy that he had been allowed to go. He confirmed the fact that he had a wonderful time with Big Thunder and relayed the information that he had been given to say hello to them and that he was proud of them for teaching him in a manner where he would receive a desirable and beneficial education.

"That's fine, son. You be sure to tell him that we would still like for him to come and visit us so we can meet him and talk to him. We would be more than happy to have him come for supper some night. He seems to be such a nice man," Angela told her son.

"I did tell him, Mom, I begged him," he said. "But I don't know. I would love to have him to come and visit, also," he told her. "He did say that the next time that I came into the woods that he would let me know when he would come to have supper with us. I promise that I will do my best to make certain that he will come to pay us a visit" he assured his mother.

# CHAPTER
## 8

Jere had just finished eating his breakfast of oatmeal with honey and Josh had asked for another cup of coffee when Jere's sharply tuned ears perceived the unmistakable sound of a motorboat coming up the river. From the sound of it, it was getting pretty close to the proposed landing site down the hill from their cabin.

A moment later, Josh turned his head to one side, indicating that he had also heard the motorboat, which was definitely coming up the Grays River and getting much closer to the spot where their landing would be. Josh had actually shoveled out a slip deep enough for a boat to pull up to the bank alongside the edge of their property down at the river.

He and Jere took off in a pretty quick walk down the hill, and before they had reached the river they could see a boat pushing a wake at a pretty fast clip. The man in the boat suddenly throttled down and headed into the slip and improvised boat landing that Josh had dug out with his shovel.

"Howdy," the man said to them as he held up his hand and waved before his boat reached the shore. "Do you folks live around here?" he asked.

"Sure do, mister," Josh answered. "My name is Joshua Langford and this is my son, Jeremiah. We live in the log cabin there almost to the top of the hill. My wife, Angela, is up there now. Would you like to come up and visit for a spell?" Josh invited him to the cabin. "I think we still may have two or three cups of coffee left in the pot and it's still on the stove," he said to the stranger.

"Well, thanks for the offer," he replied. "But I don't really have the time. My name is Ben Ferguson, and I have a place of business down the river at Rosburg. I had heard that there was a new family that moved in somewhere up here, but I never saw anyone coming downriver in a boat, so I got to wondering if you might need one to travel on the river. I'm in business to sell new and used boats, and I'd be happy to try to make you a deal on one that would satisfy you. I have a wide variety of watercraft and it might be possible to find one that would fit your needs, Mr. Langford," he tempted them.

"I'm glad to know you, Mr. Ferguson; just call me Josh," he answered. "Yes, I'd dearly love to have a boat, although I'm not certain I can afford one. I'm know boat prices can get to be pretty steep in some cases, and I'm a man of very limited means," he explained.

"Just call me Ben," he answered. "Well, yes, prices can get to be pretty steep, but like I told you before, I handle used as well as new boats. Since you don't have any way to motor downriver, why don't I take you and your son with me on a ride down to my place of business and allow you to look the merchandise over? If you don't find anything you like or can afford, then I'll be glad to bring the two of you back here to your cabin. I think the boy might enjoy the ride, wouldn't you, son?" he asked.

Jeremiah answered, "Yes sir, I certainly would like that, sir." He was anxiously awaiting his father's reply to the man, and he hoped it would be in the affirmative.

It was quite evident to Josh that Ben was a very experienced salesperson from the way he presented himself to them and from his approach to the young boy for some help in appealing to his dad. "Let me and Jere run up the hill to tell my wife where we are going, and we'll be back down here in a few minutes to go with you," Josh told Ben.

They were both winded from running up the hill, and Angela didn't know if they were injured or what had happened since they burst through the door breathing hard.

"What's wrong with you two?" she demanded to know. "Are you hurt? What's wrong, Josh?" she asked again.

When Josh finally got his breath, he told Angela all about the man selling boats at Rosburg and that he and Jere were going to take a trip downriver with him to look at a used boat or two. "I will need you to get me the twenty-dollar gold pieces out of the coffee can to carry along with me, just in case," he told her.

Angela brought the can and its contents. He opened it and got five twenty-dollar coins out, closed the lid on the remainder, handed it back to Angela, and said, "This ought to be a'plenty, if the prices are right," he told his wife, kissed her, and told her to wish him luck. "Would you like to come with us?" he asked as an afterthought.

"Oh, no," she said. "I'd just be in the way. You two go ahead and take the trip. I will stay here and guard our cabin while you're gone," she said jokingly. "I want you two fellows to have fun," she said and presented them with a beautiful smile.

Josh and Jere ran back down to the boat. They would be able to catch their breaths as they traveled downriver to the boat dealership.

Josh unlashed the line from the sapling, tossed it in the bow, and pushed off from the shore. He jumped on the bow, crossed over the seating area, and sat down. Ben put it in reverse and slowly backed out to midstream. He then put the prop in forward gear and gave it about half throttle.

"Josh, you and Jeremiah hang on tight now," he warned. "Here we go," he told them as he shoved the throttle forward. The bow came completely out of the water and the boat lunged forward like a rocket. Jere loved riding this monster. He was thrilled at the opportunity to ride a fast boat. He hoped his dad was able to buy one for them. He was already thinking that he would like to take Big Thunder for a ride.

Ben handled the boat with ease, and it seemed he was very proficient at it. Before Josh could get comfortable they were already pulling up to Ben's dealership. He eased the boat up to the dock where he had other boats tied up, got out, and invited Josh and Jere to walk along the planks with him to see the many boats he had for sale. As they walked, Josh would ask Ben the prices of certain boats. He didn't always know the exact price of every boat without looking it up, but he pretty well knew very close to the true price. Josh would shake his head at the price of one and they would walk on to another one. Josh had almost already come to the conclusion that he most definitely would not be able to afford anything that Ben had for sale there at the marina.

"How much do you want for this one, Ben?," Josh asked of a sleek-looking red and white boat that appeared to be somewhat seaworthy.

Ben answered, "I'd have to have about one hundred and fifty dollars for that one, Josh, but it would be a bargain. That would be a fine boat for traveling the river, and it would also take to the Columbia like a breeze," he assured Josh.

Josh shook his head and told Ben he wouldn't be able to afford anything quite that expensive but if he did buy one it would have to be able to run on the Columbia.

"I have an old inboard motorboat around here at the back of the dock that you might be interested in," Ben said. "I haven't been able to get it to run, but otherwise it's a fine boat with a solid hull and a powerful inboard motor that runs on tractor spirits instead of the high-priced gasoline," he was trying to interest Josh in an old piece of junk that he wanted to get rid of. He had hidden it around in the back so no one could see it.

Josh followed him to the rear dock where the boat was. He unlatched the metal hood cover over the engine room and peered inside. It really did appear to be a solidly built boat. It didn't seem to have any water leakage around the keel or prop shaft.

"Tell me one thing: What good would a solidly built boat be to a man if it doesn't have an engine that will start?" he proposed this important question to Ben. "I don't intend to have an old mule walking along the bank pulling it with a rope," he jokingly said. "When you say she won't start, does that mean that you have been attempting to start her and haven't succeeded yet?" he asked of Ben.

"Well, yes and no," Ben admitted. "I don't really know anything about an old inboard engine such as the one in this boat, so I don't really know if it will run or not," he confessed. "I figured that maybe if you knew anything about her, I could let you have her real cheap and I would tow it upriver to your place so you could work on it in your leisure until you got her running," he told them.

"Tell you what, Josh," Ben said quickly. "I'll take forty dollars for her just as she sits in the water and I will tow her up to your landing in the next couple of days so you can start working on her," he promised.

Josh said, "I don't give two hoots and a holler about a fine boat with a solid hull and a powerful inboard motor, if the dad-blamed thing doesn't run."

Josh knew that Ben must be ashamed for customers to see the boat and that was the reason for having it hidden in the back. Josh had already surmised that Ben was actually trying to get rid of the boat any way he could. He would probably have allowed someone to just take it and get it out of his way if they agreed to tow it off.

"I see that I have a customer who needs my attention, Josh," Ben said. "Excuse me for a few minutes. You and Jere go ahead and look her over all you care to while I'm showing this gentleman some of the latest models we've just received. Be with you in a little while," Ben told him. Josh looked toward the front of the marina and saw a gentleman who was dressed in a suit and tie waiting there.

Ben winked at Josh and said very softly, "This gentleman is looking for an expensive rig to buy, and he will take possession of it right away. Sorry to have to leave you in a hurry like this," he apologized.

"Take your time," Josh told him. "I understand."

Josh immediately began to look over the engine room. He wasn't worried about the hull. It seemed to be in solid condition and since it had been sitting in the water for some time and was still afloat with no sign of leakage in the bilges, he was impressed. He did notice one thing that he liked. He saw a bilge pump that would come in handy if the hull ever started leaking. Another thing that he was happy about was right in front of his eyes. It had a Continental Red Seal engine in it—a sign of luxury if ever there was one. Of course, he recognized that the boat would be considered an old tub by any sane reasoning. He would like to verify that it was a genuine Continental Red Seal engine, but he was certain that no other manufacturer would dare use that trademark. He then found the brass nameplate riveted to the engine that assured him that it was genuine. It stated that it was manufactured in Detroit, Michigan. He was also aware of the fact that it was an air-cooled engine and wouldn't have to be prepped for below-freezing operations. He knew that those water-cooled engines had radiators and hoses that sprung leaks and in general just plain rusted out. He liked the looks of that jewel.

It appeared to be a pretty powerful one cylinder engine. He searched for a spark plug but found instead a firing pin that had to be heated and inserted into a receptacle in the cylinder head while hand-pumping a shot of fuel against the hot pin to cause it to fire. He found the hammer that evidently had been used for the purpose of knocking the latch loose and locking it. He knocked open the latch that had been tightly closed on the pin. It appeared to be in pretty fair shape, though it was heat-pitted a bit. It would last at least another year or more if properly taken care of and not overheated with the blowtorch.

He was now wondering about the piston rings. He attempted to move the flywheel with an iron bar that was specifically used for that purpose and felt the heavy resistance instantly, indicating a very good compression in the cylinder. He then assumed the rings must have been in good condition.

He wondered about the rudder and prop but didn't know how he could get them inspected without getting wet. He also wanted to check the forward and reverse gears to see if they were tight but decided that was impossible, too. He had just about covered everything he had wanted to see and had actually been surprised at the overall good condition of the vessel. Of course, he still didn't know how much more money it would take to put the boat in a decent runnable condition if he bought it.

He had brought five twenty-dollar coins with him, just in case he might happen upon a good deal. He left another five gold coins in the can at home as he wasn't about to spend their last hundred dollars on a boat.

Ben had finished with his genteel customer and returned smiling. He must have made a very profitable deal with that man. Ben said happily, "Yes sir, Josh, ain't she a beauty? I feel like you could make a regular yacht out of this little gem with just a little bit of fixin' up. Yes sir," Ben said one more time. Ben sounded like a super salesman who was ready to strike while the iron was hot. He was ready to consummate a deal with Josh.

Josh said, "Well, you know, Ben, a boat can look sharp and beautiful all she wants, but if she can't get you up and down the river, then what good is she?" he wanted to know. Josh figured he might have been a bit sarcastic to Ben, but then, he was trying to make a deal with a consummate salesman who knew all the ropes and he didn't want to give any concessions that he wasn't forced to give, he figured.

"Well, I suppose I'll have to agree with you about that," Ben admitted to him. "Yes sir, you are absolutely right, so what kind of offer would you like to make me right now, sir?" he asked Josh.

Josh didn't answer but appeared to be in deep thought. He continued to remain silent for some time.

Ben looked at him and broke the silence by saying, "Tell you what, Josh. Since I have been trying unsuccessfully to get rid of her for some time now, I'm going to make you an offer that you won't be able to refuse," he said.

Josh looked at him but didn't say anything. He was waiting for Ben to make such a deal. Ben had just admitted that he had been trying for some time to get rid of her and Josh knew that he had the salesman backed up in a corner, now.

"I'll take thirty bucks for her just like she sits in the water night now," he said to Josh. "Yes siree, I'll make you a fine deal for just thirty dollars. How does that strike you, my good man?" Ben asked. "Let's shake on it," Ben said as he extended his hand.

"Well, I don't really know, Ben," Josh answered. "She may have to be towed everywhere she travels. Now wouldn't that be a corker?" Josh asked.

"If you can just put in a little bit of work on her, she'll make you a good boat for traveling up and down the river," Ben said to him. "What do you say?"

"I say she may never run a lick, and you know it," Josh answered him. "I should probably have my head examined, but I'm going to offer you twenty dollars for her right now, just as she sits in the water," Josh told him.

They shook hands on the deal and Josh handed him a gold piece. Ben said he would have to go to the office to make out the bill of sale and bring him a receipt.

Josh figured that Ben probably didn't have one red cent invested in the boat, since it was likely a trade-in from another customer. The gold coin was pure profit and Ben was probably glad to have someone to remove that piece of junk from his marina.

"Where can I buy some tractor spirits?" Josh wanted to know.

"I'm gonna be good to you, Josh," he said. "I will fill the fuel tank on your boat to get you started out right, and when you run out of fuel you can come on down here to see me and get your tank filled again," he promised them. "You should buy a two-gallon kerosene can to keep in your boat and maintain it full of spirits, just in case you run out somewhere on the river before you can get to a fuel pump."

Ben then headed for the office to fill out the paperwork on the boat. Josh removed the blowtorch from the side of the hull, pumped it up and struck a match to light it. He adjusted the flame until he had a blue tip coming from the burner. He knocked the pin out of the cylinder head, held it with a pair of tongs and touched the blue tip of the flame to the glow plug to heat it up. When it had reached a color that was between bright red and white hot, he socked it into the receptacle, locked the latch down with the hammer, and turned the torch off. He had the flywheel prepositioned to the white mark, indicating the piston was just above dead center, hand-pumped a charge of spirits into the cylinder head, and moved the flywheel just a bit with the steel rod. It moved less than six inches before it fired off like a pistol shot. Jeremiah jumped like he was hit in the head.

When the engine started on the very first attempt, Jeremiah's eyes almost popped out of his head. They were as large as half-dollars, and he was smiling from ear to ear. The engine was running smoothly and throated superbly at one quarter throttle. Josh allowed the engine to warm up at quarter throttle and then moved the throttle back and forth a few times to notice that the engine revved up and responded nicely.

When the engine had warmed up sufficiently he pulled the throttle to about one eighth and placed it in forward gear. The prop moved the water under the hull and pulled the lines taut that were tied to the pier. He then reversed the propeller and witnessed the accomplishment of the very same thing from the opposite direction.

Josh laughed out loud, banged his fist on top of the engine cowling and said to his son, "Can you beat that, Jeremiah? We now own a fabulous motorboat for the price of a twenty-dollar gold piece." Josh still couldn't believe it, and Jere was ecstatic beyond words.

Ben had heard the putt, putt, putt from the one-cylinder engine putting away from his office. He walked up to where Josh and Jere were standing in the boat and said to them, "Well, Josh, you sure got the best of me on that one, didn't you? I'll have to hand it to you, sir. You're a pretty smooth operator," Ben told him.

"Now listen, Ben," Josh said to him. "I didn't know any more than you did if that old hunk of junk would ever run or not. You know that. So it really appears that maybe both of us came out to the better on this one. You got rid of that clunker eyesore, and we got us a boat that we can run up and down the rivers with," he said to Ben.

"You know full well that we made a deal to take it as is, Ben. I wouldn't have come crying to you if it hadn't started," he told Ben. "I would have taken it home and started working on it to get it in a running condition without saying a word," Josh said.

Ben shook his hand and said, "No hard feelings. It's all in a day's work. You win a few and lose a few. Pull her up around on the other side at the pump that's marked 'spirits' and I'll fill 'er up for you, just like I promised," Ben said, smiling as he shook hands with Josh.

After getting a tank full of tractor spirits, Josh thanked Ben, shook his hand again, and headed upriver for the cabin. It would have been impossible to describe the deep happiness imprinted on Jeremiah's face.

After motoring a while at half throttle, Josh decided to push it up slightly above the half mark. She took hold and handled like a dream. He decided he didn't want to run the risk of ruining the engine before he got it home, so he slowed it down to a still very speedy half throttle. It seemed that they were going about as fast as Ben was in his new boat as he took them to the marina and he had that throttle wide open.

Josh laughed and let out a yell that could be heard for a mile. He said, "How's that for a deal, son?" he asked. "Your mom will never believe we got such a bargain for this outstanding piece of machinery."

"You're right, Dad," Jere answered. "I don't think she'll ever believe that we got such a deal."

"Before cold weather and the harsh winter months set in, I'll use my block and tackle to pull it up out of the water, put it on skids, allow the hull to dry, and give it a paint job from stem to stern," Josh told his son but meant it as a reminder to himself. "In the next few days I will change the oil and grease every alemite fitting on her," he said. "I also intend to remove the prop, check it out, file any nicks out of it, smooth the prop with fine emery cloth, and grease the drive shaft," he said as a reminder to himself.

"This boat will last us another twenty or thirty years; maybe more we take good care of it," he told his son. "A boat owner will be reimbursed for the amount of loving care and attention that he gives to it. Remember that, son," he said to Jere.

# CHAPTER
# 9

Jere had already made up his mind to hit the bank in a dead run as soon as his dad pulled the boat up to the shore. He wanted to be the first to scamper up the hill to tell his mother of the good news, but he now found out that it would not be necessary for him to run up the hill as his mother had heard them coming up the river in their new boat and was already down to the river's edge. She was all smiles and frantically waving her hands as she greeted them while the boat was pulling into the slip near where she stood. From her perspective it appeared as though it was a huge craft and she thought they only went into town to attempt to purchase a tiny little boat. She couldn't believe her eyes when she saw that Josh had actually purchased a fine craft such as that. He was only gone for a short while that morning.

Josh slowly eased the boat into the small slip that he had dug out, not realizing that he would be needing it so quickly. Angela was standing on the bank, grinning like a Cheshire cat.

"Captain Langford, I wonder if you would mind taking me for a boat ride, sir?" she asked, as Jere stepped out on the shore to beam happy greetings to his mother.

"Certainly, madam," he replied. "In fact, I would be honored to have you come aboard my new yacht. I would like to take you and your son on a short cruise upriver to a pirate's island to see if we can find some treasure," he said to his wife. They were all smiling and laughing.

Jere helped his mother aboard, and they sat in the rear seats. Josh put it in reverse gear and eased out to midstream. He then placed it in forward gear and turned the wheel, putting them in midstream. He pushed the lever at about half throttle and headed for the island upstream. Josh wasn't sure how far he would be able to navigate the river in that direction, but he intended to find out.

If the river closed in on him and got too shallow to navigate they would just turn around and go back home.

Angela said, "Wheee-e-e-e! I like this speed, Josh, but are you sure we should be going this fast? Isn't it a bit dangerous?" she wanted to know. The boat actually was skimming along the waterway at a pretty fast clip.

"I only have it at half throttle, Angela," he said. "Would you like me to open it up to full speed to see what it will do?" he asked.

"Oh no," she pleaded. "No, please don't go any faster. This is fast enough. I don't think you should really go any faster," she begged.

Josh eased the throttle down to a crawl and pulled up to a small island in the middle of the river. He told Jere they would get out and look it over if he liked. Of course, Jere didn't have to be asked a second time. He was already to the far side of the island before Josh could tie up the boat. Angela decided that she would wait safely in the boat. She didn't care to venture out on the unexplored island.

Josh hadn't really known if there was an island in the river or not. He had simply been joking to them at the time when he mentioned it previously. Jere was far ahead of his dad in the exploration of the island. Joshua decided to christen the island and take it in the royal name of Langford the Great, in the year of our Lord, A.D. 1922.

Josh found a small tree branch with leaves on it and planted a flag on the north side of the river for all would-be trespassers to see. He said, "I name you Jeremiah Island, now and forevermore. "Hear, hear!" Josh yelled. "Know ye all men now that this island has been taken for the king. Let the captain now fire a twenty-one gun salute from the forward cannon," Joshua commanded from the top of the mountain.

"Josh! If you two kids ever get through playing, would you please come on and let's get started on our way home?" she asked. "I don't really like being out here in the river away from home in a boat that hasn't yet proven its reliability," she stressed.

They paid very little attention to her plea and kept exploring the far reaches of the small island "Hey, Dad," Jere excitedly called. "Do you think there might be some pirate's treasure buried on the island?" Jere asked his father in jest.

"I doubt it, son," he answered. "I don't think you'll find anything on this island except a few trees, bushes, and vines.

"Listen to me, you two," Angela yelled to them. "I said that this boat might not make it back to our cabin from here. We don't really know if we can trust this old Chinese junk for getting us back down the river. Come on now," she pleaded.

"I do believe we need to come back in about a month to pick the wild grapes for your mom when they get ripe," Josh told Jere. "She could make us some good grape jam to go with our hot biscuits and butter some morning for breakfast. It looks like the vines are loaded with green grapes. And look here at the wild blueberry bushes. We'll need to tell your mom so she can help us pick the blueberries when they get ripe," he said.

"Uh oh, I just happened to think of something," Josh said to Jere. "Maybe it would be wiser if we circled around the island next time to see if there is a black bear eating the blueberries or grapes. They can be very dangerous if they have a cub," he said. "I think we should get back to the boat before your mother starts throwing a fit," he said to Jere. "She may not let us come here any more if we stay too long. I'm sure glad we left the motor idling while we were gone. I won't have to waste any time heating the firing pin now," he explained to his son.

"I don't really think we should mention the fact to your mom that black bears are fond of blueberries," he said to Jere. "Just help me remember that the next time we come here we need to circle the island first to look out for animals."

Angela was happy to see them return to the boat because she couldn't hear them above the idle of the engine. She was actually having fun, but she was quite relieved when they returned to the boat. Josh backed the boat out into the river and headed for home.

"By the way, son," Josh said. "Have you thought anything about what we may be able to name our new boat yet?" he asked.

Jere answered, "Well, at first I thought about naming it Big Thunder, but later I got to thinking that maybe we should name her *Angela*, instead."

"I believe you're right," his dad agreed. Josh had been thinking about naming it Angela, also, but hadn't mentioned it. "I think your son has picked out the perfect name for our boat, don't you, hon?" Josh asked his wife.

"Well, I think it's wonderful that you would want to name your boat after me," she told them. "I would certainly be honored to have such a fine craft named in my honor. I can't think of a better tribute to be paid to anyone than that. Thank you, fellows!" she bubbled with joy at the thought of her name emblazoned on the bow of their new boat. The wind was blowing her raven hair over her shoulders and she was enjoying the time of her life with the two men who mattered most to her.

"What a wonderful day this has turned out to be for all of us," Angela sang with glee as Josh eased the boat up into the slip in front of their cabin. Jere disembarked first and then offered Angela his hand to help her to the bank. Jere then tied the rope around a sapling at the water's edge. Josh double-checked the tie and they started toward the cabin, holding hands as they climbed the hill.

"You never did tell me how much you paid for the boat, Joshua," she queried him rather sternly as though he had been intentionally secretive about it to her.

Jere held up his hands and said, "Don't tell her, Dad." And to his mother he said, "It's a secret, Mom."

"Oh no, son," Josh said. "We have to tell her. It's as much her boat as it is ours. And it was as much her money that bought it as it was ours. We have to tell her," he told his son.

Angela said impatiently, "I'm still waiting."

"I'm sorry hon," he told her. "I really am. I just forgot to tell you. We were so excited about getting the boat that I completely forgot about it, Angela. I'm sorry. Hon, it cost us twenty dollars. Can you beat that?" he asked. "It only cost us one gold coin for that beautiful boat! I couldn't believe it either."

"I don't believe you, Joshua Langford," she retorted. "Show me the other four gold coins," she told him in total disbelief, challenging him to produce the other coins for her to see.

Josh reached his hand into his right front overalls pocket and produced the coins, which he then handed to his wife. He said, "Please put these back in the coffee can."

Angela almost fell backward when he produced the coins. "You weren't fibbing! You actually did get it for twenty dollars. I can't believe anyone could buy a beautiful running boat like that for twenty dollars. There must have been some mistake," she said to him.

He replied, "Well, hon, it's a long story, and I will tell you all about it some day. It really was a deal that was on the up and up, and it is not a stolen boat. I have the bill of sale to show that I purchased it. Signed, sealed, and delivered. Besides, I have a verifiable witness right here beside me who will attest to everything I have just told you," he informed her and finally convinced her.

Josh told her that he would need to use some of the money later to buy some twenty-D nails to use to fasten his dock together. He would use twenty or so small logs to sink into the mud under the water and into the bed of the river bank. He said he would need to make a trip to the lumber yard to get some two-by-six decking planks to build his dock. He figured as long as he had to make a trip to the lumber shed that he might as well haul enough lumber to finish out the two rooms upstairs in the cabin. This would be a perfect time to start hauling lumber. He thought it might take two, possibly three trips to haul it all back home in the boat.

"Dad, how do you intend to keep someone from stealing our boat as it sits there in the river? Jere asked.

"Well," his dad answered. "I have two locks and a sixteen-foot chain. I can lock both ends of the chain to make it safe and protect it from the river thieves. I doubt if thieves would ever come up the Grays River anyway. They know there is nothing up here to steal. Those people will normally spend all of their time on the Columbia River, around the larger cities. It would actually be foolish for someone to spend much time down at our dock trying to figure out how to steal a boat such as that. They would figure on getting a rifle ball in their legs if they nosed around here very long. I think it's pretty safe," Josh told them both.

Each of them were still wondering if this bit of good fortune had actually happened to them or if it could have possibly been a dream.

✢ ✢ ✢

The kerosene lamps were burning late in the Langford cabin that night as the talk centered around the acquisition of a seaworthy craft of immense worth and value that had actually been purchased for one gold coin. The subject refused to be dropped by the trio of conversationalists that evening. The unheard-of price and the manner in which it was acquired became the only topic worthy of any prolonged conversation that night, and it prevailed over all other subjects. Angela had attempted twice to get the men to forget about their new toy for the night and go to bed. They insisted that they had more important things to talk about, and besides, Jere said he was not the least bit tired or sleepy.

Joshua had recounted so many things that he wanted to check out on the motor and hull of the craft that he was unable to keep track of all that he had mentioned. He decided to get a pencil and paper to write them down. Many of the items had to do with the luxurious Continental Red Seal engine that he was so thoroughly proud of. He told Angela and Jere that the engine had been specially built at the factory for such a boat and had not been added as an afterthought to some rich man's boat.

At a quarter past eleven Angela announced that she was going to bed. She said she didn't care if they stayed up all night or not. She reminded them to blow out the lamp.

"Good night, everyone," Angela told them. "I love you both."

"G'night Mom, love ya," Jere answered.

"Goodnight dear," Josh told her. "I love you, too. We'll be coming to bed soon."

Jere went out on the front porch one more time to look down the hill to see if the boat was still there. He couldn't actually see it, but he could see some kind of a dark shape at the water's edge and he knew that must be it. He informed his dad that it was still there and decided to go on to bed. Of course, his dad knew that it was still there, but it was reassuring to know that his son was interested in helping to protect his investment.

# CHAPTER
## 10

Josh woke up early the next morning, got out of bed, and partially dressed himself in order to build a fire in the cookstove. He got the kindling wood and stove wood from the back porch, placed them in the firebox of the Red Mountain cookstove, poured a bit of kerosene on the wood, and lit the fire with a wooden match.

Just as the fire was crackling good, he heard Angela's feet hit the floor when she got out of bed. They both proceeded to the wash stand on the back porch to wash their faces and hands. Angela then filled the blue enameled coffee pot with cool water from the galvanized steel bucket, ground some fresh coffee beans, filled the basket with the grounds, and set it on the stove to start perking.

Josh headed out the back door to the two-hole privy, which was located behind the cabin and off to the side near the barn. When he returned, Angela placed a pot of water on the stove to cook their breakfast of oatmeal. She instructed Josh to keep an eye on the water while she made her own trip to the privy.

When the coffee had perked and the oatmeal was done, Angela went to Jeremiah's bedroom to call him to come to breakfast. One of his favorites dishes was oatmeal.

"Oh, my heavens, Josh!" Angela yelled as she came back into the kitchen. "Jere is not in his bed. Now where in the world could that boy be?" she asked herself.

Josh answered very calmly, "Well, one minute ago I wouldn't have known where he might be, but I'll bet a nickel to a hole in a doughnut that I can guess within ten feet of where he is this very minute," he wagered.

Angela ran to the front door as fast as her feet would carry her. She stepped out on the front porch and yelled to her husband,

"There he is! Down at the river sitting in that boat with the steering wheel in his hands and turning it as though he was actually speeding down the river." Angela chuckled and said, "Come out here, Josh, and look at that boy having fun in his new boat."

Josh hurried to the front porch and laughed with her at the sight of their son sitting at the helm of their newly acquired watercraft. He said, "Looks like a real river captain there at the wheel, doesn't he?"

Angela said, "I sure wish we had some film in our box camera, Josh. Wouldn't that make a wonderful picture of our son? Why don't we buy a roll of film the next time we go to town?" she asked and directed at the same time. She yelled from the front porch, "Jeremiah, you get on up here to the cabin so you can eat your breakfast. Come on, son."

Jere hopped out of the boat and promptly ran up the hill to where his parents were waiting for him on the porch. He said in a very calm voice, "Hi, Mom and Dad, is breakfast about ready? I'm sure hungry."

Angela laughed inwardly and told herself that she should have known better than to get upset when she didn't find Jere in his bed. She should have known instantly where he would have been. Both of her boys were acting like teenagers now.

"Dad, how about cranking up the motor and taking us on a short cruise up the river this morning?" Jere asked his father.

"Can't do it this morning, son," he answered. "I need to do lots of work in the engine room to get her ready for the time when we make a trip on the Columbia River. We need to have her in tip-top shape for an important trip like that. We're going to have to pick up some lumber, nails, groceries and whatever else your mother may need in town," he told his son. "We have many things to do in the next several days," he said to his son, but he also wanted his wife to hear those remarks.

Josh said, "We'll need to travel on the treacherous Columbia River when we make that trip, and it can sometimes be hazardous and unforgiving. If a person should lose power in his boat in the swift currents of that perilous river, he would probably be swept into the Pacific Ocean to be lost at sea. I can tell you for certain that we do not want a failure of that engine! I'd like to put it in good enough condition that I absolutely know that I can depend on it to be reliable, tried and true."

"I'm not trying to scare either of you," he emphasized. "I just want you to be aware of the dangerous situations that can arise while boating on hazardous waters if a person should happen to get a bit careless," he told them. "That is precisely the reason why we must have the *Angela* in perfect running condition when we eventually tackle that mean river," he said as his fist hit the table.

"I am reminding you of this as much for my own edification as I am for the benefit of your instructions. I want to make certain that I don't forget the importance of what I have just told to you both and that I don't lose sight of it myself, as well," he sincerely reminded them.

"Oh, my gosh," Angela said, horrified. "I'm not certain that I want to make that trip with you if it's going to be that dangerous. I don't much like the idea of Jeremiah going with you, either. You only paid twenty dollars for that old tub. Do you really expect us to be aboard that underclassed Chinese junk traveling a dangerous river with you?" she asked.

"Now, don't get upset, hon," Josh told her. "Didn't I just tell you that I am going to spend a considerable amount of time and money getting our yacht in a perfect running condition? Just wait until I get her all spiffed up," he promised her. "You'll be so proud of her you'll be ready to go to San Francisco with her. Look, Angela, I would not attempt to take my wife and son on a trip in that boat unless I considered it absolutely safe to do so, you know that," he pledged to her.

"It'll be a fun trip," Josh was trying to convince her. "We will get all dressed up and go to town to spend the day shopping," he assured them.

"One important thing that I will need to get will be a galvanized steel five-gallon kerosene can with a capped spout so that I'll be able to keep an emergency supply of tractor spirits on board at all times," he said. "Help me remember that."

"Sure will, Dad," Jere promised. "Boy, we're gonna get that boat all fixed up so we can take a trip to Madagascar, aren't we?" he asked.

"Well, I'm not sure that we can go quite that far," Josh said. "But we can sure plan some fun trips in the rivers around here in our boat. Angela, I sure wish we had accepted those rags that your mother was trying to give us when we left Oregon," Josh told her. "I could sure use them now."

"Well, smarty pants," she told him. "I did take those rags that Momma wanted us to have, and I have them stored away in a sack in the back room. Just tell me about how many you will need, sir, and I'll be happy to get them for you," she quipped.

"I don't really know how many, hon," he answered. "I just know that I will need a big handful of them to start cleaning the grease, oil, and dirt and grime from the engine. We're going to clean it to look like new," he said. "You won't even recognize her. We'll also need some old clothes to do the work in," he advised her. "We will get pretty filthy as we attempt to remove several years grime build-up from that beautiful old engine."

Josh had plenty of confidence to go along with his determination and willingness to work. He had hopes that some day that solid determination would rub off on his son. He had ample reason to believe that it probably would. He had an extra cup of coffee after they changed into their old clothes, so Jere beat him down to the boat and was sitting at the wheel when Josh arrived. Jere was acting as though he was the skipper of an ocean-going vessel coming up the Columbia River to unload his cargo of candy at the Grays River harbor adjacent to their log cabin.

Josh unsnapped the spring-loaded clips that secured the cowling above the engine room and then placed them on the river bank. They now had easy access to the entire engine room and there was plenty of light so they could see to clean. Josh showed Jere how to dampen his rag with spirits to start wiping the grease and grime. In little more than an hour they had cleaned the engine down to the bright red paint, which looked shiny as new. It had bright green brackets bolted to it. They continued to clean, and the results were absolutely unbelievable. Of course, much of it was on their clothes, but they didn't mind one bit.

"Go easy with the tractor spirits," he warned Jere. "I don't really think we should have any problem with fumes accumulating with a good breeze blowing, but we should use it sparingly on the rags," he told his son.

"If you feel you should get out of the fumes at any time, just step out on the bank for a while," Josh told him. "I'll do the same thing if I feel the need," he told his son.

By noon they had made an appreciable achievement of reaching the goal they had set and the bright, shiny, red engine beneath all that scum they had removed was simply astonishing. It actually looked like a brand-new engine.

"It's an engine that any captain would be doubly proud of, son," Josh told him. "I can't wait to show your mom."

"What do you think that high-powered salesman would say if he could see it now?" Josh asked his son.

"I think he would probably want it back," Jere answered.

"Well, let's walk up the hill to the cabin and grab a quick bite to eat, get a drink of water, and head back to finish our job; what do you say, son?" his dad asked.

"Ready if you are, Dad," Jere responded. Jere stood back and admired the work they had accomplished in cleaning up the beautiful engine. He couldn't have been more pleased if it had been a pleasure yacht. He now wanted to be able to tell Big Thunder about his new boat. He was certain that his friend's chest would also swell with pride if only he could talk him into coming home with him some day.

They raced up the hill to the cabin, and, of course, Josh lost the race. Intentionally, it was assumed by Angela, who was waiting on the front porch with a big sunshiny smile and a pretty apron around her thin waist as they ascended the steps.

Josh said, "We're hungry, hon. Got anything to eat?" he asked.

"Of course I do," she said as she smiled. "But neither of you will get a bite to eat until you march around to the back porch and take soap, water, and a wash cloth to scrub the grease off. Only then will I put your ham, baked potato, and pinto beans on a tin pie pan and let you eat while sitting on the back steps," she unconditionally laid the law down.

"Aw, Mom," Jere said. "Do we have to sit on the back steps to eat our dinner?" he complained.

"'Aw Mom,' my Aunt Fanny," Angela replied sternly. "You will not come into my kitchen looking like that. And when you come home late this afternoon, I will have some hot water on the kitchen stove and both of you will take a good bath out here on the back porch before you come into my kitchen. I want you to be squeaky clean and smiling when you come into our precious home," Angela told them in no uncertain terms.

As soon as Angela entered the kitchen, Jere said to his dad in a low voice, "Boy, she's kinda on a rampage, isn't she, Dad?"

Angela had stopped just inside the back door, purposely, to attempt to hear what they might say about her after she left. A huge smile lit up on her face, and she could barely keep from bursting out laughing after hearing what had been said. She held her hand over her mouth and bolted to the living room so they wouldn't be able to hear her chuckling out loud to herself.

Josh never did answer his son's question but nodded his head in the affirmative and gave him a sly, quick smile.

"Angela," Josh yelled to his wife. "Dear, would you be so kind as to bring us a glass of cold water, please?" he asked very politely.

Angela opened the kitchen door to the back porch and said, "Now, what is it you two are yelling about? I couldn't make out what you were bellowing about when I was in the living room," she told them.

"Would you please give us a glass of cold water, dear?" he reiterated.

Angela brought them each a meal on a pie pan and two glasses of cold water. She then asked, "Would there be anything else you would like, kind sirs?"

Josh answered, "Well, it would have been nice if you had buttered our biscuits."

Angela replied, "I'm sorry, but you gentlemen will not be having any more butter on anything until we can make a trip into town to purchase some. We have used up the last of our butter, and we don't own a cow," she told them in a lighthearted manner.

She swirled her shiny hair sideways across the back of her shoulders by flipping her head. She smiled at her two best fellows in the whole world.

"Okay, hon," he said. "Would you please mark that down on the list of things to get, so we don't forget anything? If everything goes according to plan we will be making that much-needed trip next week," he promised. "I'd really like for you to make a list of things that we should be needing for the whole month on that tablet, if you think it's possible," he told her. "We will be needing to make a trip to town about once a month for supplies, dear," he told her.

"That was a very delicious lunch. Thank you," Josh said. "Son, don't you think it's about time we got started back to cleaning the engine room, again? We've made some good progress on it."

"I'm ready when you are, Dad," Jere informed him as they started down the hill to where their pride and joy was waiting for them. They really wanted to have her name stenciled on her, but that would require a complete coat of white before they could complete that and that could possibly take a lot of time to do.

The afternoon was fast disappearing, but the progress they had seen thus far had made it well worth the sweat that was pouring from their foreheads. Angela would be proud of the cleaning job, and Josh never imagined that such a beautiful red engine could emerge from a dismal-looking, unattractive piece of grimy machinery that had been hidden under all that dirt, grime, and grease until today. Old Blue jumped up on the bow as if to give his stamp of approval but left shortly after that to go up the hill.

Josh didn't realize until that afternoon that his Red Seal engine had a fuel gauge to indicate how much fuel was left in the tank. A fuel gauge is of no benefit if it's covered up with dirt and can't be seen.

It was near sundown when Josh told Jere that they had completed all that he had wanted to get accomplished that day. They gathered up all the rags that had been soaked with spirits and set them afire before they started up the hill.

After the rags were mostly burned up, they climbed the hill, knowing that a full tub of hot water, two wash cloths, a bar of yellow lye soap, and a scolding if they failed to use the other three would be waiting for them on the back porch.

They didn't even bother to stop at the front porch just in case it might provoke Angela's wrath once more, and they were not quite ready yet for that resurgence of criticism from her.

As soon as Jere stepped one foot on the back porch he was handed a wash cloth, a bar of soap, and explicit instructions to undress, place his filthy clothes on the wooden bench, and proceed to wash himself thoroughly and then some. He answered, "Yes ma'am," and promptly complied with her verbal orders.

"The same goes for you, too, sir," Angela said as she winked at her husband and greeted him with a smile.

"Yes ma'am, I intend to do just that," he said and winked back at her.

Angela had never heard so much whistling and singing that was coming from the back porch in all her life. It wouldn't surprise her if it called up a bull elk. She sneaked a peek through the kitchen window and smiled at the sight of her two men. She kept herself out of sight in case they might be looking. She had been in a very jovial mood since they had acquired the boat. She seemed to be a lot more happy and pleased these last few days than Josh could ever remember her being.

Angela purposely kept them waiting for their clean clothes to make certain they went over the particularly dirty places twice. She finally went out to the back porch and deposited their clean clothes. She laid two clean towels on top of their clothes and said, "I'll see you boys in a few minutes. Supper needs about ten more minutes." Angela pretended not to look at them as she put the towels down, but she stole another glance at her husband and winked at him again.

Josh thought she was acting very unusual. He thought, "That girl is sure happy about something. Maybe it's my imagination," he thought again.

"Okay, Mom," Jere said. "I'm starved. How about you, Dad?" he asked.

"I believe I could eat the south end of a northbound coon, son," he replied.

Jere chuckled at that. It was the first time he had ever heard that old adage. He tucked it away in his memory bank so that he might be able to use it some day.

The three of them enjoyed a delicious meal of salmon croquettes, white beans, cornbread, and stewed tomatoes after Josh had finished asking the blessing. It was necessary once more to forgo the addition of butter to their cornbread, but the meal was delicious, anyway.

"Dad, let's go into the living room and talk," Jere said, as though the two of them needed their space to have a private conversation away from the inquisitive ears of the only woman occupying the other portion of the cabin.

"All right, son," Josh replied. "Let me take my cup of coffee with me. See you later, hon," he said to Angela.

"Just go ahead and be that way," she said, acting as though she were miffed. In reality she was actually glad to get them out from under her feet while she washed the dishes and cleaned the kitchen. Again, she smiled and winked at her husband as the two fellows departed the kitchen for a conversation in seclusion.

Josh sat on the davenport and his son took a chair. Jere cleared his throat, as he had heard his father do on numerous occasions. Jere looked directly at his father and asked, "Dad, have you ever seen a Bigfoot out in the forest?"

"Well no, I can't say that I've ever seen a Bigfoot," he admitted. "But I did see a huge footprint on the edge of a creek bank that was supposedly made by a Sasquatch or Bigfoot, when we lived in Oregon," he confided to Jere. "Many sightings were reported around the lumber towns, but I was never in the right place at the right time. Why do you ask, son?"

"Well, I've seen one at least three times and possibly four; out there in the forest a few miles from here," he told his father. "I know that sounds like it might not be true but I'll tell you that it's the honest-to-goodness truth. I promise you, Dad," he said to his father and crossed his heart.

Josh just couldn't bring himself to believe that his seven-year-old son had actually seen a Sasquatch three or four times already. "Son, you know what happens to boys who make up stories, don't you?"

Jere very calmly asked, "Yes sir, I do. But you know very well that I wouldn't lie to you about this. Honest, I wouldn't."

"Tell me about this sighting, son," he told Jere. "I'd like to hear more about this Sasquatch you claim to have seen."

"Well, Dad, the first time I ever saw her she was coming toward me, but I guess she didn't see me until she was fairly close by as I was sitting on a log," he said. "When she finally saw me she acted a little surprised but didn't get scared and run. She just kinda made a wide circle around me and continued on in the same direction that she had started before seeing me. When she got to the top of the ridge she turned and looked directly at me, maybe out of curiosity, because I hadn't moved a bit from when she first saw me," he told his father.

"I wasn't really scared, but I was so surprised at seeing something like that, that I just froze and didn't even think of getting up off the log," he said. "It was a peculiar kind of feeling, knowing that she was looking at me with those piercing eyes, wondering what I was and wondering if I had intended to try to hurt her."

"How did you know it was a her?" Josh asked.

"Well, I didn't really know at that time, but the next time I saw her she had a little one with her and she didn't get nearly as close to me as she did the first time," Jere said. "She scampered off pretty fast that time but she never did act as though she was afraid of me."

"She didn't turn around and go back when she saw you?" his father asked.

"No, she just kept going in the same direction, but when she topped the ridge she turned around and looked at me longer than she did the first time," he told his dad.

"Son, this is some story," Josh acknowledged. "I have lived in Bigfoot country all of my life and I've never had an occasion to see one."

"That's practically the same thing that mom told me when I first told her about Sasquatch," Jere said.

"Do you mean to tell me that you've already told your mother about this Sasquatch story?" Josh wanted to know.

"Well, yes. I wanted to see how my story about Bigfoot would set with her before I said anything to you about it. I'm sorry, Dad," he apologized.

Angela then walked into the room and verified what Jere had been saying. She admitted that she was also skeptical about the story at first. Josh told Jere and Angela that he would like to see one, but that he would never kill or hurt one with a gun.

"Don't worry about that, Dad," Jere told him. "If a person carries a gun into the woods then a Bigfoot will not come close enough for anyone to see him. They can tell when a person has something dangerous with them. Big Thunder had always carried a knife in his pocket and had never seen a Bigfoot in eighty years. When he lost his pocket knife, that's when he and I both saw one at the same time," Jere said to them. "Big Thunder couldn't believe his eyes. He said he had heard stories of Sasquatch all his life and that he was beginning to doubt the authen—, whatever that word is, of what they had been telling him for all those years."

"Authenticity," his mother told him.

"Yes ma'am, that's it," Jere told her. "He was beginning to doubt the existence of a creature like that, but he and I both know that they do exist because we have seen more than one out there in the woods," he stated. "And one of them had a baby."

"This is absolutely fascinating," Angela pronounced emphatically. "Don't you think so, Josh?" she asked.

Josh answered, "Yes, it is. I somehow find it hard to believe, even now. Yet, I'm sure Jere must be telling the truth. I'm compelled to put my trust in his word."

Josh then explained to Jere that similar creatures had been reported to have existed in many countries all over the world. He said, "There were huge creatures living in the snowy sections of the Himalayan mountains known as the Yeti by Tibetans. Europeans called him the Abominable Snowman. Many thousands of verifiable sightings of the Yeti have been made by sherpas, the Tibetan laborers, herders, and packers for the many climbing expeditions that are made there each year to go up Mount Everest or K-2. Photos and castings of the footprints have been made available to scientists worldwide and accounts of eyewitnesses have been published for decades."

Josh continued, "The creature that is found today in the western mountains of the U.S. was called Sasquatch by the early Native Americans and later Bigfoot by many white settlers. There was also a creature of the southern swamp areas of Arkansas and Louisiana known as the Fouke Monster or Skunk Man, because of the vile odor that came from it. There was also one that I heard of that was reported to have been seen in extreme wilderness areas of China, but I can't remember what they called that creature. Evidently all of those large human-like animals from different parts of the world must be of the same species and related," he told his wide-eyed and open-mouthed audience of two very attentive listeners.

"Reports from all over the world told of an animal much larger than a human and possibly weighing four hundred pounds or more," Josh continued. "They were all said to have been covered with long, coarse brown hair except for the Yeti in the Himalayas and it had long white fur covering its body with the other characteristics about the same, regardless of country of origin," he further explained to his wife and son as they sat spellbound.

Josh continued with his version of the explanation. "All of the similar creatures in the world, such as Bigfoot, Yeti, and others, may have been on earth for many hundreds of thousands of years and we just had very little contact with them. They had always had millions of square miles of room to wander in and live in until man recently started encroaching on his territory. The scientific name for that huge early man-like creature is Gigantopithecus. They were thought to have lived in the early portion of the Ice Age or Pleistocene era. The one similar thing that is reported to be prevalent with all of the wild creatures of that type is an ability to exude a terribly offensive odor from some particular gland on its body when it is frightened or angered. Evidently, this offensive smell can be detected for a hundred yards or more and is truly repugnant," Josh explained.

Angela was truly excited. She said, "I'm going to write a letter to my mother and father telling them about all of the exciting things that Jeremiah has observed out in the woods around here. Of course, I'll write to your mother and father and tell them of it, too. Oh yes, and I must tell them about our new boat," she said. "Oh, there are so many things that I must think of to tell them that I'm afraid I'll forget some of them if I don't write them down on a piece of paper right now," she said nervously.

"You get the letters written, Angela, and we'll make certain that they get to the post office to be mailed," Josh promised. 'You will need to put a return address of General Delivery, Rosburg, Washington, on the envelope," he said. "I need to go up there to the post office and tell them that we will be picking our mail up there until such time as they ever start delivering on the R.F.D. route, which may be never," he told her. "I think we may have a few three-cent stamps left in the trunk in the back room," Josh told her. "You might want to check on that, dear."

Angela found the writing tablet, some envelopes, and the stamps. She settled down at the kitchen table with a kerosene lamp and told the men that she didn't want to be disturbed until she had completed writing the important letters.

# CHAPTER
## 11

The sun hadn't yet risen over the hill to the southeast when Josh lightly pressed Jere on the shoulder with his hand and whispered, "Get up, son. It's time to eat breakfast and head downriver in a few minutes."

Angela had made up her mind early that morning that she wanted to go to town to do some shopping. She had already made the biscuits and fried the hog jowl before she woke Josh.

Josh said, "Let's get up now. Eat your breakfast and we'll get an early start on the river to make your mother happy."

Jere's feet hit the floor in a flash. "I was kinda hoping last night as I went to sleep that you and Mom would decide to head for the city to try out our new boat. I got my wish, didn't I?" Jere asked.

"Yes, you did, son," he answered.

Angela was bustling with activity while she was getting everything ready to go to town. She was humming, singing, whistling, and smiling all the while she was buzzing around getting ready for the trip.

"Honest, Jere," his father said. "I don't believe I have ever seen your mother in such a cheerful mood in all my life. Do you suppose the new boat has made her this way?" he wondered.

Whatever the reason, Josh was thankful that she was as happy as she appeared for the last week or so. It had made life so much more pleasurable for them.

All three of them held hands as they descended the hill. Old Blue came down to send them off. He actually wanted to hop aboard and go with them.

After getting the engine started, Captain Langford ordered the first mate, "Cast off the bow line, mate."

Jeremiah saluted and said, "Aye, aye, sir," and pulled the bow line aboard.

Angela tied and then adjusted a bright red bandanna around her head. It beautifully complemented her raven hair. She smiled her approval to the captain and first mate as they tended to their nautical duties aboard the *Angela*.

It could not be said that the engine was purring like a kitten, since a one-cylinder engine just doesn't purr. However, the pleasing *chug, chug, chug* sound it was making evoked some pleasant memories of Josh's childhood, when he had listened to the motor at the sawmill producing the same sounds. It was a sound that denoted strength and dependability. He had almost forgotten it until they purchased the *Angela*. It made him feel right at home on the water and actually gave him a wonderful sense of affluence. His chest was thrust out farther than usual and he almost felt that he belonged to the clique.

Josh only had it throttled to cruising speed, but the red bandanna on Angela's head was blowing straight back in a beautiful, artistic mode that made Josh proud to be married to her. Her laughter must have been contagious, because the men were now laughing and singing, "I want a gal, just like the gal, that married dear old Dad!"

Angela noticed that the only time that she and her son could see through the windshield was when they were stopped. She asked Josh, "Why can't we see in front of us from the rear seats?"

"Only the skipper sitting in the front seat is supposed to see where he is going," he told her. "When I push the throttle wide open, the bow raises in the air to where people sitting in the rear seats can only see to the side," he told her. "Good boats are built that way purposely so the bow rises above the water."

Josh decided that they must have been breaking the speed limit going downriver because they were already pulling up to Mr. Ferguson's dock.

Josh yelled, "Hello there. I'd like to top off my fuel tank this morning."

Ben said, "Good morning, Josh. I see you and Jere have the boat in good running condition. It looks fine."

"Yes sir, we do," Josh told him. "I'd like you to meet my wife, Angela," he said. "Hon, this is Mr. Ferguson."

"I'm pleased to meet you," Angela replied.

"How do you do, Mrs. Langford?" Ben replied. "I know that you are proud of the trade that your husband and son made the other day on this boat."

"Thank you, yes," she answered. "I'm very grateful for having such a fine husband and son," she told him.

"And well you should be, too!" Ben told her.

"I've got about half a tank. I want you to go ahead and top it off. By the way, Ben, I wonder if you would happen to have a five-gallon can that I can buy?" he asked. "I'd like to get it filled, also."

"My goodness," Ben almost flipped over when he saw the shiny red engine now proudly and conspicuously showing itself in the engine room. He said, "It seems like you spent the better part of a month cleaning and rejuvenating this boat, but I happen to know that you've only had it little more than a week," Ben said to him as though he couldn't believe his eyes.

"It's a marvelous accomplishment, Josh," Ben told him, "In fact, I would say that it's a miracle. How did you ever get her looking this good?" he wanted to know.

"Well, it's not a miracle," Josh answered. "It took a lot of sweat, elbow grease, hard work, and a bundle of spirit-soaked rags to get her in this condition. We found a nice-looking bright and shiny engine under all that dirt and grime, though we were beginning to doubt it," he told Ben.

"Well, Mr. Langford, the man who traded it in on a craft three times the size of this never did anything to it except drive it. That's precisely the reason I never allowed him much of a trade-in dollar value on it. He's a big lumber man and he could afford it. The twenty dollars you gave me for it was clear profit. I jacked the price of the other boat up $200 and allowed him a $200 trade-in value on his old boat here," Ben confided to Josh. He added, "I'd never seen an engine like that, and I didn't even know how to start it. You and Jeremiah sure have it looking and running good, though," Ben told them.

"I'm really pleased that someone has it who appreciates her and takes good care of her as I know that you and Jeremiah will," he told them. "A nice, clean-looking boat like this reflects the character of the man who owns her," Ben told him. "I'm proud of you and your son for bringing the character out in that boat. Pull up to the third pump over there and Paul will fill it up for you," he said to Josh. "I have a five-gallon can that I'm going to give you that's in good shape. You can get it filled up with fuel to carry along with you in case of an emergency,"

Josh said, "Thanks, Ben. We're headed for Longview to do some shopping and pick up some lumber."

Ben said, "I can't imagine why you would want to travel that treacherous river all the way to Longview when you can go straight across the river to Astoria and buy all the same things. You would be wasting your time to go all the way to Longview," Ben advised him.

"Well then," Josh said. "Just tell me how to get there."

Ben explained, "First of all, you want to look out for any ocean-going vessels that might be going up or down the river. If you see one coming, it would be best to delay your trip across until the ship is well clear of your course. Next, you will need to head straight across the current from here until you reach the other shore and then head downstream to Astoria, which is about a half mile away. Don't try to pick out a target and steer straight for it or you'll miss it. Give your engine full throttle and head your bow slightly upstream until you reach the other side. You'll get the hang of it. Seasoned boaters might go with the current and allow it to carry them downstream, but I would advise against it until you get to know your boat a little better," Ben told him.

"If you ever have an engine failure on the Columbia, take your shirt off and start waving it until someone sees you and comes to your rescue," Ben told him. "If your boat passes the town of Astoria and you still don't have any power, you may end up in the Pacific Ocean with your craft swamped and capsized. Always have your life jackets on when you're on the Columbia—any time," he emphasized. "I realize that I'm not painting a pretty picture for you but I'm telling you this for your own good," he stressed. "Don't try to be a show-off on your first trip across," he warned. "Remember, you have some precious cargo aboard your vessel, and it would be wrong to assume that you know everything there is to know about the river. Be extra-cautious and don't take any chances. You seem to have a level head on your shoulders. Do as I've told you and you should be fine," Ben said to Josh.

"Last of all, keep a sharp eye out for floating debris in the river that could wreck you or tear up your propeller," he cautioned him. "Look out for logs or bits of wood in the water. You may not realize just how much striking force the old tub has."

Josh said, "You don't know how much I appreciate the advice you have given me and I sincerely want to thank you." He then fired up the Red Seal engine.

Angela said, "Josh, I'm not certain that I want to make that trip across the river now, since I've heard about the dangers," she said fearfully.

"Angela, love, we're going to be just fine," he assured her. "I don't want you to start worrying. You didn't realize that on the trip we made up here with our mules and wagon, it could have been just as disastrous if we had been unfortunate enough to have run into a different set of circumstances. Terrible things could have happened to us on that trip, but we just didn't dwell on it, hon," he said. "Trust me, dear, we'll be just fine. Trust me," he said again.

"I think it will be fun, Mom," Jere persuaded his mother back to her jolly self. "I feel like Christopher Columbus on his way to a new world in his tiny little sailing ships."

"I'll be fine, darling," she assured her husband to relieve some of his anxiety about her. She really did feel better, now. She pulled the written list out of her purse and studied it, attempting to make certain that she had not neglected to include some very important item of consequence.

As the boat cleared Grays River, Josh opened the throttle to full ahead and turned the nose of the bow slightly upstream as Ben had suggested. He never would have known or realized how beautiful the engine could sound until he opened it up full. He could not only hear but also feel the strong thrust of the engine prop against the powerful current of the Columbia. The windshield was protecting them from the air rushing over the bow of the boat. Jere was enraptured. He was enjoying the ride like no other he had ever taken before. Angela was smiling and winking at her husband again.

Her shiny black hair and red bandanna were blowing straight back from her shoulders. Josh was perplexed by the unusually happy mood of his wife recently, but he was thankful for it and glad about it.

"You had better begin turning the boat now, Dad," Jere told him.

"No son, it's not time, yet," Josh said. "You don't realize just how far we are from the other shore. It's actually a lot farther than it appears to be."

"I'll let you know when we are ready to make a turn parallel to the shore," he said. "We'll hug the shoreline until we reach the boating facilities for small craft in Astoria. I have heard that a person doesn't want to take a small boat much farther toward the ocean than Astoria," Josh said. "They say there are some monster waves out at the mouth of the Columbia that can swamp you before you know what hit you," he told them. "This is the very same river we crossed on the ferry boat with our mules and wagon when we came here from Oregon," he explained to them.

"Yes, I know, dear," Angela answered. "I was afraid of it then, too. Of course, I didn't have any option then except to turn around and go back to Oregon, and that's one thing I knew for certain that I wasn't going to do," she told him. "Our hopes were ahead of us then," she reminded him. "There was a whole new world out there in front of us then, just waiting for us to be a part of it."

Josh alerted Jere that he was ready to make a slow, sweeping arc to starboard with the craft. It appeared to Angela and Jere that it was as easy as falling off a log. Their new boat had responded to every command that Josh had given her. She was as smooth as silk and handled like a dream. He now knew that the great things he had heard about those Continental Red Seal engines were well founded and this one especially had lived up to the good name that it had been given. The *Angela* was a proud boat and still had lots of use left in her. All she required in return, was a loving owner who would treat her with affection; someone who appreciated her for her trustworthiness instead of her classic beauty.

Josh throttled down when he approached a dock with several small boats tied up to it. He didn't want to create a big wake that would disturb the other boats. He told his son and wife that common courtesy was an unwritten rule that should be applied to all people, whether on land or water.

"Always remember that, son," his father told him.

Josh pulled into a marina and chose an empty berth to slip into. He asked the man standing there if he might be able to tie up his craft for two or three hours. The man told him it would be twenty-five cents for less than four hours, thirty-five cents for all day, or free if you bought fuel at their pumps. Josh told him he had just topped off his fuel tank across the river.

"Where would the main shopping part of town be?" Josh inquired. "And where would the lumber yard be located?" he also asked.

"There is only one street in town where you can do your shopping, and it's over one block from here," he told Josh. "The hardware store and lumber shed are combined at the west end of town on the first street you come to there."

"Thanks a lot, sir," Josh told him "Angela, you do your shopping while Jere and I walk down to have a look at some lumber. We should be back within an hour," Josh told her. And then added, "Possibly an hour and a half."

"See you two later," Angela told them as she departed for the first shopping spree she had been on in over two years, when they first started saving money for their land in the wilderness.

Josh handed Angela a gold coin and two silver dollars as they parted and went separately to do their shopping. The first place that Angela stopped was an ice cream parlor. She ordered a double-dip chocolate ice cream cone and sat on the rotating stool at the counter to enjoy it.

"I had forgotten how good chocolate ice cream was," she thought as she swiveled the stool. She savored the delicious ice cream with schoolgirl pleasure, and she didn't intend to be in any hurry because she knew that her shopping wouldn't take nearly as long as what the men would take.

Josh and Jere had spent an hour at the building material, lumber, and hardware store. Josh had asked at the marina about getting a name lettered on the boat and he told him he should be able to pick up a stencil kit for painting the name on himself at the hardware store. Josh finally found what he was looking for, a fancy letter stencil kit. He found enough letters that when he placed them together they spelled *A N G E L A*. Jere could hardly wait to get the name stenciled on the bow of the boat. Josh got a pint of special outdoor gloss black that the paint man recommended. He said the people of that area used it to paint names on their boats.

Josh told him he also wanted to buy some lumber and nails but didn't have any way to transport them to the boat. The clerk told him that he would deliver them to the boat, help him load it, and tie it down for a safe crossing on the Columbia. As they left the lumber store, Josh said to Jere, "Now that's the type of business people that I will return to do my trade with."

Angela had been gone for over an hour and had spent most of her twenty dollars in one store. She told the clerk that she would not be able to carry her purchases down to the waterfront marina. He told her that they would be glad to deliver it for her as well as the other packages that she had. That solved her problem. She thought she would have to get Josh and Jere to go back to the store and pick up her packages.

When she arrived at the boat, she found them waiting. She noticed also that they had the lumber loaded and tied down. She expected them to grumble about her spending too much time at the store, but neither offered a disagreeable word.

At about that time a three-wheeled cycle with a large basket pulled up to deliver her purchases. She tried to hand the boy a dime, but he told her he was not allowed to accept it. He said that the delivery was a free service of the store. She thanked him as he departed. He said, "Please come again, miss."

Being called "miss" made her feel wonderful. She smiled and winked at Josh when the boy called her that. She retrieved the red bandanna out of her purse and restored it to the proper place on her head.

Josh went to pay the marina manager. He said, "Thanks. Come back, again. We will always have a slot open for you, and we will look after your boat so that it will not be bothered by anyone," he promised.

Josh said, "Thanks. We will probably see you in a month or so."

Josh took the bow and stern lines off and settled into the captain's seat. He already had the engine idling when Angela came back. He backed it out into the channel to head upriver on the Columbia. He would be bucking the oncoming current.

As soon as he cleared the dock area he advanced the throttle to only about three-quarters since he had a load of lumber on board.

Jeremiah couldn't get over how beautiful his mother looked as the wind blew her bandanna. Josh also couldn't believe how pretty and lovely his wife looked that day on the river. It wasn't any wonder that the delivery boy had called her "miss." She actually did look like a gorgeous young woman, not a mother, and Josh was exceedingly proud of her.

Josh felt as though he wasn't making sufficient progress upstream so he pushed the throttle up to full. He could feel the surge of power as he watched the grin slowly grow on his son's face and felt the motor's response as it fully accepted his command. When they came to the crossing point, Josh noticed that there were no ocean-going vessels in sight, so he cut across the river and headed for the far shore and Grays River. The bow of the *Angela* was ploughing slightly upstream against the current. The sturdy engine had taken the bull by the horns and pushed steadily across the river as though it didn't know that it was carrying a load of lumber and three people. Josh now had ample reason to be even more proud of this magnificent piece of nautical machinery that he had purchased for a single gold coin.

They reached the other shore without a hitch and headed up Grays River toward home. They were in such a hurry to get home they didn't even stop at Rosburg. This was the first time that Josh had the throttle wide open going up the Grays, and although she had a full load of lumber on board, she sped along the rushing current like a rich man's fancy yacht. Josh finally eased the throttle back when he saw Old Blue waiting for them at the boat landing. He must have heard them coming upriver.

Jere and Old Blue acted like they hadn't seen each other in a month. Josh helped Angela carry her parcels up the hill and told her he would go back later to unload the nails, lumber, and other incidentals.

Angela brought Josh a glass of water as he sat on the davenport. She proceeded to the back room to unwrap her packages, making lots of noise with the paper. When she returned to the living room to surprise Josh with one of her purchases, she found him sound asleep on the davenport.

She smiled, blew him a kiss, and walked softly out of the room. She then peeked out the kitchen window to see Jere and Old Blue playing in the back yard. Satisfied that Jere was all right, she decided to leave the rest of her packages in the bedroom and bring her groceries and other parcels to the kitchen table. Most of it was foodstuff. She would put away the victuals while Josh was getting his nap.

She could understand why he would be tired. He had a very difficult and tiring day. She had not realized earlier the huge amount of responsibility that had been placed on her husband's shoulders and the enormous effect of emotional stress and tension that it must have had on him.

Josh finally woke up from his nap and wandered into the kitchen where Angela was humming a tune and smiling. He sat down and asked, "Why didn't you wake me up, hon? I needed to get the lumber unloaded out of the boat."

Angela replied, "Darling, I knew you needed a nap after such a hard day on the river and shopping for lumber. A little sleep did you a world of good. You don't need to worry about the lumber in the boat. I'll help you bring it up the hill in the morning when we can take our time," she said.

He went to the back porch, washed his face and hands to wake himself up fully and said, "I'll lug it up the hill by myself in the morning. It will not be necessary for you to help me," he told her.

Angela told Josh to call their son in from outside to get ready for supper. As soon as Jere heard the magic word, supper, he automatically set his feet in motion toward the back porch.

Josh said, "I don't know how you could possibly have our supper ready when you haven't even lit a fire in the cookstove, dear."

"Well, just you wait and see, Mr. Langford," Angela smiled as she winked at him and said, "We are going to be treated with a bologna and cheese sandwich on real store-bought light bread, sir," she graciously informed her husband as he sat at the table.

"Wow," Jere hollered from the back porch as soon as he heard his mother say what they were having for supper. "We haven't had a bologna sandwich on store-bought bread in about ten years," he said. "Why didn't you tell us before now?" he asked.

"Because I didn't want you two fellows to eat it up before I had a chance to put it on the table," she answered.

After they finished eating, Jere rubbed his stomach and said, "Boy, that was just what I had been wanting for a long time, Mom. Will you have some of it left for when I go to the woods tomorrow?" he wanted to know.

"I suppose if you're going into the woods tomorrow, I can fix you and Big Thunder each a sandwich to take along," Angela told him.

"Boy, that would be great, Mom," he told her. "I can't wait to tell Big Thunder all of the good things that have been happening around here, lately," Jere excitedly said.

"Well, if you're going to announce to him all of the wonderful things that have been happening around here, then I have something else to show you," Angela smiled one of her extra special huge smiles and told them she would be back in a minute.

She returned with a package and unwrapped a pink baby receiving blanket to the astonishment of the two men, whose eyes got as big as half-dollars. Angela proudly announced, "Jere, you are going to be the proud brother of a new baby girl or baby boy, come next spring. I'm hoping we'll have you a little sister," she told him.

Josh got up from his chair, encircled his arms around her waist and squeezed her until she yelled. He said, "You caught me by surprise, hon. Congratulations to you. Well, congratulations to all three of us, really," he corrected.

"This is great news, isn't it, son?" his dad asked.

Jere didn't know exactly what to say. He was also caught by surprise. "Yeah, it sure is," he finally answered. "Can I tell Big

Thunder about this, too?" he asked. "I've got so many things to tell him that I don't know if I can remember it all."

Josh said, "I'd been wondering for the past several weeks why you were smiling all the time. I knew that there must have been something different and more exciting, but I never once suspected that we were going to have a baby," he told her. "I'm so proud of you, dear," he said and kissed her once more.

Jere didn't fully understand how she knew that she was going to have a baby in the spring, but he guessed she knew and would just leave it at that. Somehow, parents just seem to know all about things like that, he supposed.

"Josh, will you need any help from Jere when you get ready to carry the lumber?" Angela wanted to know before she would consent to allowing Jere to go to the woods.

"Let him go ahead," Josh told her. "I'll be able to carry it up the hill myself with no problems if I take my time.

"You go ahead and have some fun," he said to Jere. "Just promise your mother and me one thing, though," he said firmly. "Do try to be careful, son, and don't attempt to get near any Sasquatch. They could be dangerous," he warned.

"Yes sir, Dad. I'll be sure to be real careful," Jere promised as he started to get ready for bed. He had so many things filed away in his brain that he didn't know if he would be able to get to sleep or not. He hoped he didn't forget any of the more important items that he wanted to tell Big Thunder.

"G'night, Mom and Dad," he told them. "See you in the morning," he said as he left the kitchen area.

"Goodnight son. I love you," Angela told her son.

"Goodnight son, we both love you," his dad told him.

"I love you both, too," he told them. "Goodnight."

# CHAPTER
## 12

Jeremiah heard his father starting the fire in the cookstove early the next morning and didn't need to be called. He assumed they would be having oatmeal for breakfast.

He got out of bed, put his clothes on, and made a trip to the privy. He returned to the back porch, washed his face and hands, admired his likeness in the mirror hanging on the wall at the back porch, combed his hair, and mentioned to his mom that he was just about ready for his oatmeal.

"You're not getting oatmeal for breakfast this morning, son," she informed him, surprising both her son and her husband. "Why do you think I went to the store, yesterday?" she asked.

"Well, we didn't really know where you went, hon," Joshua answered. "We had no way of knowing about some of the other things you bought until you got home. For instance, we did not have any inkling that you had a receiving blanket until you opened the package and surprised us." Josh told her.

"By the way, what are we having for breakfast?" he inquired.

Angela was still smiling, laughing, and winking at her husband as she had been for the past several weeks. She seemed to be constantly happy since she found out that she was pregnant. She finally announced, "We're having bacon and eggs this morning for breakfast, with homemade biscuits and milk gravy. We haven't had a breakfast like that in a long time, have we fellows?" Angela asked. "But then, we haven't ample cause for a wonderful celebration like this for a long time, either, have we?" she asked and kept smiling while she was cooking their breakfast.

"You two have a seat in the living room and I'll call you as soon as I get the eggs on your plates," she promised.

The two went into the living room as ordered. Josh said, "Son, what did we ever do to deserve such a wonderful woman as your mother? She's absolutely fabulous."

"You're right, Dad," Jere answered. "Ain't she great?"

The family sat down to the finest breakfast they had had the pleasure of being served in many months. Their life had been filled to the brim with happiness ever since they had completed their wonderful log cabin. It seemed that everything had fallen into place miraculously for them as though their guardian angel was guiding them. Their hopes, their dreams, and their prayers had been fulfilled as the cabin started taking shape and had since continued faithfully for them. The family prayed together every night and read passages of Holy Scripture each Sunday morning as though they were having Sunday school and church there in their log cabin. Their prayers had been answered tenfold, and they were grateful for it. And now, they were going to be even further blessed with an event next spring that would mean the addition of a little one to the family.

Josh said, "Angela, that was the most delicious breakfast I have ever enjoyed in my whole life, dear. We want to thank you very much for taking care of us like this."

Jere said, "Thanks, Mom. It was really good. He then said, "Well, I'm outta here. See you folks later. Bye."

"Just you wait a moment, young man," Angela told him. "Hold on while I fix you and Big Thunder a bologna and cheese sandwich each to take along to eat for dinner. It won't take me more than two minutes, and then you can be on your way," she promised her young son, who wasn't especially wanting to be delayed, although he did want Big Thunder to savor one of his mother's bologna sandwiches.

Angela wrapped the two sandwiches with wax paper she had saved from the bread wrappers. She put them in a paper sack that she had received from one of the stores she had visited the day before. She told him good-bye and gave him a kiss as he stepped out the back door headed for one of his most favorite places in the forest.

"Mom, I'm gettin' too big for that," Jere said sheepishly. "I'm not a baby."

"Son, you will always be my baby, even if you get to be a hundred years old," she reminded him. "Have a good time, but be careful. Bye, now."

"Bye, Mom," he said as he headed toward the destination where he would expect to find his Indian friend.

Jere had been gone about a half-hour when Josh decided to start bringing the hardware and lumber up the hill. He decided to stack the lumber on the front porch instead of in the barn. That would save double handling. He also decided to put a few boards up in the attic in case he wanted to work on the unfinished portion of the cabin when conditions got cold outside.

Angela said, "Give me forty-five minutes and I'll help you carry the lumber up the hill. You're going to need help," she told him.

"Oh no," Josh told her sternly. "You're not about to be carrying a piece of lumber up the hill, dear. You're a pregnant woman, I'll not have you hauling lumber," Josh told her in no uncertain terms.

Josh had also wanted to get the name stenciled on the boat, thinking that if he did want to paint the whole hull, it would be no problem to restencil the name on the bow right over the white paint. The directions on the can of paint recommended that the paint should be cured for twenty-four hours before subjecting it to moisture. This should guarantee that it would not crack or peel on the boat.

Josh had carried all the nails and lumber up the hill. About half past nine it was all completed. He told Angela that since he had gotten done so quickly that he might attempt to nail a few boards in the upstairs portion of the cabin. The stairs had been completed when the cabin was built, and he had laid a few flooring planks in the attic to have some room to store their extra things. All he had to do was to remove the cover and he would have access to the upper floor. He had already installed two dormers on the south side of the roof that would allow plenty of light for him to work in the rooms.

Josh would carry ten or twelve boards upstairs, and then he would nail them. He did this until one o'clock when Angela demanded that he stop for dinner. He hadn't even thought about being hungry until she mentioned that it was past noon. He admitted that he would love to have another bologna sandwich if she'd make him one.

As he was eating the sandwich, he reminded Angela that they should go to Rosburg once a week to pick up more bologna. Josh told her, "I didn't realize how much I had missed eating a bologna sandwich until yesterday. It was certainly delicious and it brought back a lot of pleasant memories of my childhood in Oregon; wonderful memories," he told her.

Angela admitted to Joshua that she had also been craving a tasty bologna sandwich for a few weeks. That's the main reason why she had decided to buy some at the grocery while they were in town. She thought possibly that her unnatural craving might have had something to do with her pregnancy. Anyway, she was glad she got it and she was also glad that the men liked it as well as she did.

Josh polished off his sandwich, smacked his lips, wiped his mouth on his shirtsleeve (as was the habit of most men, Angela reckoned), and went back up the stairs to start nailing some more boards in place. He was the type that when he got started on something he hated to quit until he could see what it was supposed to look like when it was finished. Of, course, he wouldn't be able to complete the entire upstairs in one afternoon, but no one would be likely to tell him that.

It was getting to be late afternoon when Josh stood back and admired the beautiful work that he had accomplished in such a short time. He figured that two more afternoons should put the finishing touches to it. He knew that Angela would be proud of the fine job that he had done that day.

He didn't want Angela climbing the stairs, but she insisted that she could do anything that any other woman her age could do; possibly more, she thought. "Just because I'm pregnant, darling, doesn't mean that I'm helpless or an invalid. I intend to keep right on doing the same things in the same manner that I have always done them; no different," she asserted herself. "After all, hundreds of thousands of women in the world are pregnant at any one given time and the world just keeps on spinning," she said. "I don't intend to be declared incompetent."

Angela climbed the stairs to look at the handiwork that her husband had just completed without any help or assistance from anyone.

"Oh, Joshua," she exclaimed. "I must have married the smartest as well as the best-looking man in the world. Darling, this is just so adorable and functional that I cannot believe you accomplished this with your own two hands. It's so professional looking," she flattered him.

"Of course, I knew that you built our own log cabin, and even completed our fine fieldstone fireplace, so I should have known that this would be a piece of cake for you," she again complimented him on his work. "Oh Josh, I do love you so much, dear. And I'm very proud of you. Please don't ever forget that, darling, please!" she begged.

"I love you too, Angel," he answered. "Why do you think I work my fingers to the bone for you?" he wanted to know.

"You have made me so happy," Angela told him. "You will never realize just how much happiness you and Jeremiah have brought me since we have been married. I'll love you till my dying day," she vowed to him.

Angela had sneaked down the hill while Josh was busy upstairs, to take a peek at the newly commissioned craft, the *Angela*. She later admitted to Josh that she had sneaked a look at the name he had stenciled on each side of the bow. She said, "Josh, that is the most beautiful piece of artistry I have ever seen painted on a boat, and I'm proud to have such a fine craft named after me. It's beautiful," she told him. "Thank you for painting my name on her. I love you dear," she told him.

"I love you too, Angel," he told her.

"There, he's said it again," she thought. "He called me Angel again. And this time I heard it distinctly. I know that he called me Angel," she had decided in her own mind.

"Josh, I know that it's too early to start getting worried, but the sun is going down and it'll be getting dark soon," she said uneasily to her husband.

"Yes, dear, I know," he replied. "I worry about that boy as much as you do, but I don't suppose there's one thing we can do to get him to rush home. Evidently, he will be coming home when he gets good and ready," he said to her.

Josh continued, "I know that he's too young to be traipsing around out there in the woods, especially at night, but he thinks he is as knowledgeable about the wilderness in the back country as we are. I don't really have any intentions of going out there to try to locate him, though, since I wouldn't have the foggiest notion of where he might be or where to start looking for him. He could be anywhere in a ten-mile radius and I would not run across him. I know it will be hard for us to swallow, but the only logical thing we can do is to stay here and wait for him to come home when he gets ready to come in," Josh stated sincerely and firmly to her.

Angela's heart would be pumping overtime until such time as her precious boy had returned to them, but she figured that they should go ahead and eat their supper.

"I can fix Jere something to eat when he comes in later," she grumbled, as though Josh might have been able to be of some aid in this unfortunate turn of events that had turned her cheerful happiness into a mood of slight worry.

"Josh, I sure hope the next one is a girl," Angela said, hoping to bring some of the happy feelings back to them. "Girls are so much easier to raise than boys. They don't go traipsing around in the woods by themselves, causing their parents to lose sleep like many of the boys do," she told him.

"Maybe we will have a beautiful little girl who looks just like you, dear," Josh said to her, hoping to bring back a ray of sunshine to the gloomy kitchen. "Really," he said. "A sweet little girl would be a great addition to our family," he said to her, attempting to bring some lightness into their conversation.

"Josh, I have this fantastic feeling that it's going to be a girl," she told him. "It's a very strong positive feeling I have and I don't know what caused it. I just know it's a feeling of certainty," she affirmed.

They finished their supper and Angela washed the dishes. The later it got the more Angela wrung her hands and looked nervously toward her husband.

"I just wish I could be as calm as you are about this, Josh," she said. "I just don't see how you can sit there and not be totally disturbed about this," she told him as a heavy frown formed on her face.

"Dear, let me tell you," he said. "I am just as deeply disturbed and upset about Jere not being home yet as you are, but I know that it will not do me one bit of good to beat my fist on the table, kick a chair and shout, or to curse and yell to the top of my voice. So I just sit here in the kitchen waiting for my son, wondering what may have happened to make him late in coming home to his parents," Josh told her in terms that he hoped she would understand.

"I'm sorry, Josh," she apologized. "I know I shouldn't yell at you. Forgive me. I know it isn't your fault," she said. "I'm just worried."

"Let's go to bed, dear," she told him. "We can't do Jere any good by sitting here in the kitchen. We should try to get some rest. Maybe it would do us both some good."

Angela had been lying on her side for quite some time, unable to sleep, with tears running down her cheek to the pillow, when she thought she might have heard a noise at the back porch. She could hear her husband's rhythmic breathing, and she knew that he was asleep. She slipped out of bed and slowly found her way to the back door to look out the little window. She could see or hear nothing . . . Nothing! . . . It was very quiet.

Her hopes had been momentarily built up but soon faded when she peered out the window in the back door. She returned quietly to her bed and stealthily lay down beside her husband. She hadn't awakened him, and she was glad that at least one of them was able to get some sleep.

Angela resumed praying. Her prayers were absolutely sincere. And though they may have seemed as though they were selfish to some people, she didn't really regard them as being selfish. She actually felt much better after she had finished praying since she knew for a fact that God really does answer prayers. She was certain of it.

Angela didn't know what time it was but she knew it was early morning. She decided to get up since she couldn't sleep. It was pointless to stay in bed. She got dressed, lit the kerosene lamp in the kitchen, and saw by the kitchen clock that it was four o'clock.

Josh woke up about sunrise. He went to the kitchen, where Angela was sitting in a ladderback chair, put his arms around her neck, and said, "Angela, I understand that your world looks dismal this morning, even though the sun is shining, but I am certain there is a plausible and reasonable explanation for our son staying out all night. When he does come back home then we shall learn why it was necessary for him to spend the night out there in the woods," he told her.

Josh hugged her and kissed her lips. She needed that extra attention and loving that he had graciously extended to her. She smiled, squeezed his hand, and told him that she had felt instantly better since he arrived in the kitchen. She told Josh that she would start cooking their breakfast very soon.

Her eyes were puffy and red, her face was swollen and her hair looked like a straw mat. Josh knew that she hadn't slept and that she had been crying most of the night. She had suffered excessively while waiting for her son to come home.

She went to the back porch, took the water bucket to the back yard, and emptied it on the ground. She pumped a fresh bucket of cold water, took it to the back porch, and filled the wash basin. She washed her face and hands, poured cold water over her neck and head, and took a dry towel to dry her face, hands, and hair. She observed her new image in the large mirror that was hanging on the wall of the back porch and gave approval of what she saw. She stepped into the kitchen. She was still terribly sleepy, but she looked like a queen to Josh.

It was daylight. The sun was shining brightly, and this made them feel better. Josh told her that he was sure the boy would be coming home in an hour or so. He had an optimistic feeling about it. It was a positive gut feeling that Josh said he was unable to explain.

Josh actually did have an extraordinary amount of faith in Jeremiah's ability to survive in the woods. He was a very sensible lad about most of the things in the wilderness that most boys his age would not understand concerning the forests. Josh truly felt that when the boy got home, he would offer a reasonable explanation as to why he couldn't or didn't come back home yesterday.

The fire that Josh had built in the cookstove was getting low. Angela placed a few more sticks of wood in the firebox and stoked the coals so it would catch. When it got hot again, she decided to fry some bacon. She said if Jere didn't come home soon she would fix her and Josh a good breakfast. When she had the bacon fried, she placed it on a piece of newspaper in a pie pan to absorb the fat. She placed that pan in the oven warmer and proceeded to make some biscuits. She figured it would take close to forty-five minutes to prepare the biscuits and bake them in the oven.

At a quarter past nine she used the skillet that she fried the bacon in to start frying the eggs. Josh happened to notice that she had prepared an unusual amount of bacon, possibly on a hunch. She peeked in the oven to check on the biscuits and announced that it would take about ten more minutes to make certain that they would be browned to perfection, the way Josh loved them.

# CHAPTER

## 13

Jere had left the cabin that morning in good spirits. He could barely wait to get in the woods and meet with Big Thunder on the old log by the side of the small creek. Little did he realize when he left home that he would not be returning home in the afternoon. That's for certain.

He had been walking more briskly than normal because he wanted to get to the place where he was supposed to meet his friend. He realized, though, that he was a bit early and would probably have to wait for him to show up.

He was whistling as he walked along the path over the rise and down into the valley. Jere was extremely happy that morning, but he was anxious to reach their rendezvous point and was attempting to rush a bit too fast. He sat down for a while and rested, watching the little chipmunks and squirrels playfully romping in front of him. He caught a glimpse of a doe up ahead for a fleeting moment before she had vanished from sight.

Jere loved being near the wild animals and wildlife in the woods. His mother had advised him that morning that the smell of a bologna sandwich might entice a bear or some other carnivore if one happened to be in the vicinity. She told him that if a bear did approach him to throw the paper sack at it and back off very slowly, still facing the bear. "Then try to get behind a tree if the bear starts eating your sandwich," she instructed him.

Jere didn't know how long he had rested, but he enjoyed the solitude and the quiet of being in the woods. He couldn't tell time by the sun yet, but he knew that it was still too early for Big Thunder to be making his daily rounds through the woods. He got up and moved on, more slowly this time, relishing the beauty of the rugged hills and the streams of snowmelt water he encountered along the way. His pleasures were greatly enhanced each time he passed through that area, as he listened to the tune of the small bubbling brook. He continued on and then came to the place where he was supposed to meet Big Thunder, but his friend hadn't shown up yet. He would wait and admire the beautiful scenery while he rested.

He waited for over an hour, he suspected. When the sun found an opening in the leaves of the trees, it shone on him, making him warm and sleepy. He fell asleep temporarily. His head nodded, he jerked his head and woke up startled. He got up from the log and walked around it to wake up all the way. He went down to the brook, splashed some cold water on his face, and felt better. He sat on the log once more to wait on Big Thunder, realizing that his friend must be running late. He had been sitting quietly for some time when he imagined that he saw a wolf out of the corner of his eye. A closer look verified that he actually did see a wolf. It was White Spirit, and she was headed in his direction, it seemed.

He remained motionless, watching her every move as she continued approaching him without changing her course. He was certain that she must have scented him by now. He remembered the bologna sandwiches in the sack and thought she might have smelled them. Maybe she wanted a bite of one of them.

She was slowly edging closer and Jere was beginning to get uneasy about her intentions. She had never gotten that close to him. She walked closer and then emitted a faint sound from her mouth that sounded like woof. She moved on a short bit past him, looked around at him and again went, woof.

Jere wondered if she wanted him to follow her. He got off the log, walked toward her as she continued on for a short way and then turned around to look at him and again went woof. She then continued in the same direction and would stop occasionally to turn around and woof at him.

Jere continued to follow her for a half-hour at least, when he finally came to a small opening of a cave that appeared to have been occupied. She stood still, as if expecting Jere to understand why she had brought him there. She stared at him without moving.

White Spirit maintained her distance from the cave once she was certain that Jere had perceived the cave that she had led him to.

He thought he heard someone or something in the cave groaning or saying something inaudible. Jere approached the entrance, stuck his head in, and yelled, "Hello in there!" He waited a few seconds and again yelled, "Hello, in there!"

He stuck his head farther inside the opening and barely heard someone say, "Yes, in here." Jere was not sure what to do. He thought that it may have sounded a little like Big Thunder's voice, but he couldn't be certain. He inched farther into the cave, but it was so dark that he was unable to see anything after coming in out of the sunlight. He guessed it would take his eyes a few minutes to adjust to the darkness of the cave. He inched farther and was beginning to see better.

"Over here," a man's voice said. Jere nearly jumped out of his skin. "Over here, Little Brother," the voice said. Jere recognized the voice as that of Big Thunder, and he went over to where he was lying on a bed of leaves and knelt beside him.

Big Thunder held his hand out to the boy and asked, "How did you ever find me out here in the cave?" He was puzzled and amazed that a seven-year-old boy could find his way to his cave without knowing where to go or ever having been there before.

"First of all, Big Thunder," Jere said to him. "Let's find out what's wrong with you and see if we can help you. You must be sick because you didn't show up to meet me," he told Big Thunder. "What's wrong with you? How can I help you?" he asked.

"I'm just a sick old man," Big Thunder told him in a weakened voice that was barely audible. "There really isn't anything that anyone can do for me. When a person gets so old that he can't go any farther, he just lays his head down to die. I've gone as far as I can go, Little Brother," he told Jere.

"Oh no, you can't do that," Jere told him. "If I had a cup or a glass I would get you a drink of cool water," he told the old Indian.

Big Thunder said, "You're too good to me, but there is a tin can in that sack against the wall of the cave and there's a small spring out in front of the cave and down the hill to the left. I certainly would appreciate a drink of cool water. I'm terribly thirsty," he said.

He said, "I'll be right back with the water." Jere laid his sack of sandwiches down, took the tin can, and left.

Jere ran down the hill to the spring as fast as he could go, and then back up the hill to the cave. He hadn't been gone more than a minute when he instructed Big Thunder to sit up so he could take a drink of cool water. Big Thunder took a few sips and said to Jere, "Thanks, Little Brother, that was sure good."

Jere felt that it was too cool in the cave for the old man and that he was probably being chilled. Jere enticed him to come outside and sit on a warm rock in the sun so he could get warmed up. He told Jere that he was so weak that morning when he woke up that he was unable to sit up.

Jere helped him walk outside to sit in the sun. Jere asked, "How long has it been since you ate?"

"I think I may have had some roots yesterday. I'm not sure," he replied.

Jere said, "I want you to sit here in the sunlight and eat this bologna and cheese sandwich while I get the rest of your can of water. When you finish with that can of water, I will go down the hill and get some more," he promised.

"You are too good to me, Little Brother," Big Thunder said again. "But you never did tell me how you managed to find me. I had never shown you where I spent a lot of my time, and I was surprised when you walked into my cave," he said.

"Go ahead and take another bite of sandwich," Jere told him. Big Thunder was relishing the flavor of the delicious bologna and cheese. He took another bite and actually smiled at Jere.

Big Thunder said, "Son, I had actually forgotten how delicious a good bologna and cheese sandwich tastes," he told Jere as he took another bite. "Um-m-m mmmmm, now that's real tasty," Big Thunder told him. "Delicious," he added.

"You won't believe me when I tell you how I found you here in your cave, Big Thunder," Jeremiah said.

"Well, yes. I will believe you, son, when you tell me how you came to find me in my cave, because I know that you are a boy who does not lie," Big Thunder said. "So, I will believe you."

"Well, I had sat on a log at our meeting place and had about given up waiting for you to come, and I thought that I might not ever see you again," Jere told him. "I looked up to see a white wolf headed my direction and then I recognized her as White Spirit. She came real close to me and I was beginning to get nervous when she went ahead of me and went woof. She went woof once more and I thought it indicated that she wanted me to follow her," he explained to him.

"I then got off the log and started to follow behind her," he said. "Once in a while she would look around at me and go woof. She would then go on and look around at me occasionally to see if I was still following her. We eventually ended up here at your cave, Big Thunder," Jere swore to him that it was the truth. "After she was convinced that I had found what it was that she wanted me to see, she left," Jere told him.

"Somehow, White Spirit knew that you were sick," Jere had assumed. "She led me to you and saved your live. She must really be a smart wolf," Jere told his blood brother.

"Yes, I would agree with you that she is one smart wolf, Little Brother," he said. "And all of the time before you had become my best friend, I thought that she was only an apparition. I didn't really think that she existed in real life," he told Jere. "I thought that she was only a ghost who would disappear into thin air. Come to think of it, didn't she disappear from you today?" he asked.

"Of course she did," Jere answered. "But she just sneaked away, not wanting me to know where she was going after she led me to you. She didn't actually vanish, she just disappeared from sight because she wants to keep her hiding place a secret from us; kinda like you, Big Thunder," Jere explained and laughed a little.

"Yes, I know you're right and I know also that you are a very smart boy, just like the white wolf is very smart," he told Jere. "Don't ask me how she knew that I was sick, Little Brother, but somehow she must have sensed it, I suppose. Wild animals do have a sixth sense that makes them exceptionally good at sensing trouble and illnesses," he told Jere. "No one really understands it, but the truth of the matter is, they really do have some sort of intuition," he assured Jeremiah.

The warm sunshine, the bologna and cheese sandwich, and the cool spring water had combined to perform something of a miracle cure for Big Thunder. He was feeling much better although, he was still a mite weak, he indicated to Jeremiah.

"It's no wonder that you don't have enough strength to walk the three miles to our meeting place," Jere told him. "You don't eat enough to keep a bird alive. I'm not surprised that you don't feel well. You're going to die for certain if you don't start eating more," Jere chided the old Indian.

"I think you either need to go home to your daughter or else come home with me to the cabin so you can eat proper food and have a warm place to spend the night out of the cold this winter," Jere told him. "You may not realize yet just how cold it's going to get later on this year. Mom and Dad have already invited you to come and eat your meals with us and spend your nights in the barn where it will be warmer and drier than your cave. Please make me happy, Big Thunder, and come home with me to our cabin," Jere begged the old Indian man. "Our log barn will be warm and Mom has already told me to tell you that she has extra blankets for you to use when you sleep out there," Jere was tempting his friend with the promises that Angela had made.

"I could also bring you cups of hot tea with lots of sugar to give you some strength when you needed it," he told him. "You could have a cup of hot coffee every morning when you wake up, and we could still come out here in the woods to have our outings once in a while to talk about the things we like," he promised. "Why don't you get your head together and start to live where you will at least be more comfortable in your old age?" he inquired of the old man.

"I know that I'm going to die, Little Brother," he said. "All of us are going to die someday, and it is now my time to die. That is a fact of life and we should not try to deny it, because it will surely come to all of us," he told Jere.

"I know that, you bull-headed old Indian," Jere acknowledged. "It's just that you could live out your last days in a more comfortable place than this," Jere told him and was beginning to get peeved at him for being inconsiderate of his own health and well-being as much as Jere thought he should have been under the circumstances.

"If you don't give two hoots and a holler for your own life, then why in the world should I care about you starving and freezing to death?" Jere was being exceptionally severe with his good friend because he really did care about him. He had borrowed the strange euphemism from what he had heard his dad tell Mr. Ferguson about the boat and he felt that it would fit in very nicely in this particular instance.

Big Thunder chuckled at being called a bull-headed old Indian by his seven-year-old friend, but he readily admired his gumption for having the audacity to say that to his face. He loved the young lad, and their conversation had proven to Big Thunder that the lad had loved him, as well. Big Thunder was well aware of the fact that his friend was interested in his health and he really did appreciate Jeremiah's interest in his physical comfort, his satisfaction, and his well-being. After thinking about what Jeremiah had just told him, he concluded that the young boy had run out of patience with him and he was willing to risk hurting the old man's feelings to shock some sense and reasoning power into his head.

Big Thunder grinned and said, "Little Brother, I should have known better than to do this to you. Forgive me, son. I apologize to you from the bottom of my heart. I didn't realize just how much I was hurting you."

They had talked and visited long. The sun was getting low in the southwest, and they hadn't really thought about the day being gone until then. They had completely disregarded the time of day that was slipping by as they enjoyed the endless conversation they had shared that afternoon in the sunshine. It would be approaching night and darkness would be coming very soon, they realized.

Big Thunder said, "You can see the sun is now beginning to go behind the hills, and it will soon be dark. I had not intended for you to stay long enough for you to be caught here at night," Big Thunder apologized. "Your mother and father are going to be angry with me for keeping you out. They may not let you come see me again. I'm afraid my apology may do no good, but I am deeply sorry for allowing this to happen to you. The only thing left for you to do is to spend the night with me and go home in the morning. Your poor mother is going to worry herself sick, but I don't feel that I would be able to walk the six or seven miles through the woods tonight. I feel so terrible, son, at causing your family to have to worry about what has happened to you. I know they are going to suffer extreme pain in their hearts tonight," he said apologetically.

"Big Thunder," Jere said. "I had already made up my mind to spend the night with you, anyway. And yes, I know that my mother and father will be worried about me, but I am going to tell them the truth when I get home," Jere told him. "I'll make them understand that it's not your fault that I wasn't able to come home tonight. I will spend the night in the cave with you and then we will both start walking to the cabin in the morning. When we get there my mother will fix both of us a good meal and you will be able to spend the night in our barn tomorrow night," Jere insisted.

"Little Brother, we'll just have to wait and see how I feel in the morning and make our final decision then," he told Jere.

"We will walk for a while and then we will rest when we get tired," Jere told him. "If it takes an hour for you to get fully rested, then we will take an hour. We will take our time so we won't be worn out when we finally get there. That's the only sensible thing for us to do," he told Big Thunder. "My mother and father will be glad to see you, Big Thunder," he said. "Not only that, they will also be very glad to see me."

"That they will, Little Brother," he agreed. "That they will. But I'm afraid they will be so angry with me that they will never allow you to go with me into the woods again," he told Jere.

"Don't worry about it," Jere told him. "They're very understanding people and they will not blame you for the fact that I decided to stay with you all night and care for you because of your weakened condition. Just try to concentrate on the good things that are going to happen instead of worrying about my mother and father. I haven't yet told you about all of the wonderful secrets that I have been wanting to tell you about. I have a great many things to tell you that we are very happy about, and we will tell you all about them when we get home," Jere promised him.

Jere was smiling as he said this to Big Thunder and it actually made the old man feel much better seeing Little Brother smile and act happy. He felt in his own heart that happiness must be contagious. It also touched a tender spot in Big Thunder's heart when Jere mentioned to him about when we get home!

Big Thunder had brought an ample supply of matches to the cave and had them stored in a Clabber Girl Baking Powder tin with a secure lid on it. Jere built a fire just outside the cave, where he noticed that many fires had previously been built on the stone buttress. He took the drinking tin to the spring and filled it with water. While he was there he satisfied his own thirst, as well. Upon his return to the cave he placed the water on a rock ledge near his friend. They laid on a bed of dry leaves that Big Thunder had brought into the cave before. They lay silently watching the flickering shadows dance around the interior of the cave walls.

Each of them were pondering the same thoughts in their minds about how Jere's parents would be wondering what had happened to their little boy.

Big Thunder thought to himself, "How in the world will Mrs. Langford be able to make it through the night, worrying about what could have happened to her young son?" He felt that she would probably think that he had gotten lost or possibly attacked by a wild animal.

Sleep was slow in coming for both of them. They were also certain that sleep would probably be nonexistent for Mr. and Mrs. Langford. Big Thunder had some idea of what the uncertainty must have been like for Jeremiah's mother. He was certain that it must have been a terrible ordeal for her to be subjected to for such a long night. She probably felt that each passing hour would have seemed like a dozen.

Jere was unaccustomed to seeing the flickering shadows dancing on the wall of the cave in such a manner that suggested to his young mind that maybe there were ghosts of Indian ancestors in the cave with them. They both must have lain awake for long time, but each respected the other's desire for solitude and didn't say anything. Big Thunder had evidently awakened at some time during the night because Jere looked up and saw him with the can of water. He immediately went back to sleep and didn't wake up until Big Thunder touched him on the shoulder and said, "Little Brother?"

Jere rubbed his eyes with the back of his hands and answered, "Yes?"

Big Thunder told him it was time to get up and wash their faces so they could start walking toward the cabin. He poured some of the water in Jere's hands so he could splash his face. Jere then went down the hill to fill the can of water. They each had one small portion of bologna sandwich left over that was substituted for breakfast. To them it tasted almost as good as bacon and eggs.

"I think we should get started, Little Brother, are you ready?" he asked.

"I think we should start right away if you feel like traveling this morning," he answered. "Let's go, then."

If he had known for certain, in advance, what yesterday (and last night) would have brought, he would have been terribly upset before he got started and might not have been able to complete the uncommon journey into the wilderness that he had accomplished.

They both walked leisurely until they reached the last half-mile of their journey and then they speeded up. Jere could not wait—he bolted for the back porch.

# CHAPTER
## 14

Angela sat down on a ladderback chair, her eyes focused on the rear-facing window as she had done many times previously. She suddenly let out a scream. Joshua wondered how badly she had been burned and ran to the kitchen in time to watch her disappear off the back porch without hitting one step with her feet. He had heard her yelling something like, "Oh, my God!" as she cleared the steps and hit the ground in a dead run toward her son.

She ran to meet Jeremiah and threw her arms around his neck, almost choking him and embarrassing him considerably in front of Big Thunder as she said, "Oh, thank you for bringing my son home. I've been praying all night that he would be just fine, and you certainly do look fine to me, son," she said as the tears streamed down her beautiful face.

Josh had arrived on the scene about that time, and Jere introduced them. "Mom and Dad, this is my friend, Big Thunder. I want to apologize to you for making you worry about me last night, but Big Thunder was very sick and I felt that I had to stay with him," Jere explained.

"Oh, my goodness, I'm so glad to see you that it doesn't matter why you spent the night in the woods last night," Angela was cheerfully telling them. "I'm so happy to have you home I can't stand still. Oh, my gosh, I've got to get the pan of biscuits out of the oven before they burn. I want you men to wash up and get ready for breakfast. We're having bacon, fried eggs, biscuits, butter, and grape jam this morning. All three of you look as though you could use a good breakfast," she excitedly told them. Angela was wringing her hands, smiling, laughing, and talking at the same time.

She looked at Big Thunder and Jeremiah and asked, "When was the last time you two had something to eat?"

"Angela, if you don't quit talking and get breakfast on the table, it's going to be dinner time before we get to eat it," Josh said jokingly. Josh found out that he could also laugh since his son had come home.

Angela ran up the back steps like a schoolgirl and on into the kitchen. She had the plates and cups full of food and coffee by the time the men had washed up.

Josh extended his hand to Big Thunder. "I'm happy to meet you, Big Thunder, my name is Joshua Langford and this is my wife, Angela," he said as they shook hands.

"I'm very happy to meet both of you," he told them. Angela hadn't given any of them an opportunity to speak before that.

"Mom," Jere started to say something but was cut off by his mother.

"Take your time and eat, son," she advised him. "We will have the rest of the day to talk. You three need your food, and I intend to see that you get it," she scolded them.

Joshua had eaten two eggs, Jeremiah had two, Big Thunder took one, and Angela had one, also. She told them that she would fry more eggs if they wanted them, but they all said they had enough. Angela was delighted to see them have a good appetite as she watched them putting butter and grape jam on their biscuits. It made her feel very proud of her cooking.

After having looked the two of them over very carefully and inspecting them very closely she finally decided that Big Thunder and her son looked pretty darn good after having spent the whole night in the wilderness outdoors. Jeremiah reminded her that Big Thunder had spent every night for the last five months in the wilderness, and he probably looked as good now as he did when he first started it.

"Big Thunder, I'd sure like to tell my mom how it had come to happen that I spent the night with you in your cave when we finish eating," Jere said to him. "And then I will have lots of other things that I need to tell you and show you after I get through with the explanation about last night," he said to Big Thunder.

"Son, I'm certain that Big Thunder must be tired after trekking arduously through the woods this morning with you," Angela told him. "I think he should be allowed to rest in the living room on the davenport instead of following you around. You are a lot younger than he is, and you don't feel the need to rest as much as he does. Let's allow him to rest and take a short nap for a while, and then you may tell him about all of the wonderful things you have to say," she told her son.

"Oh no, Mrs. Langford," Big Thunder said to her. "I don't really need to lie down," he insisted. "I only need to sit for a few moments and then I will be rested enough to go again."

Jere's father said to him, "Son, let's go down to the boat and bring up the rest of the packages that I left down there the day before yesterday. I think I had four or five items that I never brought up the hill to the house," Josh told him.

Big Thunder was astonished at the conversation that was being held between Jere and his dad. He asked, "Did I hear you say something about a boat?' Did you acquire a new boat, Little Brother? Did you forget to tell me about that?" Big Thunder inquired.

"Well, my dad bought us a used boat down at Rosburg last week, and I meant to tell you about it in the woods. Since I found you not feeling well, I figured it would be best to wait until we came home," he told him. "I mentioned to you that I would tell you some secrets later and that was one of them. I'm ready to help you now, Dad," Jere told him.

Angela asked, "Big Thunder, why don't you come into the living room and sit for a while on the davenport while I wash the breakfast dishes and clean up the kitchen?" She led him to the davenport and fluffed up a large pillow for him.

"Mrs. Langford, I don't know when I have had the pleasure of eating such a fine breakfast as the one you prepared this morning," he praised her cooking. "I want to thank you and your family for allowing me the honor of having breakfast with you. Thank you so very much. I really appreciate that," he assured her.

"You're very welcome, sir," she told him. "I'm glad that my son was able to find you so that he could bring you home with him."

Big Thunder admitted to her that it had been months since he had had a good cup of hot coffee for breakfast. He told her that he thoroughly enjoyed the coffee. He told her that it seemed to have an enormous amount of healing power in it.

"You are so fortunate to have such an honorable young son, Mrs. Langford," he told her. "And you have every right to be proud of him. I would like for you to answer one question for me, though," he said. "I'm curious to know how it happened that you knew to have breakfast cooked and ready for us when we walked up to your cabin this morning?"

"Just call me Angela," she told him. "It's not necessary to call me Mrs. Langford. We are friends and my friends have always called me Angela."

"Thank you, Angela," he expressed his gratitude. "I'm so glad to hear you call me one of your friends. I, too, consider your family to be my friends and I hold your family in very high esteem. I am truly fortunate to have your son as my friend and for him to have enough intelligence to follow White Spirit to where she led him to my cave, saving my life," he told her. "There is no doubt in my mind, whatsoever, that I owe my being alive and here today to that wonderful son of yours," he confirmed this fact to Jeremiah's mother. "I can truthfully say that I also owe my life to the white female wolf known to us as White Spirit, since she led your son to my cave," he told her.

"It was really uncanny how White Spirit knew to lead your son to my cave, where I lay sick and very close to death," he continued. "I know for a fact that she led him to me because I had never told him or shown him where my cave was. He couldn't possibly have known," he said as Angela listened attentively to the story that was beginning to amaze her and was sounding more like a fairy tale than any true story she had ever heard in her life.

"I can hardly believe what you are telling me," Angela said to him. "Do you expect me to believe that a wolf led my son to the cave where you were lying sick miles away from him, without him ever knowing the location of your cave?" Angela then asked him in disbelief.

"That is the absolute truth," he vowed. "Neither your son nor I would try to tell you a lie about this, and you can believe every word that I have just told you. Ask Jeremiah," he insisted. "He will tell you the truth, also."

"Well, I do know that he told me about the white wolf that he had become very friendly with and her name was White Spirit, but I didn't realize that she was so smart that she would be able to lead him to you," Angela replied.

"I shouldn't have told you this story, because Jere really wanted to tell you himself," Big Thunder said. "I wonder if I could make a pact with you for you to pretend that you had not yet heard the story before when he starts telling it to you and your husband," He said. "I really forgot about him wanting so badly to tell you and now I've gone and spoiled it for him," Big Thunder apologized.

"I will act surprised and amazed and never let on that I have heard the story before," she promised.

"Thanks, Angela, I didn't want to spoil his fun of telling it to you and Josh."

Angela said, "And now, to get back to the question that you had asked, about my having breakfast ready for you. I don't really know what you might call it, Big Thunder. Maybe it's a mother's intuition, I don't really know. All I know is that somehow I was compelled to have the biscuits done and the bacon fried when you two walked in from the woods. I agree with you that it was a strange coincidence that some people might call impossible, but it actually did occur that way. I must go wash the breakfast dishes and clean the kitchen while you sit here and rest a spell, Big Thunder," she told him. "I'll see you a little later."

Jere and his father were down at the boat retrieving the few final things that he had left there. Jere spotted the newly stenciled name on the bow and said excitedly, "Wow, Dad, you've painted the new name on the boat. That looks great. Does Mom know about it yet?" he asked.

"Yes, she sneaked down here yesterday while I was busy working in the attic and took a look at it," he said. "She liked it very much and said she was proud of it."

"Great," Jere said. "I'm sure glad we decided to name it after Mom."

"Son, this package that is wrapped is a birthday present for your mother," he said. "Her birthday is next month, on October 27th, and I want you to help me remember it. This is a pretty red sweater that she will be proud of. I happened to see it in the Mercantile Store with the price marked down, so I just couldn't resist buying it for her," he said to his son. "The salesman said they were getting in the new styles and this one was left over from last year. I snatched up the bargain and he gift wrapped it for me. Not a bad deal for one dollar. Let's hide it in the barn until next month," he suggested.

"Dad, you really have a knack for making deals," his son told him.

"Okay son. Let's head up the hill, hide this in the barn, and do some more talking with you and Big Thunder," he recommended.

After coming from the barn they entered the back door of the cabin where Angela was cleaning the floor of the kitchen. "Ssshhh-h-h," she said to them as she put one finger in front of her mouth to warn them to be quiet. "Big Thunder is asleep on the davenport. You two sit out here and I'll pour you the last cup of coffee from the pot so I can clean it out," she told them.

Big Thunder had a very refreshing nap for almost an hour. When he arose from the davenport he went to the kitchen and announced, "Thanks for everything, good people. I'm happy to meet the parents of my best friend, but I must be heading back to my cave now that I am rested. I hope to see you again soon and I want to thank you ever so much for the fine hospitality and the even finer breakfast," he said as he held out his hand for them to accept his handshake.

"You will do no such thing, Big Thunder," Angela ordered. "You will spend the rest of the day with us and sleep in the barn tonight under some warm blankets.

"You just go back in there and sit down until we have a chance to talk with you and my son about some of the important things that both of you have been wanting to tell us about," she commanded him. "Since we had such a late breakfast, it may be two o'clock before I have our dinner ready," she announced to them.

"I really don't want to impose on you good people any more," he said. "You have already been too kind to me."

"No more of this nonsense," Angela told him. "You just go back in there and sit down. I'll call you if I should need you to do anything for me.

"Josh, why don't you go in there with them and hear some of the stories that Jeremiah has to tell about being out there in the wilderness," she suggested. "Big Thunder may have some stories to tell you, also," she said as an afterthought.

Big Thunder directed his comments to Angela, "I actually think it was you, young lady, who saved my life. I don't think I would have had the strength to make it through the night if it hadn't been for that bologna and cheese sandwich that you made, which your son brought to me in my cave. That was the prescription that revived me and made me well again," he told her as if he were certain of that fact.

The three men went to the living room and sat down. Joshua then heard the amazing story of a white wolf leading his son to a dying Indian man in a cave far away in the woods. Jeremiah told the story while Joshua sat wide-eyed and slightly unbelieving until Big Thunder verified every last word of what Jeremiah had been saying. He knew that his son wouldn't lie about it, yet it was so astonishing that he thought that they must have been dreaming about it. Big Thunder convinced Joshua to the point where he actually said that he believed it fully. As Jeremiah told each portion of the story about the white wolf leading him to the cave where Big Thunder lay dying, the old Indian nodded his head in affirmation to Joshua every few moments to verify the facts.

Jeremiah would long remember that amazing episode with the albino wolf that had fatefully and surprisingly occurred during the early years of his young life. He was also doubtful that anyone would ever believe his amazing ordeal and the truthful account of his encounter with a wolf that proceeded to save the life of his good friend. Jere actually doubted that Big Thunder would have lived another day in the cave had he not been able to find him and care for him. It's certain that his weakened condition in the damp cave would only have deteriorated to the point where he would not have been able to move out to the spring to get a drink of water or anything to eat.

Joshua, Angela, and Jeremiah all entreated Big Thunder to stay the night with them and sleep in the barn. They finally persuaded him with an earnest argument concerning the coming winter with its icy, freezing conditions that would not only be uncomfortable for him in the woods but would in all likelihood be a life-threatening ordeal for him to have to suffer through for at least three months. He had wanted to return to the cave that night but it was much too late for him to even think about attempting a seven-mile trek through the woods in the dark of night without a lantern or a light of any kind. It would even be difficult enough for a sick man his age to make the trip in daylight and utter madness to even consider it at night. A person could step into a stumphole at night and break an ankle or leg, making it impossible to carry on any farther until someone happened to come along to help him. Since the woodlands in that area were mostly uninhabited, it would be unlikely for anyone to be expected to come along at all. In all probability, he would simply be left there to die if he were unable to crawl out using his hands and knees. Angela finally convinced him to spend the night in the barn.

He eventually consented to spend one night in the barn if she would allow him to pay them back for the meals and bed by doing some work for them. Angela promised him they would discuss it the next day, and Jere was thrilled. "That's settled, then," he said. Angela gathered up some warm blankets so he could take them with him to the barn when he got ready to go.

Jeremiah said to his mother and father, "Do you think I might be able to spend the night in the barn with Big Thunder? You never know when he might need some help," he said pleadingly to his parents.

Angela said, "Jere, he may not want you out there bothering him when he is trying to sleep. Have you stopped to think about that?" she asked.

"Oh no," Big Thunder rebutted. "I would love to have your son as company to spend the night with me in the barn. You don't have any idea of the many pleasant conversations that we carry on with. An old man and a young boy have so many important things to talk about when they are alone, with no one else around to make them feel embarrassed. Sometimes I lie awake two or three hours before I fall asleep. I don't like to contradict your wishes, Mrs. Langford, but I would truly enjoy having his company in the barn with me tonight," he convinced her.

"Please call me Angela," she reminded him. "Oh, I suppose if Big Thunder doesn't object to having him then I have no reason to. What do you think, Josh?"

Josh replied, "I actually think it would do both of them a world of good to spend some time together without any interference from anyone."

"We do have so many things to talk about and so little time left, Angela," he told her. "I certainly appreciate your offer to let him spend this precious time with me. You have no idea how much this really means to me," he told her.

Josh said, "I imagine Jere still has a lot of things to tell Big Thunder about getting the boat, going to town, and dozens of other things that he will think about when they get started talking. I'm sure, also, that Big Thunder has many things to tell his Little Brother," Josh said to all of them.

That was the only time that Jere could remember that his dad had called him Little Brother. Josh had paid particular attention to Jere as he uttered the words, and he thought he detected a slight twitch in his face. Jeremiah wondered if his father actually knew the meaning of blood brother the way the Indians used it in a ceremonial tribute to a person of high esteem. He also wondered if his father had suspected the ritual that the men must subject themselves to in order to become blood brothers in the tribe. Jere was fairly certain that he did know after he shot a curious glance toward him when Big Thunder had called him Little Brother in his father's presence. He never mentioned it to him, though.

Angela said, "Jere, have you told Big Thunder the good news that you are going to be the proud brother of a little sister or brother next spring?"

"No ma'am, I haven't told him yet," he said. "I was hoping you would tell him."

"Well, congratulations to all three of you," Big Thunder applauded and smiled. "I must think of something that I can make for the baby from his adopted uncle. I will set my mind to it and think of something before the baby gets here," he promised. "Tell me when the baby is due," he told her. "I must find the proper wood to use to make her a present. I don't know why I said 'her.' We don't have any idea of what it's going to be, do we?" Big Thunder asked.

"You are correct, Uncle Big Thunder," Angela told him. "But I believe that it's going to be a girl, also. I've had that proud feeling from the very first that it was going to be a baby girl. I want her to be cute and lovable so Jeremiah will have a pretty little sister and Joshua will have a pretty little daughter. She is due to arrive next spring," she confirmed that fact to them again.

Joshua said, "You two may want to spend some time here in the cabin while we have the lamps lit, if you like," Josh told them. "When you get ready to go to the barn, I will help you carry your blankets and equipment down there as you go."

"Thank you for offering to let us stay, but I think we will go ahead and get situated for the night before it gets dark," Big Thunder said. "I also want to thank you for the delicious meals you have served. I shall always treasure the friendship and kind generosity that your family has extended to me, and I will be indebted to you forever for the gracious manner in which you and your son have received me. Folks, you have a fine son," he told them. "He could have gone off and left me in the cave to die, but he elected to stay and spend the night with me, nursing me back to health, knowing all the time that he was putting his parents through a miserable, sleepless night. He knew what he was doing, but you had no idea of what he might be doing. His mind was thinking as though he were a grown person," Big Thunder boasted about the superb attributes of their son.

He continued, "I know that it must have been a heart-wrenching night for both of you and I want to sincerely apologize for causing you to go through that terrible ordeal. I hope you will be able to put a lot of trust in the decisions that he must make in the future, because he has an uncanny ability of judging right from wrong and has a good head on his shoulders to make the proper decisions," Big Thunder bragged some more on their son and his best friend.

Angela filled a quart mason jar with water and put the lid on it. She gave it to Jere and the blankets to Joshua so he would carry them to the barn. Josh saw them safely into the barn and told them that there was a pile of tow sacks in the corner that they could use as a makeshift mattress. He left the barn and returned to the cabin, leaving Old Blue there to guard the barn door dutifully until they emerged the next morning to go up the hill to the cabin to eat breakfast.

"Darling, I can't believe it," Angela excitedly told him. "Just think! We can have our second honeymoon tonight. Isn't it wonderful? This will literally be the first night we have had to ourselves since Jere was born, seven years ago," she reminded him. "They couldn't have presented me with a better present. Last night doesn't count because we were so upset about him," she said to him.

Angela encircled his neck with her arms, wrapped her legs around his waist, and kissed his lips long and lovingly. She released him and said, "I can guarantee that you will not regret letting Jere sleep in the barn tonight with his friend," she promised. "I'm going to heat some water on the kitchen stove for a bath," she said. "Don't you dare peek in on me while I'm taking my bath in the kitchen, dear," she winked at him as she vanished into the kitchen, closing the door behind her.

Josh knew very well that her "don't you dare" actually meant that she was inviting him to look in on her as she was taking her bath. Josh had learned all of her little wily tricks.

Angela had completed her bath and poured hot water for Josh. He undressed, stepped into the tub, and commenced his bath when the kitchen door opened. Angela winked at him, smiling, and said, "Turnabout is fair play." She was still laughing and winking when she blew him a kiss from the doorway, saying, "I love you, sweetheart."

"I love you too, Angel," he said.

"There, he said it again," she thought. He actually called me Angel, and I know I heard it this time. She smiled one of her most wicked smiles, winked at him, and went to the living room to wait for him to finish bathing.

Josh completed his bath and entered the living room to sit on the davenport. He had no sooner sat when Angela got up from her chair, crossed the room, and slunk into his lap. She slowly wrapped her arms around his neck, put her lips close to his ear, and then whispered, "Darling, do you think it's too early to go to bed?"

"I don't really think so, hon," he answered. "It's already dark outside and since the two in the barn don't have a lamp or lantern, I'm certain they're already in bed," he told his wife as she squirmed on his lap.

She whispered to him, "Let's blow out the lamp and go to bed, then," smiling a most beautiful smile as she unwrapped her left arm slowly from around his neck and rose from the davenport to precede him into the bedroom, casually dropping her eyelids in a sexy manner and smiling at him while glancing over her left shoulder and beckoning him to come on in to her bedroom with her right index finger.

# CHAPTER
## 15

"Big Thunder?" Jeremiah said very softly.

"Yes, Little Brother?" he answered very faintly.

"Are you asleep, yet?" Jere wanted to know.

"No, Little Brother. Why do you ask?" the old Indian man wanted to know.

"Did I tell you that we explored an island in the Grays River last week as we took our boat out for a ride?" Jere asked him, although he knew that he hadn't.

"No, you didn't mention it that I can remember," he answered.

"Well, I must have forgotten to tell you about it," Jere said. "It had slipped my mind and I just now thought about it. Maybe you don't want to talk, though," he said. "Maybe you had much rather go to sleep now."

"Oh no, Little Brother," Big Thunder told him. "I would love to carry on a conversation with you for two or three hours," he admitted. "But I hate to keep you awake that long. I'm not even a tiny bit sleepy yet. I will probably stay awake yet for a long time and nothing would suit me better than to carry on a good conversation with my good friend, that is, if it is all right with you. Are you sure you're not sleepy?" Big Thunder asked.

"Not at all," Jere answered. "I probably won't start to get sleepy yet for another couple of hours, and if I don't have someone to talk to, I would just lie here awake and stare at the rafters," Jere confided to him.

"I especially like talking to you because we have so many interesting things in common to talk about," Big Thunder said. "I am totally sincere when I tell you that I enjoy hearing you talk about yourself and your family."

Jeremiah bent his elbow and propped his head up in his hand facing the old Indian as he started talking. Even though it was dark outside there was still enough light for them to see one another faintly since their eyes had become adjusted for the darkness. Big Thunder rolled sideways so he could face Jeremiah directly. He didn't want to miss a single word that Jere would be saying to him.

Jere started, "One day last week we heard a motorboat coming up the river, so we ran out on the front porch to see it. It pulled up to the bank down in front of our cabin. We went down to see this man named Ben who said he owned a boat business in Rosburg and asked Dad if he would be interested in buying a boat.

"He rode me and dad down the river in his boat and showed us several that he had for sale. Dad told him that he couldn't afford a boat that expensive, so he took us around to the back and offered us one for sale cheap, but he didn't know how to start it. Ben had to go around to the front to talk to another man while Dad looked it over. When Ben got back he said he would take thirty dollars for it. Dad said he would give him twenty, so Ben took it. While Ben went to the office to make out the bill of sale, Dad got the boat started. Ben filled up the fuel tank and we came home in it. Boy, it really is a sleek boat now since we cleaned it up and worked on it," Jere said proudly.

"Anyway, when we got home, we picked up my mom and took a spin up the river to where we found this island," Jere said. "We officially named it Jeremiah Island and planted a flag on it. Well, we didn't exactly plant a flag, we planted a limb with leaves on it. That's the story of how we found the island that we named in my honor," he said.

"I could listen to your stories like that all night long, Little Brother," Big Thunder assured him. "I'm tempted to think that you must be of Indian ancestry because of the way you tell a story. I enjoy listening to you talk," he told Jere.

"Well, I never told you this before," he said. "But I really do have Indian blood in my veins; I mean other than the fact that we are blood brothers. My mom is the daughter of Rising Moon Peterson, who was half-Indian, so that makes her one-quarter Indian. So, you see, Big Thunder, we truly are Indian blood brothers. And I am really an Indian, just like you," Jeremiah said proudly.

Big Thunder listened intently to that bit of information. "Now I have one more reason to be proud of you for finding me in my cave and saving my life. I told my daughter, Little Flower, that I had accepted that certainty of the end of my life. She kissed me and I walked off into the woods, but as fate would have it, my spirit was not yet ready to ascend into the heavens. It must have been preordained for me to come in contact with my blood brother before it became necessary for me to depart this world. I shall never forget your friendship," Big Thunder told him in a quivering and trembling voice that undeniably betrayed his emotional feelings for the young lad who was his best friend.

"I will gladly take your kind and considerate nature with me to the grave," he said to Jere. "And I shall forever be grateful to White Spirit for leading you to me in the cave that fateful day, just in time to keep my soul from ascending into the great beyond, up there in the heavens. I would never have been allowed the honor of meeting your fine family if you had not been able to find me. I've never been this happy in my lifetime, Little Brother," he told Jere, and he meant it.

"I not only have a blood brother, I also have a grandson," he chuckled as they lay on their makeshift mattresses there in the barn. Jere could faintly detect a sparkle of something shiny on the side of Big Thunder's face and suspected it was probably tears.

"I would like to tell you something else, Little Brother," he said to Jere in a very solemn voice. "Since you are of Indian ancestry and have saved my life, you have now become eligible to wear the eagle feather at the next powwow of our Indian nation. It will be a great honor for me as well as for you to wear this symbol of life that means so much to the Indian people of my generation," he said very seriously. "I have an eagle feather hidden away in my cave that I will give to you the next time we go there," Big Thunder revealed to him.

"I will be most proud and happy to wear it, Big Thunder," Jere assured him. "Does your daughter know that you are still alive?" he asked.

"No, she wouldn't have any way of knowing whether I had passed on or not," Big Thunder answered. "I would like to be able to let her know that I am still alive, but there is no way that I could make that long journey on foot. It would take about two days to get there and two days to get back if I had to walk, since it would be necessary for me to rest at frequent intervals," he told Jere. "I think it would be best not to say anything to your mother about this just yet," he urged the boy.

"I don't really think that they would have any objections to my helping you find your daughter to tell her that you're still alive, but we should probably let them get to know you a little better before we suggest anything like that. However, I really do think that you should tell my folks about having a daughter who probably thinks you are dead."

Big Thunder said, "You're right, son. Some people are not aware of the old Indian custom of walking off into the wilderness or into the desert without any food or drink and going far enough away just to lie down and die peacefully. That has been a custom for many centuries and may still be practiced by some tribes here," he said.

"I can imagine that your daughter would be surprised to learn that you are alive and well, Big Thunder," Jere told him. "But I think she would be even more surprised to find out that you have a newly acquired family, also," he said.

Big Thunder chuckled. There hadn't been many times since Jeremiah had known him that Big Thunder chuckled or smiled. It just didn't sound like him when he laughed quietly at what Jere had just told him about acquiring a new family.

Big Thunder appeared to be in serious thought because he was taking longer than normal to reply to Jere. He acted as if he was dumbfounded at what the boy had just told him and didn't quite know how to answer. His replies were usually prompt and precise, but it was evident that he needed more time to think about this statement.

"You know, Little Brother, that's one thing that had never entered my mind until you mentioned it," he finally said. "I knew the day that we performed the ritual in the woods that we were blood brothers, but it never dawned on me that someday I might be telling my own daughter that I have a young brother out there in the wilderness somewhere," Big Thunder said, and he laughed once more about how unusual it would sound.

Jere enjoyed hearing Big Thunder laugh. Evidently he had not had much to laugh about since he first went into the woods over five months ago. He vowed to try to get him to laugh more. He had heard somewhere that laughter is good for the soul. Jeremiah believed that wholeheartedly.

"I'm certain that your daughter is a wonderful woman, and she probably misses you very much," Jere told him. "I would love to meet her sometime."

They were both silent for a while. Jere figured that he must be in deep thought about his daughter, Little Flower. He didn't want to talk and disturb Big Thunder's thoughts. He decided not to say anything until Big Thunder broke the silence.

After waiting for some time, Big Thunder asked, "Are you asleep, Little Brother?"

"No, I was just lying here doing some heavy thinking," he told him.

"So was I," he answered. "But I felt that you might have fallen asleep and I didn't want to disturb you. But then I thought you might still be awake," he said.

"I had been thinking about making a trip to your daughter's house," Jere said. "I have decided that it would be smart to put it off until after winter is over, since it might be dangerous for you and I to make a trip like that in winter. Why don't we think about trying it next spring when we can make it without any danger of blizzards or ice storms?" Jere suggested.

"You are a very thoughtful young man," Big Thunder agreed. "I praise you for considering that most important circumstance which might upset some well-laid-out plans for a journey through the forest. It would not be wise for me to attempt to prove to my daughter that I was alive, when in fact, I would be dead. You have a good head on your shoulders and I admire you for it," the old man told him. "I know that you were considering my well-being in your thoughts about waiting until the winter months were over. Blinding snowstorms can blow in from the northwest so very fast and take the lives of people who are not prepared for it, son. You are very smart to bring up this very important factor," he acknowledged.

"Big Thunder?" Jere said in an inquisitive manner.

"Yes, Little Brother?" he answered softly.

"Do you think we will ever see White Spirit again?" Jeremiah asked. "I would sure like to see her again, wouldn't you?"

"I certainly would, son," he answered. "I'd like to see her again and thank her for saving my life and for bringing me all of the joys of living with a wonderful family such as yours," Big Thunder asserted firmly.

"I wouldn't be at all surprised to know that she is out there constantly looking to find out if we are well," he told his young friend. "Someday soon I would love to go out there by the little creek to wait for her and see if she will show up. She probably knows already that she has been thanked, and I'm certain that she feels that she has been properly rewarded," Big Thunder said.

Jeremiah said, "If we will wait three or four days to ask my mother about going out there in the woods to see if we can find her, then she will probably grant us permission to do that," Jere figured.

"We shall wait and see, son," Big Thunder told him.

Big Thunder lay quiet for some time, not uttering a sound. The steady tempo of his breathing was light and evenly spaced, indicating that he had probably dropped off to sleep. Jere lay there looking at the rafters for a few minutes longer, thinking, and then evidently dropped off to sleep himself.

# CHAPTER
## 16

Angela was the first to wake up the next morning. She jumped out of bed as swift as an antelope, got dressed, went to the back porch, quickly washed her face and hands, and then hurriedly built a fire in her cookstove. She made her usual morning visit to the outdoor privy and upon returning found Joshua in the kitchen.

"It's barely daylight, Angel," he told her. "Why are you getting up this early? Why didn't you wait for me to build the fire for you in the cook stove?" he asked.

"Darling, you just go right back and get in bed," she ordered. "I am going to serve you breakfast in bed this morning. I'll bring it in to you when it's ready," she promised. She smiled and winked at him and said, "You can catch a few more winks while I'm fixing your breakfast."

"Oh no, I can't let you do that," he protested. "I don't want you to serve me breakfast in bed. I am perfectly able to get up and eat my breakfast at the table."

"But I want to," she cooed. "We are on our second honeymoon and I want to prove to you just how much I love you. Why won't you allow me to do this for you, sweetheart?" she asked in a seemingly hurt voice. "I love you, dear."

"Angel, I love you, too," he told her admirably. "But I want to get up and help you get the breakfast ready. When it's just about done, I will run out to the barn and holler for those two boys to come on in," he told her.

Angela smiled and thought to herself, "There it is again. He has called me Angel twice this morning already. I dearly love to hear him call me that. I do hope he did it on purpose."

"All right, dear," she conceded. "You can help me out this morning, but I really wanted to give you a treat for our honeymoon," she whimpered, as if seeking some sympathetic cajoling from him.

He answered her obvious plea with a huge hug and a sweet kiss. Evidently that was what she had intended for her goal to be since she smiled and looked sweetly up into his face and said softly, "I really do love you too much."

After thinking about it, he couldn't argue that point.

"We're having flapjacks and maple syrup this morning," she announced. "I'll be ready for you to go down and yell at the boys in about ten minutes. That's just about the time the bacon will be done and the coffee finished perking," she told him.

Josh walked over near the stove, placed his arms around her waist and said, "I really do love you more than anything in the world and I want you to know it."

Those were precisely the words that she had been wanting to hear and anxiously awaiting. He had just made her day. She rewarded him once more with a kiss.

Jeremiah thought he must have been dreaming. It sounded as though someone was calling his name from a far distance. When he opened his eyes he wasn't quite sure where he was. Then he remembered that he and Big Thunder had spent the night in the log barn. He realized that it was his dad's voice outside the barn calling them to come to breakfast.

"Yes, Mr. Langford," Big Thunder yelled. "We are awake now, and we'll be coming up to the cabin right away."

They each took turns using the privy and then ascended the steps to the back porch, where they washed their hands and faces. Angela noticed that Big Thunder appeared to be feeling much better that morning now that he had been allowed a good night's sleep under the warm blankets and away from that damp cave he had been sleeping in. Jere also looked chipper and cheerful after having been allowed to spend the night in the barn with his friend.

"Good morning, fellows," Angela smiled and said cheerfully, acting as though she couldn't have been any happier. Actually, that wasn't far from the truth.

"Good morning Mr. and Mrs. Langford," Big Thunder said in what seemed to be a very jovial mood. He was smiling for once, which was a very good sign.

"Good morning to you," Josh said and again told him that it was not necessary for him to refer to them as Mr. and Mrs. Langford, but instead as Josh and Angela.

"We must have been sleeping pretty soundly this morning," Big Thunder said. "I had a very good night's rest, thanks to the warm blankets that we covered up with. I feel much better this morning than I have in a long time, thanks to you good people," he said.

"You two go ahead and sit down," Josh instructed them. "We're having flapjacks and maple syrup this morning. Angela found a gallon bucket of pure maple syrup in Astoria the other day and latched on to it like a duck on a June bug. She also found a half-gallon jar of honey."

Angela said, "As soon as Josh returns thanks, we will start breakfast."

After Josh had finished with prayers Jere resounded with a loud, "Amen! Mom makes the best flapjacks in the world, and I know they'll be good with that maple syrup."

Genuine maple syrup was fairly expensive, and Josh usually frowned on it when Angela wanted to buy some, but since he was at the lumber shed when she saw it, she didn't need to ask him about it. There was no way he could crank up the boat and take the syrup back to Astoria, anyway.

Angela said, "Here are your flapjacks, and I'll get the bacon out of the oven warmer. Pass the butter to Big Thunder, Jere, and I'll pour the coffee."

When Big Thunder sat down at the kitchen table that morning, he looked directly into Angela's eyes and said, "I have noticed that your face has a much more radiant glowing smile this morning. I am pleased to know that you are feeling exceptionally well and happy this morning," he said to her.

The back of Angela's neck reddened slightly as she smiled and said to him, "Why, thank you, sir. I feel just wonderful this fine morning."

She was hoping that Big Thunder and the others hadn't noticed the slightly embarrassed shade of red that had slowly flamed across her face and down the back of her neck. She kept smiling and the blush on her face got warmer. She excused herself and went to the back porch for a drink of cool water and to get some air in an attempt to cover up her state of embarrassment. She had not the slightest idea of why she had been embarrassed at what Big Thunder had said, but there was nothing she could do to alleviate the situation. She returned to the kitchen and gave the flimsy excuse that she had been eating too fast. She decided that even though Big Thunder was an old man, he was certainly cunning and sly. He must have enjoyed making her blush at the thoughts of last night and had a good laugh to himself, also. Angela initially wanted to kick his shin under the table but then found it to be quite amusing, herself.

Breakfast was a huge success. Angela received many compliments from everyone that morning. She was completely overwhelmed with a multitude of flattering remarks about her flapjacks and bacon, her delicious coffee, and generous hospitality. She thanked them profusely and once again felt the warmth of the blush invade her face and neck. She really couldn't understand why she had been so chagrined that morning. After all, she was certain that the ones who were sleeping in the barn could not even have suspected how she may have flirted and been playfully romantic with her husband. She felt that Big Thunder was intentionally trying to see if he could cause her to be embarrassed with his witty remarks. She suspected that he could be slightly mischievous, much like a young boy. That caused her to love him even more.

Angela served notice that she had used up the last of the bacon that morning and told each of them to remind her to get more eggs and bacon when they went to town. Josh pointed out that it might be several days yet.

Josh went down the hill to the boat. Jeremiah and Big Thunder went to the barn while Angela remained in the cabin to wash and dry the dishes, sweep and mop the floor, and clean the remainder of the cabin in general.

Big Thunder told Jere he had noticed that there were many peanuts that needed to be picked off the vines in the barn and he felt it would be a perfect day to accomplish this. Jere agreed that it would make his father happy. They knew that it would mean sacrificing some of their mattresses, but it must be done. They decided to take one tow sack from each pile and use them to store the peanuts in. They would tie the sacks to a barn rafter with baling wire to keep the mice and rodents out of them. After about two hours Jere's fingers were getting sore, but if Big Thunder's fingers were hurting he didn't complain.

Josh detoured by the barn on the way up the hill to tell them that dinner was ready. Josh thought it was high time they started referring to them as men instead of boys. He praised them for the job they had done with the peanut vines. He said, "I didn't know what you two might be doing this morning but I'm glad you decided to pull the peanuts. You've done a fine job, men," he said. "Thanks."

"You're welcome, sir," Big Thunder acknowledged. "We enjoyed doing it for you. It kept our minds occupied."

Jeremiah smiled and heaved his chest out because his father had classed him as a man along with Big Thunder.

Angela was wearing a pretty apron with frilly lace binding around the outer edge. She was also wearing a big smile while welcoming the men to dinner. Josh had never seen her happier than she was now, and he attributed most of it to the expected arrival of the baby. She was not only jubilant but was also pretty and graceful. She enjoyed cooking the meals for her men. She derived a lot of pleasure from watching them enjoy her delicious food. It made her happy when they complimented her on her culinary abilities. She accepted their compliments gracefully and acknowledged them with a smile and a courteous thank you.

"Josh, I need you to find me and Jere another job this afternoon," Big Thunder said. "I figure we will be finished with the peanuts in about an hour."

Josh said, "Some time back, Angela was wanting some pine nuts for the things she was baking. Do you think you two could find the large cones that produce those good nuts and harvest a good supply for her?" he asked them.

"I know exactly what to look for," Big Thunder told him. "We will take two tow sacks with us to put the pine cones in and then bring them back to the barn to extract the nuts later."

Angela said, "Before you tie those sacks of peanuts to the rafters in the barn, I want you to bring me one large pan full so we can have parched peanuts after supper tonight. Some people call them roasted peanuts but I have always called them parched peanuts."

"Likewise," Big Thunder replied. "And I just love them. You folks are spoiling me terribly. I'm not used to being treated so well as this," he confessed. "Some day when I return to live in my cave in the woods, I will have forgotten how to survive in the wilderness."

"Big Thunder, as long as we live in this cabin, you will be welcome to stay here, and you will never be forced to live in the woods, again," Angela promised him.

He and Jere returned to the barn to finish pulling the peanuts from the vines and then took Angela the pan full she had requested. "Mom, we're going to the woods, now," Jere told her. "We're going to find some pine nuts and we'll be back as soon as we fill up two sacks. Bye, now."

They stopped at the pump to get a drink of fresh water, then started out on their search for the cones that produced those delectable pine nuts. They wandered in circles looking for that particular type of tree. Suddenly, Jere decided that he was lost. "That's nothing to be ashamed of, Little Brother," his friend told him. "I've been in that predicament many times myself, and I know that it's a weird feeling when you first discover it. Don't worry about it, though—I can find my way out of here," he assured Jere. "We should sit and rest a while, though," he said. "I'm beginning to get a little tired. Let's sit on this log for a bit."

They had been sitting quietly for some time. It was a habit that each of them had acquired, and they respected each other's wishes. That ability to sit with a friend and be comfortable just being with him without saying a word had endeared Jere to Big Thunder as much as anything else, he supposed. They were admiring the glorious beauty of the landscape when Jere whispered, "There she goes. She has the little one with her now. She is leading it by the hand and it has grown quite a bit."

Big Thunder's eyes were not very good any more and he asked Jere, "Where, son?"

Jere replied in a whisper, "Look at my finger pointing to the top of the ridge and to the left of that big rock."

"I see them," Big Thunder whispered to Jere. "What a magnificent sight for us to be able to witness, Little Brother. Lots of people won't believe us."

Jere said, "I'm sure glad we came out here looking for pine nuts. Otherwise, we would have missed the mama Sasquatch with her little one."

The old man said, "We may not ever have another opportunity to observe something like this. I am awestruck. How many people will believe that we have seen a mother Sasquatch leading her small one by the hand?" he asked.

"Let's keep this a secret between us," Jere begged. "It might bring some harm to them if the wrong person heard about it. I'm sure the Bigfoot saw us because she looked right at us as she angled off down the hill. She didn't seem the least bit scared. Of course, she was a quarter-mile away and may have seen no need to be concerned," Jere said to the old Indian.

✠ ✠ ✠

Josh had been back at the cabin over an hour when the men came in lugging two sacks full of pine cones. They told Josh they could have been in sooner but they'd had to stop and rest twice. It was just now sundown and not dark yet. Angela had supper ready when they arrived. She said the pine cones would be all right on the back porch until they could take them to the barn.

All of the men bragged on the cook again that night. Angela just smiled and accepted the compliments graciously. If a person didn't already know, he might think that Angela was a schoolgirl. She looked that young and strikingly beautiful.

"Mom, do you think I could spend the night again in the barn with Big Thunder?" he asked. "I imagine he would get lonesome out there by himself with no one to talk to," he told his mother.

"Ask your father, son," Angela instructed him.

"Unless Big Thunder has some objection, I don't see any harm in it," Josh told Angela and Jeremiah.

"Oh boy, that means I get to spend the night with you again, Big Thunder," Jere told him excitedly. "We can have some more good talks."

"That will be fine, little brother," Big Thunder said. "I just hope I don't get in the middle of a family squabble over this."

"Don't worry about that one smidgen," Angela said to him. "We're not about to have a squabble over that."

After supper the men went to the living room and Angela washed the dishes. After she had finished cleaning the kitchen she took a pan of parched peanuts into the living room and told the men to help themselves. She had brought another large pan for the disposition of their hulls. All of them found the peanuts most satisfying, even Angela. She had held off eating very many of them since she didn't know if there would be enough for everyone, but when the men had finished and rubbed their tummies, indicating they were full, she took the pans back to the kitchen and ate her fill of peanuts. She could hear the men discussing important issues in the living room but couldn't understand the content of the conversation.

The two barn dwellers finally decided to call it a day to head for the barn to get some much-needed rest. They were both tired after walking for several miles in the forest that day. They said their good nights to the Langfords and headed for the barn.

Angela said, "Good night, men. Sleep tight."

By now it had become readily apparent that Jeremiah was to be considered a barn dweller with his best friend, Big Thunder. No one could have been more pleased with this arrangement than Angela. She continuously reminded her husband that they were on their second honeymoon and that she was enjoying every precious minute of it. She could scarcely wait for the two barn rats to scurry down the hill so she could literally jump into Josh's lap and caress him with her arms lovingly wrapped around his neck. She was very generous with her warm, voluptuous lips pressing against his as she thoughtfully reminded him, "Darling, just think. We have the rest of the night to ourselves again. Isn't that wonderful?" she asked as she lovingly and tenderly kissed him again. "I can't believe those two are actually presenting us with another night of bliss together." She smiled, giggled, and kissed him again.

Josh couldn't get over the fact that she was acting more and more like a young schoolgirl who had a crush on some boy. He felt that he was indeed fortunate to be that lucky boy.

As usual, the two men sleeping in the barn were spinning tales as soon as they hit their tow sack mattresses. Jere heard the rain starting to fall on the tin roof and asked Big Thunder if he had heard it also.

"I hear it now," he replied. "Well, I guess I know what job we will have tomorrow, Little Brother."

"What?" Jere asked.

"We will be picking the pine nuts out of the cones that we harvested," he told Jere. "We will do it here in the barn while listening to the music the rain makes as it hits the roof. I have many pleasurable memories of when I was a young man hearing the rain pelting a tin roof. I would be shelling walnuts, pecans, or picking the peanuts off the vines, or maybe some other chore that couldn't be done outside in the rain. It's been many moons since I've heard the delightful, constant drum of raindrops."

Jere could tell that the old man's voice was breaking from recalling the pleasant and wonderful memories of the past. There was enough light that he could see a tear as it glistened down Big Thunder's cheek.

Big Thunder and Jere talked about many more things that night before finally giving way to a sound sleep as the noise of the rain on the metal roof lulled them into a relaxed state of wondrous slumber.

Angela was the first one awake the next morning, as usual, and she felt wonderful. Normally she would allow Josh to get up and build the fire in the cookstove, but she decided that she felt so good that she wanted to do it herself. As she got out of bed, it woke Josh up. She told him it had been raining and that he might as well sleep in that morning.

"When I get our breakfast almost ready, I'll wake you up in time to go to the barn and wake the rest of our family up," she told him.

He rolled over on his side and was instantly asleep again. Angela couldn't keep from noticing a small smile adorning his face as he was peacefully sleeping while the rain was steadily coming down on the roof of their log cabin.

Breakfast that morning consisted of biscuits, butter, and honey or biscuits and milk gravy. Each of them relished the wonderful breakfast again and told Angela so.

Jere couldn't wait to get started on their new assignment that morning. He was to be in for a big shock on the job that he had thought would be a simple breeze.

Big Thunder said, "First, I will whittle out two wooden pick handles, drive two nails into them, and file the nail heads off to a sharp point. This will make a tool for removing the nuts from the pine cones. When we finish, your mother needs to bake them in the oven for a bit so they will last without turning rancid. In cold weather, they can be stored on the back porch in a can with a lid on it. This retains the true flavor and keeps them as fresh as the day they were picked from the woods."

The two of them worked all day, with the exception of going to dinner, and had only succeeded in completing one tow sack full of cones. Jeremiah had not realized how tedious and demanding the job would be and how damaging it could be on their nails and cuticles. He had imagined that they would finish off both sacks that day. He was terribly disappointed, but Josh praised them and said that they had done an excellent job of removing the nuts and they should feel proud. Angela told them she needed a cup full of nuts to roast and put into two sweet potato pies that she would bake in the next three or four days. She said that they could have them for supper some night, soon.

It seemed to be a foregone conclusion that Jeremiah was now living in the barn with Big Thunder. The ritual had been the same each night about getting permission to sleep in the barn when Josh said that they might as well make it a semi-permanent arrangement. If he decided to change his residence, he could say so and be reinstalled in his room at night any time he chose. That seemed to be satisfactory with everyone present.

"Mom, do you think it would be all right for me and Big Thunder to go into the woods in the morning?" Jere asked his mother.

"I don't think it would be advisable for you to go into the woods this soon after a rain," she told him. "It's likely to be very muddy in the woods and besides, I had wanted us all to go to town in the morning to do some shopping," she told them. "You and Big Thunder can go into the woods on Saturday."

"Yeaaaayy," Jere cheered. "All right! We're gonna take the boat for a cruise down the river. Wait till you see how she runs, Big Thunder. It's really awesome to watch her skim over the water like an otter," he excitedly told him. "Maybe Dad will allow us to explore our own private island when we get back from town," Jere said hopefully.

"He probably will, Jere," Angela told him. "When we finish with our shopping in Astoria, the only thing we will have to do is fill up the kerosene can at the boat marina and fill the boat with tractor spirits. We will head back upriver so you fellows can explore the island, unless your dad has other plans," she told them.

Josh told them that the paint lettering on the boat should be cured enough to make the trip to town. He was glad that Angela had ordered them to make this excursion. He was just itching to get his craft back out on the open water once more. Josh was really a fine skipper, even though he was self-taught. He was going to be delighted to be at the helm again to show off his nautical expertise.

Big Thunder said, "I have never before ridden in a power boat like the one that is moored down at the river. This will be some experience for me, Little Brother. I trust that I will like it."

"You will," Jere told him. "I can guarantee that you will like it and once you have ridden in our boat, you will want to keep on boating from now until kingdom come," Jere assured him.

# CHAPTER
## 17

Angela carried some wood from the back porch to make a fire in the cookstove. It appeared to her that it was going to be a fine day—cool, no wind, clear. She thought the oven would be hot enough in fifteen minutes for her to start making the biscuits. She would have biscuits, white gravy, butter, grape jam, and eggs for those who wanted them. She would remind the men that she still needed bacon when they did their grocery shopping.

She called to the bedroom, "Come on, Josh, it's time to get up and yell at those two down in the barn. This is the day we're going to town."

Josh had been sleeping soundly, but the minute he heard the magic word, town, he jumped out of bed. His feet hit the pine flooring with a thud.

Angela went to the back porch and yelled loudly down to the barn, "Come on men, we have to eat breakfast before going to town. Last call," she hollered. She went back into the kitchen and looked out the side window in time to see her son bolt out of the barn door and start for the cabin as if his shirt had been on fire.

Angela met him on the porch and said, "Why didn't you wait on Big Thunder? He might have needed help," she told him.

"I'm sorry Mom," he answered. "I guess I just got in too much of a hurry when I heard that part about going to town."

They all waited for Big Thunder to sit down before Josh offered thanks. As soon as Josh said A-men, Jere picked up a biscuit, buttered it, and put a spoonful of grape jam on it. After he had finished the second biscuit, he asked to be excused from the table. His mind was not on breakfast. In fact, all of them were thinking about the trip.

Angela gathered up the dishes, put them in the dish pan, checked the fire in the stove, closed off the damper in the stovepipe, slid the air draft vent closed at the firebox, and told the men she would be along very soon. Joshua picked up the kerosene can, which was almost empty, and asked Angela to bring along a gold coin. Josh told her he had to go on down to the boat to fire up the blowtorch so he could heat the glow pin. He arrived at the boat ahead of everyone.

Josh had the engine ready to start when Angela came running down the hill.

"OOooohhh, my lord, Joshua!!" she wailed. "OOooohhh, Joshua, I can't believe this," she told him. "Oh, darling, isn't that sweet of you? I love you!"

Everyone except Josh thought she had gone bananas. They were wondering what terrible malady had suddenly stricken her to cause her to start acting that way. Jere was even concerned that they might not be able to commence the trip to town. He helped Angela aboard the boat, and she gave him a long, tender kiss. It was still not clear to the rest of the crew what had transpired to make her act that way.

"Oh, you are a dear, Joshua," she said, with a heavenly smile on her face.

"Dad, what in the world is she talking about?' Jere wanted to know. He was being left in the dark on that bit of privileged information and he was getting curious.

Josh explained, "Well, I painted the 'A' off the name on the boat, and it now reads Angel instead of Angela," he told them. "I was amazed that no one had noticed that the name was changed. It seems that Angela was the only one with sharp enough vision to notice it," Josh said. "I guess she likes it," Josh said.

"That's sweet of you, darling," she said, "Thank you for being so thoughtful and wonderful. You don't know how much I appreciate that," she said sincerely.

"You're welcome, dear," he told her. "My thoughts were only of you when I hit upon that brainstorm. I just had to do it for you, Angel," he said. "I'm glad you like it."

"Oh, I do, dear," she said. "And thank you so much for thinking of me."

"Jere, remind me to pick up a roll of film this morning," she told him. "I'd like to take some pictures of the boat with our family sitting in it. Each one of us can take turns snapping the pictures of the rest of us," she told them. "And since we don't have any pictures of Big Thunder, I'd like to get one or two snaps of him and Jeremiah together," Angela expressed her desire.

Everyone was aboard and seated. Josh eased out into midstream and then put it in forward gear. He pushed the throttle up to just over half and left it there. Rosburg was in view in no time. Big Thunder couldn't believe that a boat that size could run so fast. He was amazed at the amount of speed that Josh could summon from his craft.

Angela had told Josh earlier that she didn't need to go to Astoria. Josh told her that he could also purchase what he needed in Rosburg and then they wouldn't be required to cross the Columbia River. Josh pulled up to the fuel pumps and told the attendant to fill his tank with tractor spirits and then fill the five-gallon can with kerosene that they would use to burn their lamps and start the fires in the wood-burning stoves and fireplace.

Ben Ferguson happened to come by the pumps to say hello. He was flabbergasted by the appearance of the boat that he had literally given away. It pained him severely to observe a thousand-dollar boat sitting there in his marina that he actually sold for a measly twenty-dollar gold coin. He shook his head one more time in disbelief.

"Ben, can I leave my boat with you while we do a bit of shopping in town?" Josh very politely asked him.

"Of course you may," Ben replied. "And there will be no charge since I saw you fill your fuel tank a moment ago."

"By the way," Josh said. "This is our friend, Big Thunder, who is now living with us and sleeping in the barn."

"How do you do, Mr. Ferguson?" Big Thunder greeted him. "I am happy to meet anyone who is an acquaintance of the Langfords,"

"I'm glad to meet you, Big Thunder," Ben told him. "Maybe we will see more of you folks now since you have that sleek-looking boat to travel downriver in."

Josh said, "Yes, I expect you will see quite a bit of us now that we have a reliable mode of transportation."

Josh headed in the direction of the post office while Angela and her two helpers were looking for the grocery store. The first thing Angela noticed, however, was the drug store with an ice cream parlor on one side. She felt that they should stop in and pay a visit. Each ordered a double dip cone of different flavors and returned to the board sidewalk to enjoy them while sitting on a wooden bench that advertised the prices of haircuts and shaves at a local barber shop.

Big Thunder was enjoying his cone as much as any little kid would have, and there was a noticeable gleam in his eye and a spring in his step that had not been there before. His health had improved appreciably since he had taken up residence at the Langford barn. He seemed to be recuperating daily, partly because of his association with his young friend and partly because of the healthy meals he had enjoyed at Angela's table. He loved Jeremiah as if he were his own grandson and the partnership they had formed was unique. His jolly attitude was probably also a contributor to his recuperation, too.

The clerk at the grocery store had offered to deliver their purchases to the marina, but since there were three of them, they decided to carry them, instead. Josh was waiting for them to return. He had picked up one letter from Angela's folks and another from his family. He had also bought a large salmon from a fisherman who had come by the marina while they were gone. Big Thunder agreed to wrap it with clay and bake it under hot coals of fire in the back yard, as the Indians had always done it.

They stowed the groceries and Josh heated the firing pin with the blowtorch. He had never had the reliable Red Seal engine sputter and die on him. It had a beautiful sound to it that clearly cried power. He loved to hear the melodious sound of the engine with the unique bell tone ring that it had when it was wide open at full speed. It was music to his ears, and he was a proud skipper.

After they had gone about a quarter of a mile, Josh pushed the throttle to full open and felt the bow reach for the sky like a young horse turned to pasture. The powerful engine was still wide open as they passed the Langford cabin a few minutes later. Angela waved to it as it disappeared in a flash. Josh throttled down as he caught sight of the island up ahead. He circumnavigated the island completely to see if any wild animal such as a bear might be visiting ahead of them. They knew that any black bear could be dangerous if it was surprised, especially if it was a mother bear with cubs.

Satisfied that it was safe, Josh allowed Jere to step out on the bank and secure the bow line to a sapling. Jere felt big now that his father was delegating more responsibility to him. He left the engine idling as the four of them disembarked to go on an extended tour of Jeremiah's island.

After Jere had explained everything to Big Thunder's satisfaction about the many things to be observed and explored and had completed touring the sights they headed back to the boat for a short trip home. Josh was at the wheel when Jere let go of the bow line and hopped into the boat. Josh reversed out to midstream and then eased it forward for a leisurely trip down to the cabin. Josh slowed the boat to a crawl and eased into the dug-out slip. Jere made fast the bow line to a sapling and locked the lock in the security chain. Everyone helped carry the groceries up the hill, but Josh had the hardest job of all. He had to carry the heavy can of kerosene. He was winded when he finally reached the back steps.

Angela built a fire in the stove to heat some water. She had to wash the dishes she had left behind that morning. Big Thunder carried a load of wood to the back yard in order to build a fire. He would let it burn down to the point where there was nothing left but red-hot coals. He would then place the clay-covered salmon in the coals until they had almost disappeared.

Josh, Jere, and Big Thunder went to the barn to inspect the steel traps that had lain unused for the past seven months. Josh sent Jere to the kitchen to get a bit of lard from his mother with which to lubricate and rustproof the traps. The weather was beginning to get cool and it would soon be time to start trapping the fur-bearing animals that roamed in great numbers in that portion of the wilderness. Big Thunder told Josh that he was an experienced trapper and skinner and that he would love to go with him to set out his traps when the weather turned cold.

Big Thunder told him, "Thanks to you people and especially your son, my health has now improved to the point where I am able to do things that I like to do, like trapping and fishing. So I would like to help pay you folks back for allowing me to stay here and for being so good to me."

"You don't need to feel that you owe us one penny, Big Thunder," Josh said to him. "We love making your life more pleasant, and we also love having your company with us. Jeremiah especially loves having you with us."

"I would really love to help you with the trapping, Josh, if you don't mind," he said. "I am an expert in the field and I can help you make a lot of money this winter running the trap lines that we have set out. One very important thing is knowing where to set the traps. My health is good now, and I want to do this for you," he told Josh.

"That's settled then," Josh confirmed. "We will work together this winter and I will be glad to accept your advice on the intricacies of steel trapping. I'll be pleased to have you beside me, Big Thunder," he assured him.

What Josh really wanted to do before the winter weather set in was to explore the upper reaches of the Grays River to see how far it would be navigable with his boat. That would be an invaluable aid to him when he started laying out the boundaries of his trap line. He told Big Thunder he would draw a map of it on a piece of tablet paper and he intended to design it where they would be able to run the traps and make it back home in one day without having to stay out in the wilderness during the night.

Josh asked, "Is it true that Angela said you two were planning a trip to the woods tomorrow?"

Big Thunder said, "That's right, Josh. Unless there is something you would like for us to do, instead."

"No, that's fine," Josh concurred. "I was just wondering if you could keep an eye out for some mink signs along some of the creeks as you walk about. If you do find some signs, make a mental note of the location for me, please."

"We will certainly do that for you, Josh," Big Thunder agreed. "Won't we Little Brother?" he asked Jere.

"We'll be glad to, Dad," Jere said.

"Fine," Josh replied. "Then the day after tomorrow the three of us will take a trip up the Grays River to see if we can find the headwaters, or at least as far as we can travel safely in the boat, when the water may get too shallow to float us. Agreed?"

"Agreed," they chimed simultaneously at that wonderful prospect.

"Josh, I think I may know where the Grays River eventually leads to out there in the woods," Big Thunder said. "If this is the same river that my people used to call Nintuck, then it leads into a lake about ten or twelve miles from here, and then the lake continues on for about another mile. I believe that it is the same river. If it is, then my daughter lives only about one mile through the woods from the edge of that lake. If we got an early start one morning we could travel to the end of the lake and then walk to my daughter's house so we could visit her. If you would be so kind as to do me this favor, I would certainly appreciate it," Big Thunder asked Josh.

"Why, of course we will, Big Thunder," Josh told him. "Would you want to remain with your daughter there when you return to her house?" Josh asked him.

"Oh no, Josh," he replied. "I will explain to her that I love her but that I have found a new family to live with and would be returning with them. I will tell her that I am going to be helping you on your trap line to assist in paying for the things that your family has done for me. I have a very good professional skinning knife that I will want to pick up when we visit her. It will be a valuable asset to us this winter, " he stated.

"Jeremiah and I will be happy to take you to see your daughter, and we will also be happy to meet her," Josh told him.

They had hung all of the steel traps back on the nails in the barn and proceeded to the cabin. Josh said, "Angela, would you remind me to get the two barn rats up early in the morning so they can make a very important trip, please? And would you also make breakfast early, so they might be on their way to the woods on a very important mission for me?" he politely asked her.

"Your wish is my command, sir," she sweetly replied and smiled the assurance of her love for him.

"Thanks, dear," he said to her. "They are going to make a trip to the woods for me to see if they can find any mink signs along the creeks they have been exploring out there."

Big Thunder's clay-wrapped salmon had been slowly baking under the hot coals of the fire for over two hours. He judged that it was now time to rake it out of the coals and let it rest for five or ten minutes before breaking the clay with a hammer to expose the succulent meat. He had also wrapped four potatoes in clay to bake at the same time as an added complement to an already fine supper. Angela had prepared a pot of butter beans and pulled some green onions out of the garden. Josh and Big Thunder both said the green onions, or scallions as some people called them, would go perfectly with the salmon.

Josh and Angela said they couldn't recall when they had enjoyed a meal as much as that one. They were simply delighted with the smoky flavor of the salmon. Big Thunder agreed.

Josh said to everyone, "Tomorrow night we will all need to go to bed early to get a good night's sleep, Angela, we need you to wake us up early to make a long trip up the Grays River. We're going to explore the upper reaches of the river to consider the laying out of a trap line there this winter. Then we will walk with Big Thunder through the woods for about a mile to visit his daughter," Josh said.

"I'm sure we will be gone all day, hon," Josh told Angela. "Maybe you can make us some sandwiches to take along with us? I think we should also take a kerosene lantern along in case it's dark when we return home. It will be difficult to judge just how long we will be gone," he explained to Angela.

"Sounds as though you three are going to have lots of fun the day after tomorrow," Angela said. "I just want you to be very careful and return safely to me," she cautioned.

"I suppose we need to retire early tonight," Big Thunder said. "We have a very important job to do for Josh, tomorrow," he said.

No one enjoyed their early bedtime as much as Angela. She was quite satisfied that the situation had been worked out. The two had unknowingly presented her with an ideally perfect arrangement for her second honeymoon, which she felt she duly deserved.

They had said their goodnights to one another, and the two barn rats had retired to their tow sack mattresses. Needless to say, Jeremiah and Big Thunder didn't gain anything by retiring early except for a longer rest. The talking bug had evidently bitten them both. Their many and varied conversations ran rampant for at least the first three hours after they had laid down on their makeshift beds.

Big Thunder spoke first. "Little Brother, my professional skinning knife is at my daughter's house. It's the best skinning knife I've ever seen. I traded four beaver pelts to an old Frenchman for it many years ago, and it served me well for many years before I got too old to trap in the wilderness by myself," he told Jere. "But what I really wanted to tell you that's most important is the fact that I want the knife to be yours when I am finally called to the great beyond. It will be yours to remember me by, and it will serve you well and last you all the days of your life, also," Big Thunder told him.

Big Thunder continued in the darkness of the barn, "Another thing I want to pick up at my daughter's house is the bear claw that belongs to me. I want to give you that as a token of our friendship. It would be a great honor for me to have you wear it around your neck, as I used to wear it," he said. "It is threaded with a length of rawhide."

"Big Thunder, I will treasure the bear claw and the skinning knife," Jere told him. "I only hope that it's fifty years before it passes from your hands," Jere sincerely wished.

"Little Brother," the old man told him. "Without wanting to give you more than you can carry, I also want to give you a silver and turquoise arm bracelet. If you should ever be fortunate enough to be invited to attend an Indian powwow, wear it on your arm. You could wear it in my honor and to perpetuate my memory when I am gone," he said to Jere. "It is emblazoned with a thunderbird, which is hand-carved into a piece of turquoise. It is truly a most magnificent piece of fine jewelry," he told Jere.

"I am trusting that these token gifts will partially compensate you and your family for the unselfish contributions you have all made to my health, comfort, pride, and well-being since I have become associated with you all. You all have greatly contributed to bringing me back up to being a man again," he said to his best friend.

"I will be happy to wear your sacred ornaments with great pride," Jere told him. "And I will forever cherish the wonderful memories of your advice, your kindness, your special friendship, and the willingness to share your vast knowledge with me and my family, and the wonderful memories of the good times we spent together in the forest with our many wild animal friends," he said sincerely.

After discussing many other subjects and striking up several more personal conversations, Jeremiah got to wondering if they would be able to spend the cold nights of the bitter winter season in the barn, when the weather really turned miserable and cold outside.

"Big Thunder, do you plan to have us stay here in the barn when the weather turns very cold outside this winter?" he asked.

His friend replied, "Why, of course, Little Brother. When one gets used to the cold gradually, like we're going to do, you don't even notice it that much. The wild animals that sleep in the wilderness gradually accustom themselves to the cold weather and therefore don't mind the bitter cold. Besides, we will have plenty of warm blankets to cover us and a barn to keep out the wind and snow, sleet and rain from penetrating our warm bed," Big Thunder assured him. "We will be just fine here."

That finally seemed to end their conversations for the night. Everything was very quiet and peaceful. Each of them had not even realized that the other had fallen asleep.

# CHAPTER
## 18

After eating a hearty breakfast the next morning, Jeremiah and Big Thunder set out for the woods. They were really on a pleasure hike into the wilderness, but they also had an additional task to perform for Josh that day. They didn't really consider it a task or chore because it would be an undeniable pleasure to search for signs of mink playing along the streams they would visit.

They had walked about two miles into the woods when Big Thunder decided it was time to sit and rest for a bit. They chose to sit on a fallen tree trunk about fifty yards from a creek they were thoroughly familiar with. After sitting quietly for about ten minutes, a family of minks concluded that it was quiet enough to start their playing once more. They were playing and romping along the water's edge and were soon chattering away at one another. Their soft, rich, dark-brown fur made an exceptionally beautiful as well as fully functional warm coat to ward off the bitter cold weather that would invade the Northwest in the wintertime. They each agreed that this creek would be one likely spot to note for Josh to set out one or more steel traps that winter and would notify him on their return.

Suddenly, the entire mink family made a hasty retreat to a hole in the side of the creek bank. They disappeared swiftly, as though they might have been chased by something or were afraid of something. Big Thunder had commented that this was a most unusual behavior for the mink family to all scamper away at one time. He had never witnessed such behavior with minks. A quick glance around indicated that nothing could be seen close at hand in the woods that would have intimidated them.

Without any other warning, there was an unusual noise that sounded almost human but was unintelligible, emanating from somewhere in the woods. The strange sound was below the normal range of the human voice, and the tone was completely unlike any other they had ever heard. They surmised that this was probably why the minks had scurried into their hiding place in the bank as though their tails were on fire. They had evidently heard those noises with their keen hearing when Jere and Big Thunder hadn't yet heard them.

They sat on the log, dumbfounded, staring at each other questioningly. Both sat transfixed, as if frozen on the log. Once more the noise was heard coming from an animal or whatever it was. This time it seemed to be coming from over the left shoulder of Big Thunder. It bellowed out something incomprehensible. Big Thunder raised both of his eyebrows as if to say, *I don't know what it is, either.*

Jeremiah was actually afraid to move a muscle, and Big Thunder's reaction of surprise and bewilderment had caused him to freeze on the spot. Neither had spoken a word while searching the expressions on the faces of one another that might give some clue as to the nature and origin of the sound. Although it had probably only been twenty or thirty seconds at the most, it had somehow seemed more like twenty minutes since they had first heard the weird and unidentifiable sound.

Big Thunder whispered to Jere, "Do you smell that awful stink?"

"Yes," Jere whispered back to him. "Do you have any idea what it might be? It's getting stronger."

"Well, yes, I do know . . . now that I've had time to think about it," Big Thunder whispered again. "But I was completely stumped at first," he admitted.

Before Big Thunder could explain, the loud and unintelligible sound was again emitted from somewhere behind of his left shoulder, much louder than before. It seemed that it might have been similar to laughter mixed with some low-pitched guttural sounds from the throat, alternating in frequency.

Jeremiah whispered to Big Thunder, "I'm really scared," he admitted.

"Little Brother," he answered in a calm voice. "If I have to, I will sacrifice my own life to save yours, although I don't really think it will come to that. As I started to tell you, I was certain that

I knew where the sounds and stink came from," he told Jere. "I am basing that on the hearsay from some of my ancestors," he continued. "My grandfather, the old shaman of our tribe, passed along a lot of information to his people about the Sasquatch. His contention was that the male Sasquatch could at times issue forth warning sounds when he encountered something or someone in his own private territory. In his eyes, that person or that animal was trespassing on the region that he had marked out with his urine and had claimed for his own," Big Thunder quietly explained to Jeremiah.

The old man continued, "The old shaman said it was never known whether a female Sasquatch had the ability to communicate in this manner. He said he didn't think they were able to issue warnings from the throat, but then the females didn't ordinarily claim a territory like the males did."

Big Thunder cocked his head to one side and listened intently for a few seconds. Hearing nothing, he continued, "My grandfather said that the male Sasquatch was also the only one who had the ability to emit that distasteful and repelling odor that we had been smelling. Evidently this is another of his warning procedures to invite something to leave his domain. I think that vile smell can be used to mark his territory by rubbing small bushes in his area. This was supposed to also keep out intruders," he said to Jere.

Big Thunder cupped his hand to his left ear and listened for a few moments. "I think he has already gone past us, though I never did see him," Big Thunder said.

Jere said, "I never did see him, either, Big Thunder, and I have very good eyesight. I have heard that if they don't want you to catch sight of them, then you won't," Jere said to his friend.

Big Thunder answered, "I am positive that the male Sasquatch probably made a wide semicircle around our position, refusing to show himself, yet letting us know that we were trespassing upon a portion of the forest that he had already claimed as his own and intended to let us know about it. He's on top of the ridge now. I can hear him up there. He is much more cunning than the females at keeping a distance between himself and humans, yet staying completely out of sight. He is much more unfriendly," Big Thunder assured Little Brother.

"Whew," Jere breathed a sigh of relief. "Boy, I'm sure glad that's over," he stated. "I was beginning to get worried, Big Thunder, and I wondered if we had finally encountered something that meant to hurt us. I must admit, I was really scared and I was beginning to shake."

Big Thunder replied, "I'll have to admit that it also unnerved me at the beginning. I was never more surprised by anything in my whole life. I wasn't considering that anything such as that could happen to us while we were sitting on the log, minding our own business and watching the minks. It certainly is a weird feeling to have something like that thrust upon you out of the clear blue sky without warning," he said.

"I can tell you that I have never heard any weird sounds like that before, and I will never forget them as long as I live," Jere assured Big Thunder.

Big Thunder told him he was glad that they were both fortunate enough to have heard the sounds and smelled the stench together, so they would be able to substantiate their stories to those who might be interested in hearing them. Many times a person will be alone when something such as that happens, and his story will not usually be believed unless it can be verified by another person who was present at the same time.

"Little Brother, we have accomplished at least one thing that we came for," he said. "We have not only found some mink signs for your father but we have also seen some live mink as well. We can report that we have at least one creek on which to lay out his trap line that should be fairly productive," he said.

"I don't like to mention this now, Little Brother, but we need to cross over the ridge and go to the valley on the other side to check out a creek over there," Big Thunder said. "We really need to cross over exactly where that Sasquatch went," he told Jere. "Do you feel like going with me?"

"I'm game to go anywhere that you want to go, Big Thunder," he said. "As long as I have you with me and I have faith in the Lord, I will go," Jere told him.

"I think we have seen the last of the male Sasquatch today," he told his friend. "I don't anticipate any danger, son. I wouldn't lead you anywhere that I wouldn't lead my own child, and we do need to find some more mink signs for your father."

"Then let's get started," Jere quickly told him.

The incline to the top of the ridge was pretty steep and tough going, so Big Thunder was winded when they reached the apex. Jere suggested that they rest a while before descending to the creek. Big Thunder told Jere he was thirsty. Jere suggested that he would go to the creek and get him some water, but the old man decided he could wait until they got to the creek. He just needed to rest for a while to get his breath back.

They had rested for about ten minutes and had scarcely started descending toward the valley below when both of them heard the strange sounds coming from the top of the next ridge. They hadn't expected to hear from that same animal again and quite frankly didn't know whether to keep descending to the valley or not. It seemed quite clear that the male Sasquatch didn't want them in his private domain, and he was warning them again to stay out. Evidently they were considered unwelcome guests.

They decided to sit another five minutes to see if the animal would move on. After sitting for a while they decided to start again. They had no sooner started than the same eerie sound penetrated the forest. It seemed now that he was coming to meet them, since it seemed like he was coming down the near side of the ridge and getting closer.

Jeremiah begged Big Thunder to turn around and go back the way they had come. "Big Thunder, this is his territory and he owns it. It seems that he wants to defend it. I think we would be wise to turn around and move completely out of his territory. If we don't quit following him, I'm afraid that he may want to hurt us, and we certainly don't want that," Jere said seriously.

"I think you're right, Little Brother," Big Thunder agreed. "It's perfectly clear to me that he does not want us in this region of the woods. He has offered us a clear sign to stay away from him and his area of domain that he has claimed. I'm with you. I think we should heed his warning and return to the other valley immediately."

They turned and ascended the ridge quickly, then went down the other side to the valley below. They knelt down and drank their fill until their thirst was quenched. Big Thunder felt that he needed to rest for another thirty minutes before attempting the last part of the leg home. They had hurriedly come down the hill and he was winded again.

Jere said that he would have one of the most unusual stories to tell his parents that they could ever expect to hear. He wasn't certain that he would have bothered to tell it if Big Thunder had not been along to verify it. His mother especially had previously had some serious doubts about him telling the absolute truth at times.

They walked along the edge of the creek for a while before veering away from it in the direction of the cabin. They observed a multitude of mink slides and tracks all around a dead tree that had fallen into the water across the creek. It had made a perfect playground for them to romp and play on and around. They decided that this would also be a perfect place for Joshua to put some of his steel traps this winter.

Jere allowed his mind to wander back to the strange episode earlier in the day. Actually, his mind had never strayed from the occurrence the whole time they had been steadily walking toward the cabin.

"Big Thunder, do you actually think that male Sasquatch would have challenged us if we had decided to continue on down the hill to the creek?" Jere inquired of his Indian friend.

"I suppose we will never know," he replied. "But I think we made the proper decision by allowing him to claim and occupy his rightful domain there in the forest. I can abide by his decision that it is rightfully his to guard against intruders upon his territory. He gave us fair warning to keep away from his area, and we didn't heed his warning, at first. He had every right to challenge us, I'm certain of that," he stated unequivocally.

When Jere came within sight of the log cabin in the distance, he started running for it. He could not wait to be the first one to tell his mother of the exciting experiences they had undergone out in the wilderness that day. He had since changed his mind about what he had told Big Thunder in wanting to keep that episode with Sasquatch a secret. Jeremiah was all out of breath when he finally reached the back porch. His mother had seen him running and figured that something must be wrong

"Jeremiah Langford, you should be ashamed of yourself for running off and leaving your friend to walk in alone. I want you to apologize to him when he gets here," she ordered him. "Why didn't you wait on him?" she asked.

"I'm sorry, Mom," Jere replied breathlessly. "I was in a big hurry. I'll apologize to him when he gets here," he promised.

It was quite evident to Angela that Jere couldn't bear waiting to tell her some bone-chilling story about what had happened that day. She could tell that he was sitting on pins and needles, itching to tell her something about their exciting day in the woods. Angela said to him, "Now, you just wait until Big Thunder gets here and gets his breath before you start telling some wild story about the woods. I don't want to hear two versions of a story."

Angela then poured each of them a glass of cool water and told them to sit on the back porch to cool off and get their breath before attempting to communicate their wilderness adventures to the family.

# CHAPTER
## 19

It was Angela's birthday, October 27, 1923, and Josh had already made arrangements with Big Thunder and Jeremiah to bring her birthday present up from the barn to give to him before breakfast. The men assembled on the back porch to wash their hands and faces while the beautifully wrapped present was placed on a pile of wood. Josh peeked inside the door to make certain that Angela was still busy, then hid the present behind his back as they entered the back door singing happy birthday.

She was completely surprised when Josh produced the professionally wrapped birthday present from her loved ones. She smiled and cried simultaneously as she started tearing the paper away from the gift. The tears would not stop. "Oh, thank you so much for remembering my birthday," she said before she even knew what was in the package. She tore open the paper to discover the beautiful red sweater inside the box.

"Oh, my darling Joshua," she cried. "Thank you so much. I love you," she said. "From the bottom of my heart, I thank you," she said again. "All of you!"

They all chimed in unison, "You're welcome, and happy birthday!"

After breakfast was finished and the birthday greetings completed, Josh went down the hill to the boat ahead of the other two in order to get the firing pin hot and to check the boat over. This would be the day they were going to try to find the headwaters of the Grays River. When Big Thunder and Jere arrived at the boat, he had the engine idling and was ready for Jere to cast off the bow line and push the boat away from shore. Josh reversed to midstream and then headed upriver. The boat sliced through the cold water like a hot knife through butter, and the captain was extremely proud of his luxurious nautical machine.

Josh noticed that there were numerous bends in the river as they motored upstream, but in a short time they were entering the lake Big Thunder had told them about. He recognized the location of where they were, and it was now obvious that he had known all what he was talking about.

Big Thunder said to Josh, "Go to the northeast corner of the lake and find a good shoreline to tie up the boat."

Josh followed his expert advice, and they were soon walking up the hill and through the woods toward Little Flower's house. When they finally came to a clearing in the woods Big Thunder let out a loud yell, "Hellooo-o-o, there." They kept walking in the direction of the house and he yelled again, "Helloo-o-o in there."

A beautiful lady with shiny black hair came out on the front porch of the dwelling, jumped off the porch, and ran as fast as her feet would carry her toward Big Thunder. She hugged and kissed him saying, "Oh, my father, you have finally come home."

Little Flower was crying, tears streaming down her face. She said, "I actually thought you were a ghost when I kept hearing someone say, 'hello there,' because I recognized your voice. I had actually thought you were dead though."

Big Thunder beamed one of his seldom-seen smiles at the sight of his daughter. He said to her, "This my new family. This is Joshua Langford and his son, Jeremiah, who saved my life. This is my daughter, Little Flower," he said to Josh and Jere.

Informal greetings were exchanged, and they were invited into the house to sit and wait for her to fix them something to eat. They told her that they had sandwiches in the boat and declined to eat with her. Little Flower said her husband was hunting and wouldn't return home until at least nightfall. She had so much wanted them to meet him.

"I am going to go home with my new family, Little Flower," he told her. "This in no way means that I do not love you, my dear daughter, it's just that I am so happy with them that I wish to spend the remainder of my days here on earth helping and living with them. This is my little brother, and we are the same as one, Little Flower," he said to her. "He is my pride and joy and I am especially fond of him."

When they had completed visiting with Little Flower, Big Thunder then picked up the items of significance that he had wanted to get at her house. As they were returning to the boat through the woods, Big Thunder told Jeremiah to remember the route well. He told him that it might be that he would need to use that information at some time in the future. It would be wise for him to pay attention and remember it.

All of that walking had made them hungry. They hurriedly gobbled up all of the sandwiches that Angela had prepared for them when they arrived back at the boat. Big Thunder couldn't thank Josh enough for allowing him to see his daughter once more while he was alive. He never thought that he would ever see her again when he walked off into the woods that day to die, many moons ago. She, too, never thought that she would ever see her father again. Father and daughter would both remember the kindness of Josh and his son as long as they lived.

Big Thunder had brought back his treasured skinning knife, the silver and turquoise arm bracelet, and the bear claw strung on a rawhide necklace. The treasures would be presented to his blood brother very shortly.

The tasty sandwiches were quickly finished with gusto, and Josh set his sights for the opposite side of the lake and the entrance to the Grays River. He slowed down at the narrow slit where the lake emptied into the river and then opened it up full for the trip to the Langford cabin. The trip downriver was enjoyable and uneventful. The boat handled like a dream and their primary goal had been accomplished with no mishaps.

Angela was very happy to hear the boat coming down the river before it had turned dark. She had worried that it might be after nightfall when they returned home. She remembered hearing about the dangers of boating on the rivers, and it tugged at her heartstrings each time they made a journey in the boat. She knew that Josh was a good skipper, but she had felt a bit uneasy that morning when they left. They could not see her as they left that morning, but she waved her hand until they were completely out of sight. Upon their return, she always rewarded her family with the best meal she knew how to cook. Supper that night was superb, as usual, and the family was again greatly thankful for it.

It seemed that all of the members of the family were tired that night and had opted for an early retirement after supper. Even Jeremiah, who was always ready to keep going, had said that he wanted to go to bed early. The usual parting remarks were made and the men shuffled off down the hill toward their private nightly retreat.

As usual the next morning, Angela was the one who was bright, cheery, full of vim, vigor and singing about what a beautiful morning it was. Josh wouldn't have been able to sleep if he had wanted to, having to listen to the joyful sounds of her singing that could be heard for a quarter of a mile. Jere and Big Thunder had even reported that they could hear her singing down at the barn that morning.

After a filling breakfast of hominy grits, butter, and maple syrup, bolstered by a cup of hot coffee, Jere and Big Thunder got permission from Angela to once again head for the unknown reaches of the forested hills and valleys. They made a bee line for the usual meeting place far back in the woods by the small stream.

"Little brother, don't be in such a hurry," Big Thunder begged him. "I can travel for long distances if I take my time, but if I am rushed, I will not be able to travel very far. We will arrive there in plenty of time," he said to Jere. He was breathing hard.

"I'm sorry, big brother," he apologized. "I wasn't thinking. My mind was completely away from what I was doing. I promise to take a slower pace from now on. I keep forgetting that you are not a young man."

Big Thunder noticed that this was the first time he had ever called him big brother, instead of Big Thunder. He was pleased to hear himself referred to as a brother.

"I understand, son," he told Jere. "I used to be a young man, myself, and I have been known to be guilty of that very mistake. Don't worry about it. I am now getting stronger and stronger as the weeks go by, thanks to you and your family," Big Thunder acknowledged to his friend.

"Suppose we take a rest, now," Jere suggested. "We are more than halfway to our meeting place, and we have lots of time left."

"Good idea," Big Thunder concurred. "That would be nice. Let's pick a log to sit on while we talk and get the wind back in our sails," Big Thunder said.

It was unusually quiet when they sat down, and Big Thunder noticed it. He wondered why the little chipmunks, birds, and squirrels were not making their usual chatter. After sitting for several minutes, the birds had evidently gotten used to their presence and started singing again. Soon it was so noisy that they could barely hear one another talk from opposite ends of the log.

Suddenly, Jere was almost jolted out of his skin. A white wolf was bearing down on them in a full run and was heading directly for the log. The wolf veered away at the last minute, moved out in a wide semicircle around them, and returned toward them from the same direction as before, still in a full run. Jere recognized her as White Spirit and was then satisfied that she probably wanted to play with them.

She came to a full stop at the outer limit of her orbit and looked back at them without moving. She then came at them again in a full run, veering only at the last second to avoid a collision with the log. You could almost see her laughing as she continued to tease them with her antics. Her mischievous pranks were so outrageous they were comical. She was having the time of her life by playing with them, but she wasn't the only one enjoying that strange interlude. Jere was having as much fun as she was. It seemed evident that she had wanted the boy to chase her through the woods, although she couldn't have realized that he would have been at a great disadvantage in the running department.

"White Spirit wants us to play with her, Big Thunder," Jere told him.

"Little brother, I have never before had the occasion to observe anything quite as incredible as what we have just witnessed," Big Thunder attested to him.

"At first, I thought she was going to attack us, but when I found out for certain that it was White Spirit I felt at ease, because I knew she would not hurt us," Jere confidently explained.

White Spirit turned around and looked at them one more time before trotting slowly up the hill to the top of the ridge. She turned around again as she reached the apex of the ridge, as if to say, "so long," and then disappeared over the ridge.

Jeremiah said that he had never had very much affection for wolves until he met White Spirit. She was so smart and understanding that one could not help loving her. Jere vowed that she would be his friend, forever. Big Thunder said that he loved her because she was intelligent enough and kind enough to want to save his life. He said that she was smart enough to figure out how to proceed in order to rescue him, with Jere's able assistance. Her act of kindness had then allowed him to cherish the love and admiration that he had found with his newly acquired family. Jeremiah also vowed to be eternally grateful to White Spirit for her kindness and devotion, her generosity, and willingness to playfully contact them in the wilderness. She had become a special friend to them both, and they treasured her benevolent nature.

The two then walked on slowly to their private meeting place by the creek and saw signs of where they had visited previously. The prevalence of mink tracks was also noted and filed away in their minds to report to Josh. They sat down, rested and reminisced, and had several meaningful and memorable conversations of experiences they had both enjoyed while visiting their private sanctuary there in the woods.

After resting sufficiently, they decided to return to the cabin. They had totally enjoyed their eventful trip into the woods that day and wanted to tell Josh and Angela all about their unique experiences.

Big Thunder asked Jere, "Do you see those mackerel-looking clouds floating in from the northwest, son?"

"Yes sir, I see them," Jere acknowledged to him.

"All right, pay attention," he said. "There will be a snow in this area within the next three days. Mark my words!"

"You seem to be pretty certain about that, Big Thunder," Jere said.

"Mark my words, son!" he told him. "That's all I'm going to say."

They continued toward the log cabin, observing the natural beauty of the woods, the surrounding hillsides, and valleys as they walked and talked.

They were already approaching the back porch of the cabin when Angela stepped out the door and said, "I can't believe that you two are back already. Did you not have a very good time today?" she asked in a concerned tone of voice.

"Oh yes, Mom," Jere answered his mother. "We had a wonderful time today. It was swell. We even got to see White Spirit again," he excitedly said to her. "That was really the high point. We had been hoping to see her but wouldn't mention it for fear that we might jinx it."

Angela could tell instantly that they had both thoroughly enjoyed the day and were slightly more than just excited about the outcome of their excursion in the woods.

"Mom, she is the smartest, most wonderful wolf in the whole world," he assured her. "She is also the most beautiful snow-white wolf you have ever seen in your life."

"I wouldn't know, son," she replied. "I have never yet seen a live wolf in my entire life. I have seen pictures of them, though, and I do happen to think that all that I've seen pictures of would be considered beautiful," she agreed.

"You could never imagine how beautiful this wolf is until you happened to see her for yourself," Jere convinced her. "She has a beautiful white coat. She has the weirdest looking eyes you have ever seen. They are beautiful, yet they look haunted. Her eyes make it seem like you could actually peer into her soul. I love her more than any animal I've ever seen, besides Old Blue, of course," he interjected. "She loves me, too," Jere told her. "I can tell."

They proceeded to the living room to sit and rest. Big Thunder was tired. Josh had just come from the boat and plopped down on the settee at the front porch. Angela could see him from the window. He seemed to have some papers in his hands. She went to the front door and asked curiously, "What are you reading, dear?"

Josh answered, "Would you believe that while lying there on my back in the engine room of the boat that I noticed a clump of papers stuck between the one of the ribs and the hull that turned out to be an owner's manual for the Red Seal engine? I'm going to read it," he said to Angela. "Hopefully it will give me some pointers and information on how I can keep it in tip-top running condition," he said.

He remained on the front porch until he was finally called in for supper. He told them that it was a most interesting and helpful book of facts and helpful hints that he was glad to have available to him for advice for how to maintain the ultimate performance of that great engine.

At the supper table, Big Thunder gave him a well-received report on the prevalence of mink signs they had witnessed around the edges of the creeks they had visited. He told Josh he was confident that there were more creeks in the area with families of mink in them as well as the streams they had already seen. Josh was elated over this information.

Big Thunder was surprised and overjoyed as he sat down at the supper table and noticed they were having rabbit and dumplings. He told them about the men in his tribe catching a six-hundred-pound sturgeon fish in the Snake River when he was a small boy. He said it was a female and she had two cast-iron kettles full of caviar in her. They feasted for days.

Josh told them that he had found many rabbits in an area of the woods that had been burned over about four or five years ago. The ten or twelve acres was completely bare of large trees but had lots of grass growing in the area that had probably been denuded by a fire started by a lightning strike.

Again, the men praised the cook for preparing such a delicious meal, and once again Angela graciously accepted the compliments and applause with shy honor. The old Indian told them that he was grateful to the Langford family for spoiling him perfectly rotten, as he had put it.

Angela told Big Thunder that she had a denim jacket that Joshua had outgrown that she wished to give to him. She told him that the buckskin shirt he was wearing was beautiful and was also very functional, but he needed to change it out now and then. She convinced him that she could clean his buckskin jacket with a stiff bristled brush and hang it on the clothesline to air out and soak up some sunshine, making it much nicer.

Big Thunder said, "Angela, I want to thank you. You folks are being too nice to this old man, but I do appreciate it."

"Josh, it's going to start getting colder at night, now," Angela told him. "We may want to think about giving the men in the barn more blankets to cover up with," she suggested.

Big Thunder assured Angela that they would yell for them in plenty of time to avert a catastrophe of cold shakes in the barn. He said it could be that they would be required the following night since he knew for certain that a cold front was moving in from the coast out of the direction of northwest.

No one asked how he knew that the cold front was moving in, but they figured he knew, anyway. They exchanged good-night greetings to one another, and the two friends proceeded out the back door to the barn.

Big Thunder woke up the next morning feeling the cold, hearing the wind blowing on the side of the barn and seeing the darkness of the clouds that were steadily approaching their area from the northwest. He was absolutely right about the cloud formation.

They noticed that a heavy blanket of snow had covered the tops of the mountains in the distance that morning. It indicated the beginning of the trapping season and an opportunity to bring in some much-needed cash to the family coffer.

Within two weeks, winter had set in decisively. The snow was beginning to get deep. The trap line route had already been established, and they were now running them with much more than average success. Big Thunder really did know what he was doing in the business of trapping as well as skinning and boarding. Josh realized that he was an experienced trapper. He had shown Josh the ropes about successful trapping in a very short time. If Josh had been trapping by himself, he wouldn't have had a fraction of the pelts that he now had drying stretched out on boards. Big Thunder had been a godsend for the family from the very start.

Big Thunder and Jeremiah woke up one morning to hear the sound of a rifle shot in the woods. It sounded as though it might have come from somewhere near the river. It was already daylight, and no one had come to the barn to wake them up. They jumped up and faced the north wind to the privy and then quickly darted for the back porch. The wash stand and water bucket had been moved into the kitchen to keep the water bucket from freezing. Angela had only just lit the fire in the cookstove and it was still cold in the kitchen. She informed them that Josh had gone hunting before daylight and hadn't come back. She said she heard a shot and supposed he had been the one who had fired it.

Josh yelled from the back yard at about that time, and Jere went running out to see a huge buck deer lying on the snow, already gutted out. He came into the kitchen and asked Big Thunder if he would help him skin the hide and quarter the carcass after they ate breakfast.

"Nothing would suit me better," he said. "I would also like to take some of the venison meat to make pemmican with it, if you will let me."

"Oh, absolutely, Big Thunder," he answered. "I love pemmican, but I don't have the recipe for making it."

"After today you shall have the recipe for making the finest pemmican that has ever been made," he promised. "I will have to find some hemlock to make the fire so we can smoke and cure the meat properly. I will also need to fine-grind some of those dried red peppers strung up on the back porch. That will make a nice seasoning."

"I can hardly wait!" Jere said.

Winter continued unabated, and the trapping business was booming. Big Thunder and his young partner continued to sleep in the warm barn, even though it was bitterly cold outside, with ample coverings of blankets to keep them cozy.

Their hides had to be taken to a fur dealer in Astoria to get the best prices. Josh could have sold them at Rosburg, but it was much more profitable to boat across the Columbia River and sell them at Astoria. The money kept rolling in from the sale of furs, thanks mostly to the expertise of the old Indian man and his knowledge of trapping, skinning, and boarding. Without him it would only have been a mild success. An unskilled skinner could ruin a pelt to where the dealer would only offer half the price it would normally bring. Big Thunder was considered a professional skinner, and his pelts were sought after by the the fur dealers in that area.

Successful trapping continued with Big Thunder still in excellent health, feeling well and enjoying the trapping. He was happy with his new life at the Langfords. He was pleased that the money had kept rolling in like it had. Jere was happy to have Big Thunder to buddy around with, and Angela was happy to have Josh alone with her all night long, every night.

Big Thunder was wishing they could extend the winter months for longer. He would be happy to live in an environment such as that year-round, but winter was beginning to release her hold and warmer weather would soon be peeking its head above the snow. He and Jere had not seen White Spirit or Sasquatch since the early part of winter. Jere had wondered if the wolf was lonesome for their company in the woods. It seemed that she had liked him, especially.

Angela was getting as big as a barrel with her pregnancy, but she was still as beautiful as ever. If anything, she was even more beautiful. She wasn't too far from birthing now. She was bright and cheerful constantly. She never had a down day. They all loved being near her and relishing her delightful disposition. She had supposed that Josh would need to go into town to bring a doctor or a midwife out to the cabin when her time was due. She hadn't really thought too much about it. Her mother had told her numerous times that things always seem to work out, and Angela had evidently always believed in it.

Josh, Jere, and Big Thunder returned from a very profitable trip to Astoria one morning. They had gone to sell the hides and furs they had trapped, skinned, and dried previously. Joshua brought the money to Angela when they came into the cabin, telling her to put it in the coffee can in their secret hiding place.

Angela said, "Josh, I'm afraid it's going to be necessary for us to find a different place to hide the money. The coffee can is full and running over. I am going to put it in a three-pound lard bucket with a lid on it, but you will need to take some baling wire to hang it from one of the upstairs rafters since I'm getting too big to climb the stairs," she instructed him.

"All right, hon," he told her. "I'll take care of that little problem when you get it ready for me." That was one problem he wished he had more of. He didn't mind dealing with that one at all.

Josh and Jere were running the trap lines, and Big Thunder had been putting in lots of time skinning and boarding the hides and pelts. He would loved to have gone on another trip with them on the trap line, but he couldn't afford to give up the available time that he had for skinning out the pelts. His skinning knife had been a lifesaver. Without it, their fur business would not have flourished as much. Winter would soon be coming to an end and it definitely would have to be considered a very highly successful fur-bearing season. They had made enough money already to last them the remainder of the year, and Big Thunder still had several skins boarded that would be sold later as they dried. In addition, they could still trap a few more animals before the end of the season. The pelts that were now on boards had been trapped at the coldest part of the winter and would be considered prime because of the heavy, full fur that was more shiny and much more beautiful than the fur on the animals that were trapped earlier that season before the weather got extremely cold.

Big Thunder was happy and smiling because he was now doing what he enjoyed most. His health had improved to the point where he seemed to be in very good physical condition for an eighty-four-year-old man. His skinning technique and expert help had meant the difference between success and outstanding success that season. Josh, Angela, and Jeremiah never failed to take the opportunity of telling Big Thunder how much they really appreciated all of the great help that he had been to them since he had come to live with them. But then, he told them that he appreciated them twice as much.

# CHAPTER
## 20

Spring had arrived in the beautiful green hills and valleys, after a cold, snowy winter that seemed as though it would never end. When it got a bit warmer, Josh said he was going to pull the boat up out of the water on runners and let it dry so he could refresh it with a much-needed coat of paint. That would not only make it a more beautiful boat but it would protect and preserve it as well.

Before he pulled it out of the water, he would need to check with Angela to make certain that she had all of the things she would need for the pantry for at least a week. He figured that it would need two days to dry, one day to paint, at least three days for the paint to dry and cure, and another half day to launch her back into the water, again. Before pulling it out of the water he would also need to run the trap line to pull all of the steel traps in from the creeks and woods. Josh still had the map of where they had placed them. He wanted Jere and Big Thunder to go with him to retrieve the traps as it would give Jere some much-needed experience that he would find useful later in life.

Josh said, "Let's take the boat tomorrow and pull in all of the traps from the line before the weather gets any warmer."

Big Thunder and Jeremiah said it would be fine with them since they had both been wanting to go for a boat ride anyway.

"Fellows, let me tell you that this will not be a pleasure cruise," he stressed. "This is going to be more work than we have done for a while. It's not going to be easy. First, we will pull in the traps. When we get them to the barn, we will clean them and rustproof them with lard. We will store them in the barn for use next winter again," Josh explained to them.

Everyone was ready and willing to get started the next morning, and things started out well for them. Jeremiah couldn't wait to start hauling in the traps. He soon found out that the traps were chained to something to keep the animals from pulling them away and escaping, losing the trap. Josh usually lost one or two traps a year, but that was mainly from rusting out or wearing out. If the trap gets rusty, the spring loses its tension and will allow an animal to free itself. He countered this by putting his traps in hot water for a few minutes and then covering them with a thin coating of lard while they were still warm to protect them from the dampness that caused the rusting.

Jeremiah was getting tired as well as bored long before lunch and tried to get his father to quit and come back tomorrow. Josh told him he wasn't about to quit the trap line until every single trap had been retrieved and was in the boat. This chore was very important to ensuring the lasting quality of the steel traps, and it needed to be carried out promptly when started.

"Son, you just sit in the back of the boat," Josh told him. "Big Thunder and I will finish getting the rest of the traps in the boat."

Jere decided that he wasn't about to admit that an old Indian man could stay longer and work harder than he could, so he said he was ready to complete the job they had started.

Big Thunder said, "I knew you were too proud to be called a quitter when you once started something."

They were slightly late in getting back to the cabin for dinner, and Angela told them she would warm it up for them. She had already eaten, as she had to eat for two now.

Big Thunder was more than just fond of Angela's cooking. He was one of her best customers. He had gained so much weight now that not even his own daughter would recognize him. He appeared to be a fine specimen of health, and he admitted that he now felt much better than he had in years.

Angela said that she enjoyed cooking if she could feed someone who loved her food and paid her adequate compliments on her expertise at the kitchen stove. Big Thunder was always paying her a compliment—not only on her cooking but also on her wholesome attitude and her wonderful friendship and companionship.

By late afternoon they were storing steel traps in the barn with a shiny fresh coat of lard on the surfaces to prevent them from rusting. Angela had just completed her grocery list for Josh to take to the store the next day. She declined the invitation to go herself, because she felt it might not do the baby any good. In fact she was beginning to get somewhat uncomfortable now, and she doubted that she would even be able to get in the boat even if it became necessary for her to go to the doctor's office.

She told Josh that she felt like when it was time for the baby to be born, he should go into town and fetch the doctor and bring him back to the cabin. Josh said he wasn't at all sure if the doctor would make a house call up the river.

"Oh well, I suppose we'll just have to wait and see," she told them and didn't seem too concerned about it.

After breakfast the next morning, Joshua and Jere made the boat trip to town for groceries while Big Thunder stayed behind to look after Angela in case she found that she needed help while they were gone. The first place they visited was the paint store. Josh told the salesman he wanted to paint his boat. The salesman told him he would need some white lead and boiled linseed oil to mix with it. He told Josh when he had it mixed sufficiently in the bucket for him to squeeze a small amount of Prussian blue from the small tube that he bought, to mix with it and stir completely one more time. He told Josh that the small amount of Prussian blue would make it much whiter than white and much prettier. He instructed him to allow three days for drying, four if it was cloudy. The manager at the paint store told him the paint was fully guaranteed not to peel or crack for two years, and if it didn't prove to be satisfactory he could bring the can back for a refund. Josh reckoned that was a pretty good guarantee. Josh paid for the paint, thanked the man for the advice, and headed for the grocery store across the street to pick up the essentials that Angela had requested.

They were then on their way to the boat when Jere decided he needed an ice cream cone. That accomplished, he was happy and smiling. He only wished that he had been able to take one to his mother without having it melt.

Josh had the fuel tank filled to capacity, heated the firing pin, took the pair of tongs and placed it in the receptacle, knocked the wedge tight with the hammer, and started the engine. He eased out into the current and headed upstream. He pushed the throttle about three-quarters full and heard the engine's resounding rhythm while she easily sliced through the current as if she knew the way home. The wind in their faces felt good, and they were soon pulling up to the Langford Place.

After dinner Josh asked Jere and Big Thunder to help him bring the boat out of the water on the skids so he could allow it to dry thoroughly before painting the hull. He had cut nineteen saplings that were about two inches in diameter to act as rollers when they winched the boat out of the water. He tied his block and tackle to a tree and started pulling the boat out a little at a time on the rollers. They repeated this procedure about five times before they had the boat high and dry. Josh said he would allow the boat to dry until morning before he started scraping and wire-brushing the hull. He had three brushes, but he doubted if he could count on Jere to do a good enough job to allow for a good paint job.

After the third day the paint had cured well in the beautiful sunshiny weather, and it really looked like a new boat. Josh said that since he was in no particular hurry to get the boat back in the water, he was going to allow it one more day to fully cure. He felt that it would serve to make the paint last longer. Angela was admiring the boat from the front porch and said the new white skin on it made it look beautiful. It was so bright looking in the sunshine that it almost hurt her eyes.

The next day they launched the boat by allowing it to roll down the saplings until it reached the water with the help of a push by the men.

Angela told Josh at the dinner table that she would like for him to stay close around the cabin the rest of the afternoon. She told him she thought that her time was getting very near. "I will need for you to make a quick trip down the river to fetch the doctor when my labor pains start getting close together," she said. "Big Thunder had told me some time back that it would be born on the night of the full moon, and that's tonight, Joshua," she reminded him. "Do you think Big Thunder knows what he is talking about?" she asked.

"I wouldn't be at all surprised to find out that he actually does know what he is talking about, Angela," Josh replied to her. "But I was looking at the Black Draught calendar in the kitchen and it gives tomorrow, May eighth, as the date for the full moon instead of the seventh, dear," he told her.

Angela went right away to the kitchen to check with the calendar, and sure enough it reported May eighth as the night of the full moon. "I was mistaken, dear. I'm sorry," she told him.

"That's perfectly all right, Angel," he told her. "Anyone can make a mistake," he smiled at her and she blew him a kiss.

That afternoon and night went by without a hitch. Angela was feeling well the next day when she woke up. She said, "Well, this is supposed to be the day according to Big Thunder, but I actually feel just fine. I don't really feel like it's going to be today or tonight," she reassured him.

Josh answered, "Well, nobody knows when it's going to happen except the baby, and it will make up its mind to arrive when it's good and ready to be born."

They had eaten dinner with no apparent change in the condition of the patient, and everything still seemed to be going well, considering Angela's oversized condition and her inability to move about freely. The three men spent most of the afternoon dawdling around the area of the barn with Josh looking in on Angela hourly to check on any changes. The last time he looked in on her she was crocheting a pair of pink booties. Josh chuckled at her insistence that it was going to be a girl. He hoped that she would not be greatly disappointed and hurt if it happened to be a boy.

Josh was beginning to get nervous. He returned to the barn and told them that he had forgotten to get his cabbage plants while he was in town. He said they should have been planted in the ground already.

Angela called from the back porch late in the afternoon, "Josh, maybe you should go to town and fetch the doctor for me. My pains are getting closer together and I think it may be born tonight."

Josh answered nervously, "All right, dear. You know better than I do. I'll take the boat then and go after the doctor. I'll try to be back as soon as I can."

Angela said, "Bye dear. Now, don't go at breakneck speed for the doctor. Just take your time and be careful. I don't want you to have an accident on the way so the doctor can't make it out here at all."

Josh said, "Right. Bye."

Josh thought it would take forever to heat the firing pin. It finally got hot enough to place in the receptacle, and he started the engine. He eased out to midstream, changed gears, and pushed the throttle wide open. The bow reached for the sky and he was skimming the waves like an old salty sailor.

Angela knew that Josh hadn't been gone very long but she thought she heard the sound of a motorboat coming up the river. She thought, "Thank goodness, that didn't take very long at all."

Joshua hit the front porch in a run and told her that the doctor had gone on a call up the Columbia River about twenty miles to deliver a baby and would not be back that night at all. He then broke the news to her that there was no other doctor in Rosburg.

"What are we going to do?" Angela wanted to know. "I don't think I will be able to handle this by myself. I'm getting scared," she said, almost in tears.

Big Thunder said, "Little brother, come with me to the boat. We must go and bring my daughter here to deliver your baby," he said to Angela. "Josh, bring me a kerosene lantern. I have seen you operate the boat so many times that I know how to do it, and I'm going after Little Flower. She doesn't have any children of her own yet, but she has acted as midwife several times to many other women. Let's go, son! We need to get there in a hurry," he said to Jere.

They were out the door and down the hill before anyone could even think to voice an objection.

"Josh, do you realize just how far it is to his daughter's house and how long it will take for them to get there?" she asked. "And what if they have an accident, Josh?" she asked. "No one will ever find them because no one ever goes up the river." Angela was wringing her hands over that as well as grimacing with her labor pains.

Josh answered, "Yes dear. I was just thinking that." He then said, "I don't know why I let them take the boat. I wasn't acting very sanely. I don't know what I was thinking," he said. "I don't really know what we're going to do now, hon."

Angela noticed that Josh was beginning to get despondent and edgy. She also was aware of the fact that this was the last thing on earth that she needed in her condition. She needed someone with a strong will and lots of fortitude. This happened not to be Josh at the present time, and she knew it. Angela felt that she should be the only one to be allowed to be unstable at this time. She now wished that Josh had gone with Jere to go find Little Flower and left Big Thunder with her. "At least," she thought, "he wouldn't get all unnerved and shook up. He is always cool as a cucumber."

It now seemed as though hours had passed, and Angela was lying on the bed gasping for breath and perspiring profusely. Her pains would subside for a brief period and then they would strike all over again. Angela found it necessary to force the muscles of her face into contortions to help her with the pain, but this is what would throw Josh into a tizzy. He couldn't understand that this was a natural reaction to her pain, that it was not unbearable or life-threatening.

She then decided that for her own good, she needed to get Josh out of the room completely. In order to do that and to get his mind off her, she told him to build a fire in the cookstove and start heating some water. She said, "Josh, we will need gallons of hot water when Little Flower gets here, and you need to have it ready."

That was precisely what Josh needed to do to keep his mind occupied and keep him out of the room. They would actually need the water, anyway. Angela didn't really think that Little Flower would make it in time, but she didn't say anything to Josh about it. He was unstable enough already. He was going to make certain that they had sufficient hot water available, though.

Angela felt much better now that she was allowed to grimace in pain and make a few facial expressions without Josh having a conniption. She had to smile a little at how she had tricked him into getting out of her sight for a while. She didn't like playing tricks on her husband, but it was really the best thing for both of them.

Time seemed to be dragging for Joshua. His water didn't want to boil. It seemed that it was taking forever. It didn't occur to him that the reason it wasn't boiling was because it hadn't been on the fire long enough. Josh felt that he needed to go out on the back porch to get a breath of fresh air. He was almost to the point of hyperventilating. He knelt down and steadied himself on the stack of wood with his hand and started praying that the Lord would be gracious enough to allow his wife to successfully deliver their child. Josh had already decided that it was of no consequence whether it was a boy or a girl as long as his wife would be able to safely deliver. He then added as an afterthought that it really would be preferable if the Lord could see to it that it was the little baby girl Angela had wanted so much.

Old Blue was at his side, assisting him in his prayers and as Josh said, *A-men*, Old Blue returned to the yard and Josh returned to check on Angela's condition.

# CHAPTER
## 21

Big Thunder and Jere were walking swiftly through the woods toward the house where his daughter lived. Big Thunder said, "Little Brother, I am too tired to go any further. Will you please go on to my daughter's house to tell her that your mother is having a baby and we cannot get a doctor to come? Tell her that we need her to come right away to be a midwife for the delivery of the baby. Can you remember that?" he asked.

Jere quickly replied, "Yes, Big Thunder," and took off in a dead run toward the house. He was on the front porch of Little Flower's house in no time. Jere quickly explained the situation and told her that Big Thunder was waiting in the woods because he was winded after a short walk. She picked up a bag that she kept packed for just such emergencies and in no time at all they had reached Big Thunder and immediately headed for the boat.

Big Thunder started the boat and headed directly for the outlet to Grays River. As soon as they reached the river, he immediately opened the throttle all the way. Since the moon was full they had no need to light a lantern. They could see almost as well as if it had been daylight. Big Thunder kept the throttle wide open until he could see the lamp burning at the Langford cabin. He eased the boat into the slip and told Jere to lead Little Flower up the hill. He said he would be along later when he had taken care of the boat and got his breath back.

Josh had been the first to hear the faint sound of a motorboat upstream from their cabin, but he was certain that it could not possibly be Jere and Big Thunder returning with his daughter. He assumed that it would have to be someone else. Besides, he felt that it was going much too fast for his boat, and it was also too soon to be expecting them back. It sounded as if it were getting closer but then, when it finally throttled down in front of their cabin, he knew it must be them. He heard the motor shut off completely.

The next thing he knew, Jere and Little Flower had entered the front door. She put her things on the floor and told Josh to get lots of hot water ready. He informed her that he had scads of hot water ready for her in the kitchen, and he would bring it to her when she called for it.

Little Flower said, "In that case, go outside with the other men and I will call you if I need you," she ordered him in a calm voice.

Josh sulked and went slowly out the front door to join the other men. She had hurt his feelings by pushing him out of the house while his wife was having their baby. Little Flower didn't want any interference of impropriety from an excited father when she was in the middle of a matter of importance for the mother and child.

Jere was telling his father that he just couldn't believe the uncommonly high speed that Big Thunder had coaxed out of their boat. Maybe it just seemed faster at night, but Jere was almost certain that the *Angel* had never before had that much power and speed as it had on the way to Little Flower's house. Josh explained to Jere and Big Thunder that it was very possible that the relative humidity on the river at night would have allowed for a cleaner and more powerful combustion of gases that were mixed with oxygen as it combusted in the cylinder head. Josh also told them that they were lucky to have had the full moon shining brightly as they traveled the river or else they might not have made it back to the cabin in time.

Big Thunder was very tired after walking briskly through the woods and then up the hill as they returned. He said he needed to sit and rest on the edge of the front porch. Josh sullenly moved out into the yard, still bruised from being pushed out of his own cabin by Little Flower.

Inside, Little Flower said, "I'm happy to meet you, Angela. I've heard so much about you that I feel I already know you. For instance, I heard that you were a beautiful woman, and that is certainly true. I'm also certain that the part I heard about you being such a fine woman was also true," she said to Angela in a voice that would have clearly identified her as Big Thunder's daughter. She had a decidedly feminine voice, but the inflections were the same as her father's voice.

Angela said, "Little Flower, God must have sent you. I didn't know what I would do without a doctor. I didn't think your father would be able to travel the river to your house, especially in the dark. I know that the moon was shining, but that's not like traveling in the daytime," Angela told her. "Truly, God did send his angel to see me through this blessed event," Angela told her. "I am thankful, Little Flower, that He has been so kind and generous to me and my family. This may sound selfish to you, but I have prayed that God would send me a little baby girl, a beautiful little daughter," she told her.

"You are not being selfish, Angela," she replied. "I honestly feel that God may grant your request.

Angela said, "I didn't think your father would know enough about the boat to be able to operate it going up a dangerous river at night. I'm very thankful for having him here with us, now. He is such a joy to our son. Well, really, he has been such a blessing for all of our family," she said sincerely.

"I am very proud of my father, Angela," she said. "We had given up hope on him being able to live, and he wanted to go out into the woods to die in peace like many of our ancestors had done. He was eighty-four years old at the time, and I was certain that he would not live very long, but God has found a use for him still in this world with his friends," she told Angela.

Little Flower said, "They have told me the story of the white wolf leading your son to the cave where my father was near death and of your son saving his life by giving him one of your bologna sandwiches and a can of water to build his strength and health back. Father told me that he will always be indebted and thankful to Jeremiah for giving him another chance at life with his other family in this world," Little Flower told her.

"And Angela, I will always be indebted to you for taking such good care of him and nurturing him back to good health," she told Angela. "He has now gained so much weight that I hardly recognized him tonight when I first saw him in the woods. It was somewhat dark and I could see an outline of a man, but I was sure that it could not be my father," she said to Angela. "He looks very good, now. Thanks for the wonderful care you have taken with him."

Angela's face contorted as she experienced another labor pain. Little Flower put some cool water on a washcloth and placed it on her forehead. She had started perspiring again. Little Flower told her it might be another two or three hours before she delivered, so she decided to make the men a fresh pot of coffee to soothe their nerves.

"Thank you," Angela said, "I don't know how I can ever repay you."

"You already have, Angela," she said. "And now I'm going to do something on my part to help repay you for your generous help and kindness to my father," she vowed.

When Little Flower went to the front porch with two cups of hot coffee, she asked Jere if he would like a cup, also. He said, "No, thank you, I wouldn't care for one."

Joshua was biting his nails and he asked Little Flower if she knew how much longer it was going to be.

She answered, "Who knows? This is one thing that we have no control over. The little one will arrive when it gets good and ready. Not a minute sooner, Joshua," she promised.

Little Flower went back inside to be with her patient. She said, "Angela, I told Jere and my father on the way here that my husband was killed in a logging accident near our home out there in the timber country. I haven't had time to tell your husband, and I didn't want to give you the details since you already had enough on your mind. I will tell you about it in a couple of days. Since my husband is dead, I plan to stay with you and help you out for ten or twelve days until you can get back to normal again. You're going to need lots of help in the coming weeks, and you have done so much for my father that I feel I owe you this, at least," she told Angela.

"Well, I certainly appreciate your offer to stay and help me, Little Flower," she said. "But I don't want you to think you have to because you owe me something. I will certainly need the help that you have offered because men are so helpless when it comes to doing things for a baby. You will be able to sleep in Jeremiah's room since he and your father are spending their nights in the barn," she told Little Flower.

"You act as if your back is hurting. Let me get another pillow to put behind you to see if that will help," she told Angela. She fluffed up a pillow and placed it behind her back and said, "Now, that should help your back some. Nothing will take the pain completely away, though. I have acted as midwife for thirty-nine births, so far. This will make my fortieth delivery," she revealed to Angela.

Joshua was walking around in the front yard as if in a daze. Big Thunder had asked him to come and sit on the porch so they could talk, but he declined. He was unable to sit. He felt that he had to keep walking around in circles. So he did.

Little Flower said, "Angela, I can get you a small sip of water if you like." She was licking her lips as though they were parched.

Angela replied, "Yes, please. I'd like a small drink of cool water. My mouth is so dry and hot. I feel like it would cool my parched lips." She sipped a bit of the cool water and said, "Thanks, that's much better." She closed her eyes to rest them for a while.

Big Thunder said to Joshua, "This may turn out to be a very long night, Josh. Why don't you and your son go take a cat nap in the barn, and I will come and call for you the minute something starts happening."

Both of them answered in the negative, mostly because they were afraid they were going to miss something if they wandered away from the front porch. Also, they didn't feel like they would be able to sleep, anyway. Joshua finally quit walking, probably because he was tired. He sat on the edge of the front porch and they all sat quietly for some time, not quite knowing what to say.

He had been sitting for what seemed like an hour (although it was probably more like ten minutes), when all of a sudden, there was an unmistakable cry of a baby coming from inside the cabin. It sounded as though it was coming right through the walls.

"My goodness," Joshua said. "That baby sure has a set of strong lungs. I wonder if it's a boy?" he wondered and asked no one in particular. It was fairly evident that he had actually wanted another boy, while Angela had her heart set on a pretty baby girl.

Big Thunder then took off in the direction of the barn in somewhat of a hurry. He was the one person who never seemed to get in a hurry for anything. He returned shortly to the front porch where he deposited a handmade cradle that he had fashioned from some lumber he had begged from Josh. It was made mostly from scrap pieces that had been discarded from cut-off ends that Josh had thrown away when finishing out the upstairs in the cabin. It was a sturdy, beautiful cradle that Big Thunder had lovingly crafted to make it a one-of-a-kind masterpiece. There would never be another one like it, and it would probably last long enough to raise her great-grandchildren. Big Thunder had kept his promise to Angela about making something for the baby.

They had been waiting by the front door for what seemed to be an hour for news of the baby, though it had only been a few minutes. Little Flower had needed to clean the infant up prior to presenting it to the father and also taking care of the needs of the new mother as well. Men didn't understand that it took time to take care of those things. She didn't really have the time to go to the front door to make an announcement. She had a lot more important items to care for at the present time. In due time, when the most important things had been taken care of, then she would go to the front door, make her announcement, and invite the men in to see the mother and the new baby that had just been brought into the world.

Little Flower finally took the baby to the front door, opened it, and announced to the men, "Joshua Langford, you are the proud father of a beautiful baby girl, and her name is Running Brook Langford. Your son named her while we were in the boat coming down the river to your cabin. Congratulations! Isn't she precious?" she asked while she pulled the blanket back to reveal a precious little raven-haired beauty to her father, brother, and adopted grandfather.

"She was actually born on the eighth of May, during the night of the full moon."

Little Flower had attested to that fact in the family Bible and wrote it down on the page titled "Record of Births." She had written, "Running Brook Langford, born May 8, 1924 at 11:45 p.m., daughter of Joshua and Angela Langford, and weighing approximately eight pounds. Attest this eighth day of May 1924, by Little Flower Hatling, midwife."

"You can all come in the house, now," she told them. "Running Brook is hungry, and she is going to get something to eat, which should make her a happy little girl."

Joshua hurried to the bedside of his wife, kissed the tired mother, and said hello to his beautiful new daughter. Jeremiah just walked up to the bed slowly, grinning with a huge smile and wide eyes, and said, "Can I touch her?"

His mother said, "Of course you may, son. Go ahead and touch her. One of these years she will be following you around like a little puppy dog. I know because I used to have some older brothers who would tell me not to follow them."

Jeremiah rubbed her hand lightly and smiled. He said, "Do you think she will be able to play with me next year, mom?"

"Why, of course she will, son. But not in the manner in which you may be expecting her to play with you," she told him. "It may be necessary for you to sit on the floor to play with her, mostly," she explained. "Sometimes you may be able to take her out into the warm sunshine and sit for a while, also. She would probably like that."

"Josh, Little Flower has agreed to stay on here with us to help me out for about two or three weeks or until I can get on my feet and help myself again," she told her husband, but she was really speaking to all of them. "I think it's very kind of her to volunteer to do this for all of us, and I would like to ask you men to assist her with anything she requires help with," Angela said. "Can I depend on you three to do that for me, please?" she asked.

"Why, of course," they all replied. "We will be more than happy to help Little Flower with anything that she may need help with. All she has to do is to let us know what it is that she wants and we will be right there," Josh promised. "I am so thankful that she came to help us out in our time of need, that I will gladly do whatever it is that she asks."

Big Thunder said, "I think congratulations are in order for the three of you, and especially for Angela. Congratulations!" Big Thunder said.

"Thank you, so much," Angela told him.

Joshua said, "I'm still having trouble believing that Big Thunder and Jeremiah went all the way up the Grays River, through the lake, and then up the hill to Little Flower's house during the nighttime hours as they did. On top of that, they made it back here in record time, bringing Little Flower with them in the boat," Joshua said to them. "I realize that you had a full moon to light your way, but still, that's not like traveling in the daytime. I never would have allowed them to do a fool thing like that if they had asked, but before I could come to my senses, they were already gone and running the boat up the river at full speed. I know, I could hear the sound of the engine," he said. "Oh, what a night," he said to no one in particular. "Whew!"

"Little brother, my daughter and I are going to teach you some authentic Indian dances later when she is able to spend some time away from caring for your mother and sister," Big Thunder told him. "You will need to know how to perform these in order to attend an officially sanctioned powwow when you wear your eagle feather," he told him. "Little Flower is very good at teaching dancing, and she enjoys keeping the Indian traditions of her ancestors alive. I also intend to make you an authentic Indian drum with a stretched hide over a hardwood frame before the summer is ended, and I will teach you how to play it," he said to Jere. "It will be a masterpiece that you will really be proud to play in front of your fellow kinsmen of the tribe," he affectionately told his little brother.

Jeremiah sounded very enthusiastic about learning the dances from him and said, "I'm ready to start any time, Big Thunder, and I want to thank you and your daughter for being so kind to us."

"You already have, little brother," he answered. "Many times over. And I don't know what I would have ever done in the cave except die if it hadn't been for you and your good friend, the white wolf. I would never have been able to make it without your assistance," he affectionately told Jeremiah.

✣ ✣ ✣

Little Flower had been at the Langford cabin for three weeks and had become as much a part of the family as Big Thunder had. Big Thunder had now been residing in the barn for nine months, and he was affectionately attached to the Langfords. Little Flower and Big Thunder now had no blood relatives except one another. They both loved living there with them and loved the family so much that Little Flower approached them about her and her father remaining there permanently.

Angela answered, "Why, we would love to have you and your father stay with us as long as you like! You have absolutely been a godsend to us, Little Flower. There could have been no way that I would have ever made it through my delivery if it hadn't been for you, and there is no way that Joshua and Jeremiah could ever get along without the able assistance from Big Thunder. You are both a part of this family and we love you both as much as our own kin. In fact, you really seem like our own family," Angela told her in a very emotional manner.

"Oh, that's wonderful, Angela," Little Flower told her, sounding much relieved. "I don't know how to thank you enough for what you have all done for my father," she said happily.

Little Flower told Angela that she and her husband had been renting their house from the timberman landlord who had employed her husband and that a lot of the furniture in the house belonged to her. She said she would like to make arrangements to bring her personal belongings there to her in exchange for the inexpensive furnishings that she would voluntarily leave with the house if he would be willing to trade.

"If he declines, I might ask Jere and my father to make a trip in the boat and ask them to hand carry as much as they could of my personal items and just leave the rest of it behind," Little Flower told her.

"We will ask Joshua, Jeremiah, and Big Thunder to go with you to retrieve all of the personal belongings in your house. Would you be able to go with them to make certain that they get the more right items?" she asked.

"Yes, I suppose I really should go with them so that it wouldn't be confusing about what to bring," she said. "Then, if the landlord came by there he would understand that someone wasn't stealing. If he isn't there, then I can leave a note on the door telling him that I won't be back and that he can have whatever items are left in the house and around it. I don't like that man, Angela," she told her.

"I really feel that he is responsible for the accident that caused my husband's death, though there is no way that I could ever prove it. He has been so mean and nasty to me since then that I just wanted to get away and never see him again. It gave me an excellent opportunity when Jeremiah came after me that night. I doubt if I would have ever had the courage to leave, otherwise," she tearfully admitted to Angela.

"You poor girl," Angela said pitifully. "I can't imagine anyone being so mean to a grieving widow. Forget about this man completely, and we will accept you as our own family, here." Angela vowed. "And to think, you've had that bottled up inside you for several weeks, now." Angela said, "Tsk, tsk," and shook her head.

"We are going to completely finish out the upstairs rooms this summer, so there will be enough room for you and your father to live here in the cabin with us," she said. "We love both of you and we would never allow you to depart from us," Angela promised.

Running Brook emitted a faint sound from her little mouth as if to verify what her mother had just told Little Flower, and that she, too, would be more than happy to fully accept them as her own family. The women looked at one another and chuckled as if they understood what she was trying to tell them as she had lain there listening to their conversation about her family.

# CHAPTER
## 22

Everything was beginning to get back to normal around the Langford cabin except that Running Brook was now demanding the majority of the attention of those around her. This didn't really seem to bother anyone very much since they fully enjoyed having that cute little angel with them. It seemed that everyone in the household had wanted to hold the pretty little girl constantly, and Angela had to keep reminding them that if they didn't quit spoiling her by picking her up that she was going to have to put her foot down and put an end to it. She explained that Running Brook would get to a point where she would demand to be held all the time. She finally convinced them that this would not be good for her or them.

The men had not become completely accustomed to Little Flower's cooking, but they knew better than to complain about the meals, since they knew that if she hadn't been there, they would have had to do the cooking themselves. They even made themselves mental notes to occasionally brag on her cooking to make her feel wanted and appreciated by the family so she would keep trying to improve. Slowly, Little Flower's cooking took on similarities of the savor and special gustatory qualities and attributes that almost paralleled Angela's expert cuisine. They weren't certain if Angela had given Little Flower instructions in cooking or if she had just fell into Angela's way of cooking naturally. In any event, it was something the men appreciated, and they never failed to praise her abilities as she improved. The meals were getting tastier as time went by or else they were just becoming acclimated.

Little Flower went to the back porch and yelled down to the barn for Jeremiah or Big Thunder to come up to the porch. They were almost certain that it possibly had something to do with

Running Brook, so they hurried to get there. Jere was the first to arrive since he could run. He said, "Yes ma'am?"

Little Flower said, "I wonder if you would mind going down to the root cellar to bring me three large rutabagas to cook for dinner? Also bring me four or five parsnips so I can make us some candied parsnips tonight."

That let the wind out of his sails because he was expecting it to be a message about his little sister. Jere's head dropped and he said, "Yes ma'am, I'll get them for you."

"Thank you, Jeremiah, for being such a nice young man," she told him. "I always wanted to have a son, but I suppose it was just not meant to be," she said as Jere noticed what appeared to be a teardrop in her eye.

Big Thunder sat on the back porch talking to his daughter about their stroke of luck at living with the Langfords. Little Flower said it had worked out too smoothly to be considered a stroke of luck.

"What is luck, anyway?" Little Flower wanted to know. "I think it's God's way of handling things that people wouldn't have the knowledge or the power of making it happen, otherwise," she answered her own question.

Big Thunder couldn't disagree with that. He confided to her that he had never in life been filled with so much happiness and love as after he had met Jeremiah and had then come to live with the Langford family. He told Little Flower that he now felt about twenty years younger than before.

She said, "Father, if I came here today and didn't know ahead of time that you were here, I would never have known who you were. I would never have been able to recognize you," she told him frankly.

Jeremiah returned from the root cellar with the items she wanted.

She said, "Son, I'm going to make a treat for supper tonight that you will just love. Well, really, it will be a treat for all of us. Father will love it, too. I'm going to fix a dish of candied parsnips. Have you ever eaten any, Jere?" she asked.

"No, ma'am, I can't say that I have," he answered.

"I'll guarantee that you will love these," she said.

"I'd be willing to bet a coonskin cap that he will enjoy the ones that you're going to fix, daughter," Big Thunder wagered.

They were going to have rutabagas boiled with salt pork side meat for dinner, but Little Flower said they would just have to wait until supper to try the candied parsnips.

"Father, I'm wondering if you and Jeremiah would look for something in the woods for me the next time you're out there?" she asked.

"Certainly," he said. "What would you like for us to find?"

"I'd like for you to find me one or two Indian turnips, if you can locate them for me, please," she told them. "I'd like to use a sliver of one to put in my white beans the next time I cook them. It gives them such a wonderful and unusual flavor," she told him. "If you can find more than two, go ahead and bring them. I'll dry them out and save them for later."

Big Thunder said, "I'm going to see if I can talk Joshua into buying a beef brisket the next time we go into town. If he will do that, I'll make us the best corned beef he has ever tasted in his life. I noticed a five-gallon stone crock down in the root cellar the other day that would be ideal for corning the beef. When you simmer it all morning one day with an Indian turnip in it, you will think you are in heaven when you taste it. Promise me that you will cook us some corned beef and cabbage after the beef has been corned," he said to his daughter.

"Of course, father," she told him. "All you have to do is to bring me the corned beef and I'll take care of the rest. And by the way, after you finish corning the beef in that stone crock, I'd like to use it to make sauerkraut."

Big Thunder replied, "I'll say amen to that, daughter."

Big Thunder then explained to Jeremiah that an Indian turnip is a bulb type of plant that grows in the woods and produces a small but beautiful flower from May to mid-June. It is the only time one can locate the bulb because the stalk dies down and withers as the bloom dies. It's necessary to have a long-blade knife to dig it up because the bulb is quite deep under the flower. After the bulb has been allowed to dry, it becomes hard and brittle but can be scraped with a knife over the cooking pot to enhance the flavor of almost any vegetable dish that is being prepared. The pungent, spicy flavor of Indian turnip is a little-known flavoring agent in most households. It must be used sparingly or else it will overpower the meal. It is too hot and pungent to be eaten raw, but it can be used in soups and stews, beans, and other dishes, as well.

"I want you to show me what it looks like before you dig it up, Big Thunder," he told him. "I want to be able to identify it if I happen to be in the woods by myself."

"I will be sure to do that, little brother," he promised. "We should be going into the woods in a couple of days, and this is the time of the year when we should be able to locate the blossoms easily. Let's remember to take that small spade that your mother uses to dig around in her flower bed," he suggested.

Jeremiah got a most pleasant surprise when Little Flower brought a plate of candied parsnips to the table at suppertime. Jere was the first to accept one with his fork.

"Ooooohhh, this is great. I've never tasted anything this good in all my life," Jere exclaimed to Little Flower. "I wish I had counted how many parsnips were left in the root cellar when I was down there. When can you fix another batch?" he asked her in a begging manner.

Little Flower answered, "I'll cook some more next week. I promise."

A couple of days later, Jere woke up early in the barn, looked over to where Big Thunder was lying on his bed and noticed that Big Thunder's eyes were wide open and he was staring intently toward the barn loft, not moving. The first thought that came to Jere's mind was that Big Thunder was dead. His heart started racing and he was afraid to do or say anything. He wasn't sure what he should do.

"What are you staring at, Big Thunder?" he finally asked, but was really afraid to.

"Oh, I was just lying here thinking about the wonderful life that you and your family have provided for me and my daughter," he said to Jere. A tear was running down the side of his cheek. "It must have been the will of God that sent us here to live with you good people," Big Thunder reckoned.

"I woke up earlier, Little Brother," he said to Jere. "But I saw that you were still resting well, so I didn't want to wake you up.

We have quite a long way to walk in the woods today," he reminded Jeremiah.

Jeremiah actually breathed a sigh of relief when Big Thunder started speaking to him. He had at first feared that Big Thunder had gone to the far beyond. He was terribly frightened when he first saw Big Thunder lying completely still with his eyes fixed toward the loft without even an eyelid moving.

"I had completely forgotten about going into the woods today," Jere told him. "I'm sure glad you reminded me. Let's head for the cabin to eat breakfast so we can be on our way," he said.

They jumped up and headed for the water pump to splash some cold water on their faces and hands, took a side trip to the privy, and then ascended the steps leading to the back porch to wash their hands and faces.

"Let's have some breakfast, Big Thunder. I'm hungry," Jere told him.

"I'm as hungry as a bear this morning," Big Thunder echoed.

As they stood on the back porch they could smell the bacon frying and the wonderful aroma of freshly perked coffee. "What a wonderful smell on a cool morning such as this," the old Indian told his barn partner.

"It doesn't get any better than this, Big Thunder," Jere told him.

Little Flower beckoned them into the kitchen with a nod of her head and told them to have a seat at the table. She had the oatmeal already cooked.

"I will have the bacon and eggs done very shortly, and the biscuits will be done in four or five minutes," she advised them. "You two have timed it about right to have breakfast while it's hot." She seemed to be in very good spirits.

"Good morning, daughter," Big Thunder said. "How do you feel this fine morning?" he asked her.

"I feel great, father," she answered. "You will never know how happy you and the Langford family have made me. I had already given you up for dead and I didn't have an inkling if you might have suffered or not. Please don't do this to me any more, father. I beg you. I want to be with you until the very end of your life," she begged. "I intend to try to care for you in a manner in which I may have failed you before."

"You have never failed me," he told her. "It was I who failed you. I didn't know how much anguish I was putting you through, or I never would have caused you all of that torment," he said apologetically. "Please forgive me, and I promise never to put you through that again," he assured her.

Big Thunder looked at Jere, smiled, and said, "I would never be able to leave my dearest friend in the world while I went into the woods to die, so I promise you both that I will never think of doing that again," he promised them once more.

"Don't even try it," Jere warned him.

"I give you my solemn word, so help me, God," Big Thunder said to them.

Little Flower was grateful for the partnership her father had cemented with Jeremiah, his best friend, because it had made him feel and look like a totally different man. He appeared to feel better than he had in years. He looked great for a man in his eighties.

Jeremiah had decided to have oatmeal, bacon, and one biscuit that morning for breakfast while Big Thunder chose to have one egg, bacon, a biscuit, and a cup of coffee. Angela would have two eggs over easy with bacon and one biscuit with the gravy poured over it. Joshua decided to have the same except he wanted some grape jam on his biscuit instead of the gravy. Josh then decided that he would also have a bowl of oatmeal to finish it off. Evidently, he was as hungry as a bear, also. Little Flower finally sat at the table and had her breakfast. She opted for one egg, bacon, a biscuit with gravy poured over the top, and a cup of coffee.

After breakfast, Little Flower made two sandwiches of biscuits and bacon, placed them in a paper sack, and handed them to Jeremiah. She wasn't aware of the fact that Big Thunder could get down on his hands and knees to drink water out of the creek, so she sent a mason jar full of water.

Big Thunder had already told Jere not to be in any hurry that morning as they had sufficient time to procure what they were looking for. He could walk much farther if they didn't try to hurry him. After walking for an hour they sat on a log by the creek to rest. Jere opened the jar of water and allowed his friend to drink his fill. Jere then drank from it and poured the rest on the ground. He said if they needed more he would fill it up from the creek.

They got up and walked for about another mile when they decided that it was time for them to rest again. The birds were singing, the chipmunks were playing around the stump and across the leaves. The morning was beautiful, warm and sunny, and the noise of the wild animals was quite loud and cheery. They reminisced for quite a while and came to the conclusion that the reason that the animals were extra-noisy that morning was because they were extremely happy to see their friends as well as the bright sunshine.

Suddenly the noise stopped completely. It was as though it had been turned off with a switch. There was an almost shocking silence. It was eerie. Big Thunder couldn't figure out what to make of it.

Jeremiah whispered, "What does the sudden silence mean?" Jere was afraid to speak out loud.

Big Thunder replied, "I don't really know, little brother. Let's just sit still for a few moments," he whispered. "Keep your eyes alert but let's not talk," he warned.

After about two minutes, the eerie quietness in the woods was beginning to get on Jere's nerves. He wished the chipmunks would start playing again. He then heard a soft whine behind where they were sitting. He turned slowly. His eyes were met with the stare of White Spirit looking directly at him and whining softly. She had stealthily sneaked up behind them, evidently wanting to make friends with them once again after having been absent from their wanderings for about four or five months.

Jere held out his hand and offered it to her. She eventually but reluctantly came to smell his fingers and lick his hand. Big Thunder then held his hand out for her. She then duplicated the process and gestures to him in the same manner.

Jeremiah slowly got one of the sandwiches out of the sack and unwrapped it. She smelled the sandwich before he got it unwrapped. He offered her a bite of it, and she snatched the whole thing in her mouth and wolfed it down instantly in one swift gulp.

She continued to lick Jeremiah's hand where she smelled the bacon and biscuit flavors, hoping to get some more food. Jere slowly reached into his jacket pocket and produced the other sandwich they had with them. He unwrapped it and offered it to White Spirit. She removed the sandwich from his hand without even touching his fingers, had it in her mouth in a flash, and devoured it instantly.

Big Thunder said, "The reason she is so hungry is because she is feeding the little babies that she is carrying inside her belly. Had you noticed that her stomach is extended and that her breasts are enlarged? This means that she is pregnant and is going to have little ones very soon. She will have a den full of babies sometime in the near future," he explained to Jeremiah.

Jere said, "Will she need help delivering her babies?" Jere asked Big Thunder in a serious manner without cracking a smile.

Big Thunder assured him that animals in the wild do not need help when giving birth to little ones. They very seldom have any problems with a delivery.

Satisfied that no more food was available for her, White Spirit whined once more and took off in the opposite direction. Once more the woods became noisy again, and Jeremiah then wished they would quiet down.

They had experienced such a wonderful day in the forest that they had almost forgotten the real reason for being out there in the first place, which was to look for Indian turnips for Little Flower.

Big Thunder said, "Little Brother, if we're going to look for Indian turnips then we had better get started right away. We have now given our lunch away and we'll need to wait until we get back home in order to get something to eat."

Jere told him, "I don't care if we have to do without something to eat all day; it was well worth it to have a visit from White Spirit once more. It had been such a long time since we had seen her that I wasn't sure if she would recognize us. She had remembered us though, and I'm proud of that," Jere told his friend.

"I will have to agree with you, little brother, it was worth doing without our lunch to be rewarded by seeing White Spirit again and to find out that she was going to have a family of little ones. I would dearly love to see her puppies. Do you think she will ever allow us to see them and visit with them?" he asked Jere.

"I'm not sure," he said. "I don't really think she will allow us to get close enough to them to pet them. She may not even want to bring them around close enough to let us take a look at them," he surmised.

They walked on aimlessly for another fifteen minutes when Big Thunder spotted a tiny reddish brown flower on a green stem that was about nine inches high. He called this to Jere's attention so he could come and see it.

Big Thunder retrieved the garden tool from his hip pocket and dug deep under the stem to extract the bulbous root of the plant. He shook off the dirt and placed it in his shirt pocket. Jere then spotted another one not twenty feet from the first one. They identified it and dug it up also. Jere asked Big Thunder if two would be sufficient since he didn't see any others in the immediate vicinity. Big Thunder said he would like to find one more if possible. They walked another fifty or sixty steps and found another, much larger bloom than the others. They wondered if it might have a larger bulb than the others. It turned out that it was much larger. They decided that should be plenty for Little Flower and decided to head for home.

"Ready to call it a day, son?" Big Thunder asked Jere. "Ready to start for home?"

"I suppose we really should, but I would like to see Bigfoot one more time," Jere said to his friend. "We are having such a fun day, I just hate to leave."

Big Thunder answered, "I, too, would love to see Bigfoot one more time, but I don't really think it's going to happen," he told Jere. "Had you forgotten about the metal garden tool that I have in my back pocket?" Big Thunder pointed his finger toward his hip pocket, where Angela's little spade was concealed.

"Oh, yes," Jere acknowledged. "I had completely forgotten. Oh, well. We've already had an exciting day, anyway," he said. "Do you think my mom and dad will believe us when we tell them about White Spirit licking our hands and eating our sandwiches?" he asked.

"They don't have any reason not to believe you," he answered. "Your folks know very well that you do not tell lies," he reminded him. "And besides, I will be there to verify your story"

They started for the direction of the cabin when they heard what sounded like a large animal hurriedly trampling through the underbrush, snapping small tree branches and limbs as it lumbered hastily toward them. They assumed that it must have been caused by something or someone moving swiftly and carelessly through the underbrush in a terrible hurry. The noise grew steadily more intense until it became apparent that it was a Sasquatch running, jumping, and flailing his arms at the small branches while traveling at full speed in and through the dense forest underbrush as though it may have been chased by something it was terrified of. It came to within a scant twenty yards of them and evidently paid no attention whatsoever to them being so near, or even, for that matter, to the piece of metal tool that was in Big Thunder's pocket.

As the Sasquatch drew closer, they then saw why he was in such a rush to evade his pursuers. A large swarm of yellowjacket wasps were in close pursuit, stinging and tormenting him as he attempted unsuccessfully to flee from them. They had been partially successful in forcing their stingers through the thick hair and inflicting real pain to his body, but many of them were trapped in the coarse hair and were making a buzzing noise that was tormenting to him. The noises they made in trying to extricate themselves from the long hair only tended to frighten the beast more, it seemed. Evidently that swarm was very angry at something the Sasquatch had done to them because they seemed intent on running him completely out of the country.

Yellowjackets are known to have a ferocious temper and will attack anyone who even thinks about getting close to their nest in the ground. Sasquatch's agonizing and loud grunting noises reminded Big Thunder of a wild boar hog. The old Indian knew immediately what had caused the yellowjackets to swarm and raise their ire to that severity, since he had once been in that identical predicament. It would serve as a gentle reminder to the Sasquatch to never disturb that type of hole in the ground the next time he saw one.

Big Thunder and Jeremiah both watched and laughed a little at the Sasquatch trying to get away from his attackers until they had all disappeared up the hill and over the ridge. He was still grunting and swiping at them with his hands when they saw the last of them. Occasionally he would intentionally run through some thick underbrush in a vain attempt to dislodge them from the hair on his body, but a majority of them were still in hot pursuit as he topped the ridge.

Big Thunder told Jere that he actually felt sorry for the Bigfoot because he knew of the terrible pain that was being inflicted on him. He found it to be so comical that he was unable to stop laughing about the hilarious and totally surprising incident that had just completed their already exceptional and exhilarating day in the forest. The blatant noise and boisterous activity of that unexpected event had finally subsided. They both sat down on a log to catch their breaths and rest a bit after laughing so hard and long at the comical antics of the Bigfoot. They had never, in their wildest dreams, expected to witness such a comical episode involving a Sasquatch. That unusual tale would probably be told repeatedly as Jere got older, sitting around the fireplace in later years while spinning tales with his friends and family on a cold winter night.

"Big Thunder, I've had more fun here in the woods today than I ever had in all of the previous trips. I wouldn't trade living in the wilderness for a million dollars," he sincerely told his friend.

Big Thunder offered his hand in friendship to Jere. They shook hands and walked in silence toward the beautiful cabin home nestled in the woods there in the wilderness on the bank of the Grays River. They had each known happiness, contentment, friendship and joy of the highest order that day. Their world was so minute, yet it was also so vast and immense. Their beautiful forest was perpetually renewing itself continually. It would go on forever. As soon as one tree blew down in a storm, another tree was already growing to take it's place.

Jere didn't race ahead to leave his friend behind that time. They each walked up the back steps together as Little Flower, who had seen them through the kitchen window, opened the back door to greet them.

Jere said, "Hi, Little Flower. Boy, I can't wait to tell you and my parents about the exciting things we saw out there in the woods today. "

He was almost breathless from the excitement of thinking about which portion of his story he wanted to tell them first. They were both anxious to relate the extraordinary experiences that he and Big Thunder had witnessed and had been a party to that day.

Big Thunder suggested to him, "Son, why don't we wait until after supper when we will be able to get everyone into the living room to tell all of them at the same time? Don't you think that would be a good idea?"

Jere was sitting on pins and needles wanting to tell someone about their exciting and unusual experiences in the woods, but he decided to accede to Big Thunder's wishes. He finally said, "Yes, I suppose that would be best." He really wanted to tell his version of the story to the audience at that time. Waiting until after supper seemed like a long time to have to keep his story under wraps.

# CHAPTER
## 23

The spring and summer months had been unseasonably warm and humid for that part of the northwestern United States, and the Langford garden had produced abundantly with an excess of vegetables and herbs. Little Flower was becoming experienced in knowing how to use them properly in preparing many gourmet meals. She had acquired a vast knowledge of the art of preparing and presenting food, which had been taught to her by the master chef, Angela, for the past few months. The men were now favorably impressed with her culinary abilities and magnificent meals that were presently being prepared by the newly self-appointed chef.

Big Thunder had made the promised authentic Indian drum for Jeremiah with rawhide stretched over a hickory head that was allowed to dry and shrink. He then started teaching him the rhythmic beats that were used for rituals that were sacred as the Indians danced the meaningful steps at the official Indian powwows. He and Little Flower then got together to teach Jere how to dance the special steps that he needed to know for those occasions. He had also presented the boy with a bear claw, an arm bracelet, and an eagle feather. He had already given him his professional skinning knife, which he was terribly proud of. He told Big Thunder that he would loan it to him the next winter.

Josh had obtained some fertile hen's eggs and an old setting hen from a family who lived near the Grays River just a mile out of Rosburg. He allowed the hen to set on the eggs in a nest made out of a box lined with straw on the back porch. He would build a proper chicken house and surround it with a chicken wire fence soon. Josh said they would have frying-size chickens in about five weeks and would have this hen and possibly two more laying eggs in two or three months. Three hens should keep them well supplied in fresh eggs for breakfast as well as a few that Little Flower might want to use to bake the special goodies that she was fond of making for them. The younger roosters would be used for food.

Running Brook was now beginning to eat some soft cooked foods, such as creamed and sweetened parsnips, mashed potatoes, crabapple sauce, and other cooked wild fruits that they had harvested in the woods and on the special island in the river.

Jeremiah and Big Thunder had been so busy helping Joshua with the huge garden he had planted that spring that it was imposing a restriction on the amount of time they could visit their wild friends in the forest. It is true that they enjoyed reaping the benefits of the gardening venture by savoring the delicious foods from it, but it had placed a crimp on the once leisurely lifestyle they had grown used to by traipsing around in the forest. Many of the animals had come to know them and welcome them as cordial visitors.

Although Big Thunder thoroughly enjoyed the strolls through the forest with his little brother, it was now beginning to get to the point where he was unable to make the long treks that he had once been accustomed to. He felt that he was no longer able to walk far enough to visit the cave that he once called his home. Although he still felt good, old age had crept into his muscles and had denied him the ability to make the cross-country jaunts in the forest and across the hills with Jeremiah. He hated to admit that he found it necessary to remain behind sometimes when Jere wanted to explore, but he was forced to decline many of his invitations to explore the woods.

It had become difficult for Jeremiah to understand the underlying cause for Big Thunder's reluctance to go with him. He was too young to understand that the aging process that had overcome his friend was the real reason for keeping him from accompanying Jere's trips to the woods. Big Thunder had given him delaying promises such as, "Wait until cool weather gets here. The weather is too hot now for me to enjoy it."

Big Thunder was actually thinking that he might get to the point where he would feel better and get stronger when the weather turned cool. His intentions were to be able to go with his blood brother one more time into the woods.

Jere would sometimes counter with, "But Big Thunder, I will sit you on a log by the creek and let you rest for as long as you want to. I know you would enjoy seeing the white wolf again. I'm sure that she has had her babies by now. They should be following along with her in the woods."

"Yes, I'm certain that she has had her babies by now, Little Brother," Big Thunder would reply. "And nothing in the world would please me more than to see her with the little ones. I'll bet they are precious. I'm afraid I won't be able to make it just yet, son. Maybe soon," he would promise. "I wonder if all of her babies will be white or if only some of her babies will be white?"

Jeremiah told him that he wished all of them would be white and he would love to see them. He thought that maybe the majority of them would be tan and some of them might even be black. "Wouldn't that be a corker if some of them were black, Big Thunder?" Jeremiah asked.

"Well, one never knows," he answered. "I would still love to see them sometime, little brother," he added.

Angela had regained her radiance. Running Brook was four months old, cute as a bug and rapidly growing. Angela had also resumed many of the household duties, but Little Flower had been unwilling to give up her position completely. She not only loved her work there at the Langford cabin for the sheer pleasure it had given her, but it had also given her something to occupy her mind and bring her closer to her father once more after having almost lost him. She had been very happy to learn of the unusual episode that had saved his life in the wilderness when the white wolf escorted Jeremiah on a mission of mercy. At least, she was able to share some of the pleasures of his last days tending to him and loving him as any daughter would be glad to do.

Of course, he also had the care and love of the Langford family, but it was not quite the same as a blood daughter who had loved him all of her life. Little Flower considered it a wonderful gift from the Great Spirit above to allowed her to come to the Langford cabin and joyfully spend some of her last days with her ailing father. She was thankful not only to the Great Spirit, but to White Spirit as well.

Joshua had by now completely finished the two upstairs rooms in the cabin. Angela had begged Jere and Big Thunder to consider moving from the barn into the cabin, but they declined, saying they were having too much fun staying in the barn at night. The room that Jeremiah had originally occupied had long ago been taken over by Little Flower, who desired to have Running Brook sleep in her room, as well. She said it would be handy to get up at night to tend the baby in the handmade cradle in her room. It became so acceptable for the baby that it was continued. It was supposed to have been on a temporary basis, just until Angela got back on her feet. It became permanent without anyone saying anything, and now Angela was beginning to like the arrangement and was completely satisfied with the situation.

Big Thunder and Jeremiah still enjoyed talking for the first few hours of the night after they went to the barn. They often engaged in lively conversation, which would have been next to impossible had they moved into the cabin. They were most thankful that they did not have any eavesdroppers listening in on their private talks each night. Many subjects that were discussed were of a private nature and would not have been discussed at all if they had thought someone might be listening to them.

Sometimes they were silent, which each of them also loved. Each respected the other's wishes to refrain from talking and not break the wonderful stillness as they lay on their mattresses of tow sacks. The grocer told them that he would always be buying potatoes in tow sacks and if they ran out they could always get more from him.

Angela told Joshua that she wanted him to make a boat trip to town to pick up some groceries. Jere couldn't wait to tell Big Thunder about it, but when he finally did, the old Indian declined to make the trip. Normally, he would have been ready to go at the drop of a hat, but not this time. Big Thunder told Angela that she should go with them. She agreed that it was probably a good idea since she hadn't been able to travel for several months. She felt that it could do her some good to go on a cruise with her husband and son once more. Jeremiah and Joshua both agreed.

They all woke up early the next morning to the aroma of the freshly ground coffee beans brewing in the pot and the last of the bacon being fried by Little Flower. They also had eggs, biscuits, gravy, and grape jam to go with the bacon. They were now getting plenty of eggs from the four hens laying in the nests in the chicken house. They would get one full-sized egg each day, and two or three pullet eggs. Jere had two pullet eggs and a slice of bacon with one biscuit. As soon as he got up from the table he said he was ready to go to Rosburg.

Angela said, "Hold your horses, son. There are others who are making this trip, too." She assured him they would try to be ready shortly.

Josh headed down to the boat with Jere at his heels. He got the glow pin hot, started the engine, and had it idling when Angela came skipping down the hill looking like a young schoolgirl again, with her red bandanna tied around her black hair and a pretty yellow dress. Josh gave the order, "Let go o' the bow line, mate!"

Jere replied, "Aye, aye sir!" He loosened the line and told the skipper, "Anchors aweigh, sir. Ready to depart."

Josh slowly reversed the boat into the river and then headed downstream. After a hundred feet he pushed the throttle to full speed and watched the feisty boat hike her bow into the air to push the passengers back in their seats. Angela's bandanna was flowing straight. Josh pulled up to Ben Ferguson's marina and cut the engine. Jere jumped out, secured the bow and stem lines fast, and then helped his mother out of the boat.

It was still early when they docked at Ben's place. His assistant hadn't shown up for work yet. Josh told him he didn't need to fill up the fuel tank until they returned from shopping, anyway.

Ben said, "You know it kinda irks me to see that boat and be reminded about how much of a fool I was to get myself snookered, like I did."

Josh replied, "Aw, Ben, you made a killing off the new boat you sold to that fellow as well as the twenty dollars that you made off me on this one. You wouldn't have made any money at all if you had just let it lie there in the water and rot in behind your marina," Josh reminded him.

"I suppose you're right," Ben said. "Maybe I should be thankful that you took her off my hands without charging me." He laughed.

"We'll be back after we get through grocery shopping," Josh told him. "I will want a tank full of spirits when we return," Josh said as he retightened a line before they departed the marina to go shopping.

Josh let Angela shop for groceries while he sat on a nail keg in the rear of the store. Most of the old men sitting around were shooting the breeze, so to speak, but Josh didn't dare engage in the conversation because he had already figured out that he was not in their league. They were professional tale spinners, and he wouldn't stand a ghost of a chance.

Angela and Jere had done the shopping with the help of the store clerk. When they were finished, Josh couldn't believe the monstrous pile of groceries they had bought in the little amount of time that they had been there.

Josh teasingly asked Angela, "Are you sure that food won't swamp the boat when we load it?"

Angela replied, "Oh hush, Joshua Langford. You will enjoy eating this food every day when Little Flower prepares the fine meals that you have all gotten used to. Besides, you made plenty of money from your fur trapping last winter, and I'm having fun spending it," she smiled and winked at him, flirting with him like she used to before the baby was born.

"Let's go, darling," she said. She had already made arrangements for the store to deliver her groceries to Ben's marina.

Josh noticed when they left the grocery store that the both of them had headed in opposite directions. He said, "Don't tell me. Let me guess."

Angela smiled at him and said, "You get three guesses but two don't count."

Jere laughed as his dad said, "Ice cream!"

Angela said, "How did you ever guess?" She winked.

They received their ice cream cones and started walking toward the marina.

As Ben's assistant was fueling their boat the delivery boy came with the groceries and helped stow them on board. Angela offered the boy a dime, but he refused to take it, saying, "This is part of our service and it's free. We are not allowed to accept any gratuities from our customers. Thank you, anyway, and come again, soon," he told her.

Jere asked his father if he might be allowed to take the wheel on the way home. Josh offered to give him some lessons on safe boating and seamanship starting next month and that he might allow him to take the wheel at slow speed for a short stretch on the river. At Angela's insistence, Josh told Jere, "Not yet, son."

After running full tilt all the way, Josh slowed the *Angel* down to a crawl and into the slip. They saw Little Flower holding Running Brook in the rocking chair on the front porch enjoying the breeze while waiting for the family to come home. Big Thunder was sitting on the edge of the front porch with his feet dangling off as though he was waiting for the return of his friend. Those two were almost inseparable, and it was highly unusual that he would allow Jere to go boating without him tagging along. It was very seldom that you saw one without the other. However, it could have been that Big Thunder had deferred in favor of Angela, since it had been months since she had gone to town with her husband and son.

Josh, Angela, and Jere carried groceries up the hill. Josh set his down on the front porch and went back to the boat for another load. Big Thunder offered to go down to the boat and help him carry them, but he said, "No, thanks. You don't really need to be running up and down that hill."

They hadn't yet eaten dinner, and Josh was wondering if they might have a bologna and cheese sandwich on store-bought white bread.

"Why, of course we may," Angela replied. "I'd like to have one, myself."

"Sounds like a winner to me," Big Thunder replied. "Jere, I'll never forget the time you brought one to my cave and saved my life with it." He laughed and said, "That was absolutely the most delicious sandwich that I had ever tasted in my whole life. I still find it hard to believe that the white wolf knew how to lead you to my cave where I was dying. And to think, she stayed right there with you until she made certain that you had seen me," the old man reminisced.

"Big Thunder, do you think it might be possible for us to go out into the woods tomorrow morning?" Jere asked him.

"Well, I'm not sure, son," Big Thunder answered. "We'll just have to wait and see how I feel in the morning before I can say for sure. Let's just wait and see," he said.

After supper it seemed that everyone was full and lazy. Big Thunder said, "Jere, I think we might as well head for the barn. Are you about ready?" he asked.

"I'm as ready as I'll ever be," he replied.

As usual, after Big Thunder and Jeremiah had gone to the barn to lie on their backs looking up at the barn rafters, they talked about many interesting things before falling asleep. Jere could never have talked to anyone else about some of the things that he had divulged to Big Thunder.

As they lay there looking up at the barn roof, Big Thunder said to Jere, "Little brother, I would like to ask you for a favor, if you don't mind."

"Ask away," Jere answered.

Big Thunder said, "Son, when I am dead, I would like for you to see to it that my body is cremated so my spirit will rise in the smoke and ascend into the heavens. Will you please see to it that my wish is carried out?" he solemnly asked his little brother.

"Of course I will, Big Thunder," Jere agreed. "I will be glad to grant your wish when you finally die. I'll make you a promise on that," Jere told him. He crossed his heart with his hand.

"Thank you, my son," he replied. "Once again, you have made me happy."

They both lay in silence looking up at the barn rafters. Jere couldn't think of anything else to talk about. He lay awake longer than usual that night, looking up and thinking that some day in the future that it would come true that he really would lose his good friend to death. He hoped that it would be many more years, though. Jere glanced sideways and looked at Big Thunder, but he couldn't see well enough in the dark to tell if he was asleep or not. He thought possibly that he could see the old Indian's eyes wide open, but he couldn't tell for sure. Both of them had been staring up at the loft in the barn, so it was quite possible that Big Thunder wasn't sleepy and was still looking up with his eyes wide open. Jere couldn't remember going to sleep, but it must have been pretty late. They hadn't talked any more that night.

It was barely light when Jere woke up the next morning. He rubbed his eyes and looked over to where Big Thunder was lying. His eyes were wide open, and he was again staring up at the rafters. He came to the conclusion that Big Thunder was in deep meditation and didn't want to be disturbed. Big Thunder was very still. Jere had observed that the old Indian's eyelids had not blinked.

"Big Thunder?" Jere called to him.

Waiting and hearing no response, he said again, louder, "Big Thunder."

Big Thunder's eyes were wide open, just like they were the previous night as they lay there in bed before they went to sleep, but he wasn't answering the boy's summons that morning.

Jere got out of his bed and went over to where Big Thunder was lying on his back. He touched him on the arm to wake him up, but his arm was cold and rigid and he didn't respond. Jere assumed then that his best friend was dead, but he didn't know what to do. His first instinct was to try to wake him up by shaking him, but since his arm was cold, he knew for certain that he was dead. Big Thunder must have surely known the night before that he was dying when he asked Jeremiah to grant him the wish of cremating his body. Jere decided to get his father's help.

He ran up the hill crying, "Dad! Dad! Come quickly. I think Big Thunder must be sick or something. He won't wake up." Jeremiah was crying, and tears were streaming down the side of his face. He said, "Please, God. Don't let him be dead. Oh, please don't take my best friend away from me," Jeremiah wailed with a mournful cry.

Joshua ran quickly to the barn, went inside, and returned to the cabin immediately. Upon his return, he announced to the family, "He's gone. Big Thunder is now gone from this earth." Josh hung his head down and said, "Little Flower, I'm sorry. Your father has passed away during the night."

Little Flower came over and put her arms around Josh, Angela, and Jere and said, "Please don't be sorry for him. He is happy now, and you have made his last days very wonderful and joyful. Be thankful that you have brought him back from death once so that I might be able to share in his last days, but allow him the honor of dying in peace and tranquility now. He was never loved as much by anyone as he was loved by Jeremiah. He adored your son as much as he would have his own son, and he made his last days very happy. He gave him a new life and new strength to live on to the point where he was fully ready to depart this earth. He had accomplished at the end what he had wanted to do."

Little Flower caressed Angela for an extended time without saying anything, but finally suppressed her emotions enough to say, "My father and I want to thank you for all of the love and friendship that you have so graciously given us during the last days of his life here on earth. May God bless you," Little Flower expressed her thanks to them.

Joshua said, "I have covered his body with a blanket. I will go out beyond the barn and dig a grave, Little Flower. You will let us know when it would be a suitable time to have his funeral and burial, please."

Jere said, "Dad, last night we were talking before we went to sleep, and he made me promise that his body would be cremated. He said he wanted his spirit to rise into the heavens as it left this earth."

Little Flower said, "He also asked me to make certain that his body was cremated when he died. He said that he wished for his spirit to rise into the clouds to be with our Heavenly Father, on high."

Josh said, "Then I will go cut some tree limbs to make a large funeral pyre, so we can fulfill his last wishes. If that was his request, then that is what we must do. I'll have to cut lots of timber."

Joshua worked all morning, cutting and stacking the wood on a huge funeral pyre behind the garden. Little Flower told Josh that it would be better to go ahead and have his funeral since there were no other children, brothers, or sisters that would need to attend. There would be no need to wait for the cremation.

That afternoon, Josh wrapped the body up tightly in a blanket and carried it to the pyre to be placed on top. He then dashed kerosene all around the bottom timbers, allowed it to get saturated for a few minutes, and then lit the bottom timbers with a wooden match.

The fire slowly caught and then started roaring high in the sky. The blaze started to consume the body, and they watched in awe as his spirit ascended upward in the smoke toward the heavens. Big Thunder was going to be with his ancestors in their eternal home on high.

"In the beginning, God created the heaven and the earth."

It had been truly evident for some time that God had created that special niche in the world for Big Thunder, Jeremiah, Joshua, Angela, Little Flower, and Running Brook, so that they might live out their lives in sublime happiness in their own secluded section of the woods; their own Garden of Eden in the foothills of the mountains there in Washington state. They were thankful for the small portion of eternity that had been granted them in their own utopia.

"And God said, 'Let the waters bring forth abundantly the moving creature that hath life, and fowl that mayfly above the earth in the open firmament of heaven.' And God created great whales, and every living creature that moveth, which the waters brought forth abundantly, after their kind, and every winged fowl after his kind: and God saw that it was good. And God blessed them, saying, 'Be fruitful and multiply, and fill the waters in the seas, and let fowl multiply in the earth.' And God saw every thing that he had made, and behold, it was very good."

As the smoke from the funeral pyre reached upward toward the heavens, a single cloud moved across the face of the sun and covered it. Big Thunder's spirit had reached the clouds and was then ascending into the heavens to be with his beloved ancestors.

Joshua then quoted a passage of holy scripture found in Job 14:1–2. "Man that is born of a woman is of few days, and full of trouble. He cometh forth like a flower, and is cut down: he fleeth also as a shadow, and continueth not, And as we have borne the image of the earthly, we shall also bear the image of the heavenly."

Joshua said, "He is now at peace with his Maker."

Little Flower replied, "A-men, Lord."

Joshua then read a passage of scripture from Genesis 2:7–8: "And the Lord God formed man of the dust of the ground, and breathed into his nostrils the breath of life; and man became a living soul. And the Lord God planted a garden eastward in Eden; and there he put the man whom he had formed."

Joshua then read from Genesis 3:19: "in the sweat of thy face shalt thou eat bread, till thou return unto the ground; for out of it wast thou taken for dust thou art, and unto dust shalt thou return. And, behold, I come quickly, and my reward is with me, to give every man according as his work shall be. I am Alpha and Omega, the beginning and the end, the first and the last."

Joshua said to the assemblage at the funeral of Big Thunder, "The Lord and Giver of life has graciously presented this family a precious new life as we celebrate the birth and arrival of our beloved little daughter, Running Brook. We also mark and celebrate the passing from our midst to an eternal home in the heavens above, our beloved friend, our father and our blood brother, Big Thunder. May he rest in peace. Amen."

The Lord giveth and the Lord taketh away.
The End